THE IMMIGRATION CRUCIBLE

THE
IMMIGRATION
CRUCIBLE

TRANSFORMING RACE, NATION, AND THE LIMITS OF THE LAW

Philip Kretsedemas

COLUMBIA UNIVERSITY PRESS | NEW YORK

Columbia University Press
Publishers Since 1893
New York   Chichester, West Sussex

Copyright © 2012 Columbia University Press

Library of Congress Cataloging-in-Publication Data

Kretsedemas, Philip, 1967–
The immigration crucible : transforming race, nation, and the limits of the law /
Philip Kretsedemas.
p.   cm.
Includes bibliographical references and index.
ISBN 978-0-231-15760-5 (cloth : alk. paper) — ISBN 978-0-231-15761-2 (pbk. : alk. paper) —
ISBN 978-0-231-52732-3 (ebook)
1. United States—Emigration and immigration—Government policy—History—20th century.
2. United States—Emigration and immigration—Government policy—History—21st century.
3. Immigrants—Government policy—United States—History—20th century.
4. Immigrants—Government policy—United States—History—21st century.
5. United States—Emigration and immigration—Political aspects.
6. Emigration and immigration law—United States—History.
7. Immigration enforcement—United States.
I. Title.

JV6483.K74   2012
325.73—DC23

2011036609

Columbia University Press books are printed on permanent and durable acid-free paper.
This book is printed on paper with recycled content.
Printed in the United States of America

c 10 9 8 7 6 5 4 3 2 1
p 10 9 8 7 6 5 4 3 2 1

BOOK DESIGN BY VIN DANG

FOR MY FATHER,
ALEXANDER KRETSEDEMAS, *1939–2009*

CONTENTS

TABLES

This book could be described as a research memoir that is masquerading as a macrohistorical survey of U.S. immigration policy. The critical review that I provide in the following pages has been imprinted by experiences I've had over the past fifteen years, during which I've researched service needs for immigrant communities and worked at immigration-oriented, nonprofit organizations. This personal history is, if you will, the prism of intelligibility through which the writing for this book has been filtered.

Many of the noncitizens that I encountered in the course of my research (either indirectly, through the stories of case workers and community activists, or directly) would probably not be picked as the poster children of U.S. immigration by federal lawmakers. This is not to say they were bad people. Quite the opposite, in fact. Most of them were earnest and resourceful people who had fallen on hard times. They had, in many respects, become fully acculturated to life in North America, but they had also hit a number of roadblocks in their quest for social mobility—and ended up in the ranks of the jobless or working poor. Some were individuals and families who had become homeless; others were fortunate enough to qualify for some form of public assistance but had been unable to land a secure, full-time job; and still others had been doing fairly well for themselves but had became deportable due to a minor criminal infraction.

One of the goals of this book is to interpret recent trends in U.S. immigration policy in a way that refocuses attention on the problem of immigrant marginality. Even though it is generally true that immigration is good for the U.S. economy—the economy doesn't always work in the best interest of immigrants (or of many U.S. citizens for that matter). The same can be said for recent trends in immigration policy and immigration enforcement, both of which play a role in conditioning the "utility" of immigrant populations. Because anti-immigration advocates have stigmatized immigrant poverty, welfare use, and joblessness (framing these problems as burdens that immigrants are imposing on the U.S. citizenry) the proimmigration camp has tended to emphasize the positive side of immigration. In this book, I hope I have broken this habit of developing arguments that are simply reactions to the "other side." Even though I do provide a number of critical insights into the limitations of the anti-immigration position, I am not interested in devoting my energies exclusively to challenging and reframing this position. Instead, I map a political, cultural, and economic terrain that, hopefully, provides some new insights into why so many noncitizens are in a difficult situation. My analysis also draws attention to the limitations of the mainstream proimmigration position. Many of these critical observations are informed by questions and concerns that I came across in the course of my fieldwork and also in my community outreach work (in my various incarnations as a policy analyst, community liaison, and development officer for nonprofit organizations).

For example, I came across some immigrants and immigrant rights activists who were critical of the "good" versus "bad" immigrant distinctions that were implicitly reinforced by the framing strategies of the mainstream immigrant rights movement. In some cases, these framing strategies were exclusionary toward criminalized immigrants or immigrant welfare users—but in either case they sent signals about the kinds of immigrants who were suitable (or not) as public spokespersons. Tensions also occasionally surfaced between the priorities of national-level policy advocacy outfits and community-based immigrant rights outfits, and these tensions usually reflected something about the differences in the race and class composition of these organizations (with the national policy advocacy groups being notably whiter and better connected to the social circles of the upper middle class than the community-based groups). Broadly defined, these were struggles over who got to define the issues and concerns of immigrant communities. At root, this wasn't just a problem that had do with race and class. It also had to do, more broadly, with the willingness of people to be exposed to aspects of the immigrant experience that they hadn't expected to learn about ("yes I realize that race, class, gender, and legal status matter, but I didn't realize that they mattered in *that* way").

My interest in revealing these awkward issues (the sorts of things that tend to be obscured by all sides of a given field of debate) has been shaped by the peculiarities of my personal history. I am a person of Afro-Caribbean (Jamaican) and Greek parentage who was born in Canada and first entered the United States in the late 1970s. I was born outside the United States, but all of the nations I lived in prior to landing in the United States (with the exception of the Bahamas) were majority-white, English-speaking, Western, industrialized nations. So even though I am not native to the United States, I am—in many respects—a child of the Western world. This also means that I am intimately aware of what it means to be a non-white person in the Western world. So even though my migration history is very different from that of the typical brown-skinned immigrant, I grew up dealing with the kinds of racial profiles and stereotypes that are associated with brown-skinned immigrants.

My family's first place of settlement in the United States was south Florida (and south Florida was also where I began my career as an immigration researcher). We entered south Florida months before the first waves of the Cuban Mariel boatlift (and the even more stigmatized Haitian boatlift). I became accustomed, very quickly, to being mistaken for a Cuban (and dealing with all of the political and cultural baggage that went along with this ethnic label). Having spent several years prior to that living just outside of London, England (which was undergoing its own racial turmoil, fueled by immigration anxieties and a crippling recession), I had become accustomed to seeing myself as black. But I came to learn that the rules for determining the meaning of black and white (or black and non-black) in south Florida were different than the ones I had grown up with in the UK. In any event, these are the sorts of foundational experiences that would shape my understanding of the racial subtext of the immigrant experience—and especially my interest in exploring points of intersection between the situation of immigrants, native-born minorities, and the broader U.S. working population.

Another ambiguity that has defined my immigrant experience is my location at the intersection of two very different kinds of immigrant co-horts. My family's migration to the United States in the late 1970s oc-curred several years before the current immigration boom, which didn't take off in earnest until the late 1980s. Even so, my social experience of migration is more similar to this post–Cold War era of immigration than any other. South Florida was (and still is) one of the principal gateways for these new migrant flows, and for a period of time in the 1980s and 1990s, it was one of the fastest-growing parts of the United States, containing the largest per capita number of foreign-born persons in the United States. But I did not have to struggle with the kinds of legal issues that are typical for most immigrants of this era because, legally speaking, I wasn't really an immigrant. My father had acquired U.S. citizenship through his father, who had become a U.S. citizen in the 1920s and then returned to Greece several years later.

So I had been registered as a U.S. citizen at birth (even though I did not set foot in the United States until I was nine years of age). In this regard, I was never an immigrant. I was actually born a U.S. citizen, which was made possible by an original act of migration, on the part of my grand-father, which took place at the very tail end of the last "great wave" of European migration that ended in the early 1920s. Within my family two very different immigrant experiences were at play. My mother was a "new" immigrant, who entered the United States for the first time in the late 1970s—and who had to deal with gendered and racialized immigrant stereotypes that were alien to my father's experience of the world. My father, on the other hand, was tied to an older wave of immigration (and had grown up in the United States from the 1940s onward). Both of these experiences intersected in the rather unusual migrant experiences of my siblings and myself. There is a relationship between these details of my life history and some of the issues that I tackle in the following chapters. For example, the disjuncture between the social fact of migration and the legal construct of the immigrant is one of the key themes of my analysis. This is related, in turn, to a broader interest in exploring the slippages and limitations of the law.

There are probably readers who would like to see more of my personal narrative woven throughout the book. All I can say to these readers is that, as valid as this method may be for advancing new theories, it is best left for another writing project. This book takes aim at the macrohistorical policy context. But it should also be apparent that I am not trying to bury my personal history. Instead, I have used it to guide my interpretation of this macropolicy context. What I offer, in this regard, is not a truer or more comprehensive account, but a different one—that organizes familiar information around some relatively new concerns and framing devices that stem from the experiences I've outlined here. If the book is successful in getting people to think about U.S. immigration policy in a new way, as well as, perhaps, making room for some new perspectives in the public discourse on immigration, I will be more than pleased. Either way, I have put forward my best effort.

———————

I thank the editorial team at Columbia University Press (including acquisitions editor Anne Routon, copyeditor Anne R. Gibbons, and editorial assistant Alison Alexanian) for their patience and guidance as I worked my way through the various drafts of this manuscript.

THE IMMIGRATION CRUCIBLE

INTRODUCTION

The immigration debate has a tendency to complicate the political fault lines that define other policy issues. It is not unusual for liberals and conservatives to join forces in favor of legislation to legalize unauthorized migrants. More rarely, immigrant rights activists and immigration restrictionists have found themselves joined in opposition to the same immigration laws—albeit for very different reasons.[1] Arguments for and against immigration can give rise to similar kinds of puzzling contradictions. For example, the argument against immigration has appealed to the economic interests of an embattled citizenry. Immigrants are often depicted as unproductive, low-skilled workers who are a tax burden for the U.S. middle class (Capetillo-Ponce 2008). This critique is connected to a much larger debate about the costs and benefits of immigration that has been playing out in academia and the public sphere for the past two decades.

There is compelling evidence that immigration has played a critical role in driving economic growth and workforce replenishment in many parts of the United States (Fiscal Policy Institute 2009; Dowell Meyers 2008).[2] Questions have been raised, however, over whether recent migrants are more "costly" or prone to poverty than the migrants of the early twentieth century (Borjas 1991; Portes and Zhou 1993). These questions, in turn, have generated more research into patterns of socioeconomic mobility among recent migrants and the role that U.S. policy and other mac-rostructural factors has played in shaping current trends in immigrant mobility and immigrant poverty (Bashi and McDaniel 1997; Borjas 2006; Reitz 1999; Zhou 1997; VanHook, Brown, and Kwenda 2004).

One fact is uncontestable: the expansion of U.S. migrant flows over the last several decades has taken place during a period of economic re-structuring that has downsized the social service sector and casualized U.S. labor markets. These transformations have contributed to a more intense form of class stratification and a decline in job security and real wages for most middle- and lower-income U.S. residents (Massey 2008, 113–210). This situation has not been caused by immigration but there is a relationship between this broader process of economic restructuring and the priorities that have been guiding U.S. immigration policy (Kretsede-mas 2005). So, although immigration has been a net economic gain for the U.S. economy, the costs and benefits of immigration have not been fairly distributed across the U.S. population, which is consistent with other pat-terns in the income and wealth stratification that have unfolded during this period of time. It also bears noting that immigrants (especially Latino migrants) have become more concentrated in the lowest paying and most unregulated segments of these restructured labor markets over the past two decades (Catanzarite 2000; Crowley, Lichter, and Qian 2006). Even though the socioeconomic status of many U.S. citizens has deteriorated over the past few decades, an argument certainly can be made that im-migrant populations have fared even worse and that, in some ways, they have buffered U.S. citizens from the worst consequences of these econom-ic trends.

Unfortunately, these nuances have been lost within the public dis-course on immigration, especially in the arguments that have been ad-vanced by anti-immigrant pundits. Instead of stimulating a critical public discussion about social and economic policy, the undesirable outcomes of these policies have been blamed on immigrants. So, for example, the solution to the problems of the U.S. working poor is not to improve wage levels, worker bargaining rights, and workplace safety regulations, but to stop the flow of foreign bodies entering the United States. The irony of these sorts of arguments is that they mobilize economic complaints that are not connected to a serious analysis of economic inequality.

The anti-immigration pundits who have managed to garner the most public attention (including the likes of Lou Dobbs, Pat Buchanan, and Glenn Beck) do not have an impressive track record examining the structural causes of poverty in the United States, and when they are not railing against immigration they have not been particularly sympathetic to the situation of the U.S. poor. All of these pundits approved of the deregulatory policies and public sector spending cuts that have been responsible for shrinking the middle-income stratum and expanding the gulf between the native-born rich and the poor over the last three decades.[3] As they describe it, the American middle class is not a socioeconomic category but a cultural formation that shares a common heritage and value system. Not surprisingly, these pundits also gravitate in the direction of a flesh and blood nationalism that views the U.S. national identity as a unique product of the culture and kinship networks of the white, native-born majority (Brimelow 1996; Buchanan 2007).

Arguments in favor of immigration have been complicated by a very different set of issues. Immigration is typically depicted as a good thing for pragmatic, economic reasons. The immigrant is portrayed as a hard worker who is willing to take on the jobs that the native-born, middle class does not want to do. Just as important, the immigrant is willing to patiently climb the social ladder in a way that affirms the meritocratic values of U.S. society.[4] As a result, mainstream arguments in favor of immigration can function as an apologetics for the economy-in-general. Observations about the social marginalization of some immigrant populations, new trends in immigrant poverty, or of the labor market exploitation of migrant workers have become something of an inconvenience for this position. This is partly because immigration control advocates have used these developments (including exaggerated claims about the labor-market displacement effect of low wage migrant labor) to argue against immigration.[5] Once again, all these problems are blamed on immigrants instead of the priorities that have been shaping federal policy for the past several decades. But the mainstream proimmigration position has not been especially interested in critically examining these same policy priorities.

Within some proimmigration circles, arguments about the labor market exploitation of immigrants can easily be misinterpreted as arguments that are critical of immigrant labor.[6] And even when there is an interest in addressing the labor market exploitation of migrant workers, it is often relegated to the periphery of a policy agenda that is mainly concerned with increasing the labor market supply of these workers (and is usually willing to compromise its defense of worker and immigrant rights, if this is what it takes to secure the labor supply). On balance, it has been this instrumentalist orientation that has defined the mainstream proimmigration agenda. There are some clear advantages to this pragmatic approach. The argument that immigrants are hard workers (and good for the economy) is one of the few perspectives in favor of immigration that has been able to gain traction across partisan lines in the halls of Congress. But this emphasis on the utility of the immigrant worker also makes it very difficult to address the problem of immigrant marginality—which requires a proimmigration discourse with a stronger ethical foundation and a willingness to look beyond the neoliberal common sense that has dominated federal policy for the past several decades.

For example, lawmakers who support immigration for economic reasons have also been willing to support get-tough immigration laws that appeal to the very same anxieties propagated by the immigration control movement. The end result is a policy climate that has been proimmigrant, insofar as it has consistently facilitated the expansion of migrant flows, but that has also introduced unprecedented restrictions on immigrant rights coupled with the unprecedented expansion of the immigration enforcement system (Brotherton and Kretsedemas 2008; Cole 2005). Consider, for example, that the 1996 Immigration Reform Act, which has been criticized for inaugurating the current era of get-tough immigration laws, was enacted under the Clinton administration. Meanwhile, the Obama administration has not only continued most of the immigration enforcement initiatives of the Bush administration but has also significantly intensified them (TRAC 2009).[7] Indeed, the continuities in the immigration priorities of the past several administrations have been more striking than their differences.

The implicit message being sent by these policy decisions is that immigration may not be desirable but it is most certainly necessary. Immigration may be good for the economy, but it is also important for the government to convince the public that it will not let immigration get "out of control." As a consequence, the incarceration and deportation rate for noncitizens has increased steadily over the past two decades, despite the fact that immigrant crime has decreased over the past fifteen years (mirroring patterns in the overall crime rate) and despite the fact that immigrants commit less crime than the native born (Rumbaut and Ewing 2007).

These trends draws attention to enigmas that are typical of the U.S. immigration debate. Things are not always what they seem. Economic complaints about immigration are not necessarily just about the economy and policy makers who support new restrictions on immigrant rights are not necessarily in favor of restricting immigration. One of the few points of consensus that has defined the fragile middle ground in this debate is the willingness to expand immigration enforcement.

PUZZLING EVIDENCE: THE CONTRADICTIONS OF IMMIGRATION ENFORCEMENT AND THE POLITICS OF IMMIGRATION POLICY

This book is not exclusively focused on immigration enforcement, but the analysis of immigration enforcement *is* integral to my argument about the limitations of current trends in U.S. immigration policy. This is mainly because, over the past three decades, immigration enforcement has increasingly defined the immigration priorities of the federal government. The concern for securing the border and protecting the U.S. citizenry from "predatory migrants" (including unauthorized migrants, "criminal aliens," possible terrorists, etc.) has also become a more prominent feature of the public discourse on immigration. These priorities are reflected in spending levels for border control and immigration enforcement, which dwarf federal spending on all other immigration-related programs by a ratio of approximately six to one.[8]

On closer inspection, however, the popularity of immigration enforcement is rather puzzling. The Department of Homeland Security (DHS) has become one of the fastest-growing segments of the U.S. government's public sector bureaucracy, with most of this growth being driven by the expansion of its enforcement wing (including but not limited to immigration enforcement).[9] This continually expanding bureaucracy of enforcement officers would appear to be the antithesis of the small state that has been idealized by the advocates of free trade and open markets. And yet it has become an integral feature of the U.S. government's strategies for expanding and liberalizing U.S. migration flows, despite the fact that the organizational mandate of the DHS sometimes runs counter to employer interests.[10]

Arguments against immigration have also been marshaled in support of expanding immigration enforcement. Ironically, these arguments appeal to the same kind of libertarian and conservative populist sentiments that are critical of government spending. This line of reasoning is very similar to the views of anti-immigration pundits who have been very critical of the U.S. "welfare state" but very much in favor of public spending on border control and interior enforcement. It appears that the immigration system is a kind of big government they find very appealing; so long as it can be used to effectively control immigration. But immigration enforcement has not been successful in achieving the goal that these pundits are seeking to achieve (this being an absolute reduction in immigration levels), and there is no evidence that this goal has been officially adopted by the U.S. immigration system. In this regard, the organizational mandate of the immigration enforcement apparatus does not appear to be strictly derivative of a free market ideology or the restrictionist agenda of the immigration control movement, even though it has been influenced by both sets of interests.

IMMIGRANTS AND STATE POWER:
ON THE MARGINS OF THE LAW

The expansion of immigration enforcement has been accompanied by a new field of interdisciplinary research that has examined the impact of these enforcement practices for immigrant populations (Dow 2005; Dunn 2010; Fernandes 2007; Inda 2005; Nevins 2010; Welch 2002). This book makes its own distinct contribution to this growing body of work. Unlike these prior studies, however, it does not focus on a particular wing of immigration enforcement, such as border control or immigration prisons. Instead, it examines trends in immigration enforcement that are broadly descriptive of the entire immigration system (and, in the case of local immigration laws, stretch beyond the federal immigration system). And my analysis is not exclusively focused on immigration enforcement. It situates enforcement trends within a much broader context that has been shaped by the various governing strategies, legal rationales, and discourses on race and nation that have defined U.S. immigration policy and the public discourse on immigration. The goal of this analysis is to provide some novel insights into the political process and the blind institutional momentum that has been shaping U.S. immigration policy and immigration enforcement for the past several decades. Throughout the book, I try to show how the hazards of the contemporary immigrant experience (which includes, among other things, living with an insecure legal status, the ever-present possibility of being deported, or being subjected to surveillance practices that are informed by racial profiling).have been produced by policies and practices that have become a more or less normal feature of the way immigration works today. Many of these policies and practices operate in the margins of the law. A good example is the assortment of economic interests, informal practices, and (de)regulatory strategies that has produced the "unauthorized migrant."

From the vantage point of the mainstream discourse on immigration, the unauthorized migrant is a person who has made a deliberate decision to violate U.S. law. But the illegality of these migrants must also be understood as a situation that is being systemically produced by the workings of U.S. immigration law, immigration enforcement, and local labor market recruitment practices. On one hand, labor market recruitment practices have carved out a niche for these workers in the U.S. economy and, for the better part of the twentieth century, this has been tolerated, and even tacitly facilitated, by the U.S. legal system. Meanwhile, the targeting of these populations by immigration enforcement has tended to complement (and not disrupt) the labor market dynamics driving this process. High profile roundups of "illegal workers" drive home a point that is implicit in their terms of employment (and which makes them attractive to employers)— that they are an expendable workforce that is expected to be more compliant and more productive because they are residing in the United States entirely at the discretion of the legal resident population.

The conditions that have produced the illegality of these workers can be connected to a broader set of governing strategies that have been used to regulate many other kinds of migrant populations—and other matters that extend far beyond the domain of immigration policy. All of these governing strategies operate within a terrain that lies outside the law but that has also been shaped, in part, by the law. They can be used to create a zone of discretionary authority that grants its beneficiaries broad leeway to interpret the law (or to exempt themselves from the strictures of the law) and to produce stateless conditions that render its subjects vulnerable to the sanctions of the law but unable to access the protection of the law.

My examination of these governing strategies decenters the pro- and anti-immigrant divide that has defined the mainstream immigration debate. Both sides of this debate have supported changes in policy and governing practice that have resulted in the expansion of these extralegal (or marginally legal) discretionary powers. The proimmigration side of the debate has generally favored the liberalization of migrant flows and the shift to a more fluid kind of labor market regulation. These transformations are part of a broader restructuring process that has been used to expand global flows of trade and commerce. Notably, this process of global economic restructuring has been guided by a form of state power that uses the kinds of extralegal governing practices described above.

In this case, the extralegal powers of the state would appear to be aligned with a free flow position on immigration. But the U.S. government also has a long history of cultivating zones of discretionary authority that predate the latest phase of globalization and that are more closely related to governing strategies used to control racial minority populations. In this case, the deployment of discretionary authority drifts in the direction of "states' rights" arguments, which give local authorities freedom to craft laws and enforcement practices that are not strictly beholden to federal laws and constitutional standards. These sorts of arguments are currently being revived by immigration restrictionists who want to expand the authority of state and local governments on immigration matters so that they can more aggressively pursue unauthorized migrants.

Throughout the book I observe how both of these trends in the expansion of discretionary authority have converged in the present-day immigration system and how—despite the very different sets of interests that have been shaping them—they tend to condition and reinforce one another. This explanatory focus distinguishes my analysis from prior studies of U.S. immigration policy. Even though I explore the same political terrain, I am not as concerned with describing the history of contestation that has unfolded between the various positions that have defined the immigration debate (largely because there are already a number of thorough treatments of this subject; see, for example, D. Daniels 2004; Hing 2003; Ngai 2005; Tichenor 2002; Zolberg 2008).

I am not offering the reader a chronological, historicist account of immigration policy. Instead, I present the reader with a collection of essays that examine U.S. immigration discourse and immigration trends over the same time span, but from the vantage point of several different (but thematically related) sets of concerns. Each chapter draws attention to a variety of processes that have been operating beneath the surface of the immigration debate. The histories I examine have more to do with the maturation and unfolding of these submerged processes than with immigration policy itself—and in many instances, these explanations will lead my analysis beyond the scope of immigration policy.

Chapter 2 begins the analysis with a description of the precarious legal terrain that has been produced by the last several decades of U.S. immigration policy—which I describe as a kind of de facto statelessness. The federal government has allowed unprecedented numbers of migrants to enter the United States, but under conditions in which their right to remain in the United States is never guaranteed and is conditioned by the prospect of removal. As a consequence, many of these persons are caught up in a legal limbo, having been incorporated into the social and economic life of a nation that may never grant them the right to permanent residence.

This kind of migrant experience blurs the lines between the situation of the legal migrant and the illegal alien (who are often treated as if they belong to two entirely separate populations). Many of the migrants who end up as "illegals" come from this population of noncitizens who were initially admitted to the United States on a temporary legal status. What is most important to understand about this migrant experience is that it has been directly shaped by state policy and is a product of the recruitment practices that draw migrants into the United States. One of the principal reasons why immigration enforcement has been expanded over the last few decades is to police this expanding flow of migrants who are admitted under the condition of "temporary legality."

Chapter 3 provides a theory of state power that sheds more light on the policy and enforcement trends described in chapter 2. The recent expansion of immigration enforcement is connected to a political process, dating to the mid-nineteenth century, that has steadily expanded the discretionary authority that the executive office wields over the law. From the late 1980s onward, this discretionary authority has been put in the service of neoliberal economic restructuring, but it has also been used to advance many other policy agendas.

The common thread woven through all of these governing strategies is an interest in expanding the authority of the state over the law so that it can better adapt the law to a variety of unexpected contingencies. I draw on the writing of Giorgio Agamben (2005) to conceptualize this process, explaining how it leads to a situation where the state of emergency begins to define the normal relationship of the state toward the law, rather than being an exception to the normal operation of the law. And the immigration policy decisions of the executive office have set new precedents for the exercise of this kind of discretionary authority. A good example is the role that the 2000–2008 Bush administration played in overturning prior legal precedent to affirm the inherent authority of local governments to enact their own immigration laws. I discuss the significance of this decision at the end of chapter 3. This discussion also sets the stage for chapter 4, which explores the recent history of police involvement in enforcing immigration laws (from the early 1980s to the present) and the even more recent history of local immigration laws (from 2005 to the present).

Chapter 4 takes a closer look at the policies and practices that have been used to negotiate the immigration enforcement responsibilities of federal and local authorities. The overarching goal of this chapter is to situate local immigration laws and local enforcement practices in the context of a broader history of federal-local governing arrangements that have perpetuated institutional racism. I argue that in order to develop a viable theoretical framework for explaining how local enforcement leads to immigrant profiling, it is important to understand the kinds of practices that have been historically used to marginalize black populations in the United States.

A long history of institutional discrimination in the United States has been made possible by slippages and discontinuities between federal legal standards and local practices. Much like local immigration laws, this situation draws attention to a kind of discretionary authority that the federal government has been willing to divest to local governments. As a consequence, legal precedents that appear to protect vulnerable populations from unreasonable search and seizure are undermined by the relatively wide discretion that federal authorities are willing to give local governments in interpreting these legal precedents. As it concerns local immigration laws, an unavoidable consequence of these developments is the rise of a new kind of immigrant racial profiling.

It is important to understand the constructions of necessity and of the public interest that have quietly shaped the law. These ideas and assumptions are not always apparent from the language of the law itself, but they play a critical role in shaping how the policies and practices of the state are implemented. Policy changes that expand the discretionary authority of federal, state, and local actors provide even more room for these ideas to shape the law, but in ways that allow the ideas themselves to be shielded from public scrutiny.

Chapter 5 examines some of these ideas, including several currents within the academic discourse on cultural pluralism, racial difference, immigrant assimilation, and national identity. The main goal of this chapter is to show how the dilemmas of political membership (i.e., who should be included in the nation and under what conditions?) can be informed by discourses on race and culture. I begin by exploring how these connections have unfolded within liberal thought, because of the defining influence it has had on mainstream sociology and U.S. social policy. But I also draw attention to unlikely points of convergence between strands of liberal pluralist theory, cultural conservativism, and some variants of Marxist thought that can all bend in the direction of a preservationist ethos. Even though this desire to preserve is not an inherently bad thing, it can foster a defensive posture on the subject of racial inequality and immigrant integration. When this orientation is translated into state policy and institutional practice it can lead to the kinds of worrisome trends documented throughout the book, where it appears that the mainstream society is more concerned with protecting itself from immigrant populations than engaging those populations as "future citizens."

The closing chapter explains how the issues explored in the preceding chapters relate to the current state of the immigration debate. I examine the similarities and differences between the Obama and Bush administrations on immigration policy. I also reflect on some of the governing strategies and patterns in immigrant marginality that are likely to persist irrespective of how the debate over immigration reform is resolved over the next several years.

Despite the rather somber prognosis that I deliver in the final chapter, my analysis is premised on the understanding that there will, eventually, have to be a substantive change in the priorities guiding U.S. immigration policy. Even if such a change does not seem likely for the immediate future, it is even more unlikely that the United States will be able to stumble along indefinitely under the current immigration status quo. My hope is that this book will help to foster a critical discussion on U.S. immigration policy that is not limited by the practical constraints of the present, but is more concerned with developing ethical policy solutions that can be sustained for the long term. In order to encourage these new lines of critical thought this book attempts a rather difficult balancing act, by presenting an analysis that is relevant to the present-day immigration debate but that also attempts to look beyond the confines of this debate.

2

A DIFFERENT KIND
OF IMMIGRATION,
A NEW KIND OF
STATELESSNESS

The great epoch of U.S. immigration that ended in the 1920s is often used as a reference point for immigration today. The peak levels of both these immigration boom periods are very similar and they both took shape during a period of free market optimism and aggressive, corporate-led economic growth.[1] As such, they can both be described as cyclical events that played an integral role in growing the U.S. economy.

This narrative is not inaccurate, but it obscures some important differences in the way that immigration is being defined and regulated by the state in the current era. As I explain in this chapter, there is something very different about the way that immigration works today; and one of its most distinctive features is the changing relationship between the immigrant population (or legal permanent residents) and another class of migrants categorized by the state as nonimmigrants or temporary arrivals.

The aim of this chapter is to describe this changing relationship and explain how it relates to the expansion of immigration enforcement. Admittedly, this is a rather unusual approach to the study of U.S. immigration. Most sociologists have treated immigration as a social process, not as an assortment of legal categories that have been defined by the state. The classic social science literature on immigration mainly focused on examining how immigrant populations integrated into the mainstream society (Kivisto 2005). The guiding concerns of this body of research have been pushed in new directions by the current field of immigration studies. Researchers have pointed out that acculturation is not a unidirectional process and that there is no necessary correspondence between different kinds of integration (Alba and Nee 2005). In some cases, for example, acculturation (or "Americanization") may be an impediment to socioeconomic mobility (Waters 2001). There has also been a great deal of interest in examining how recent trends in cultural and economic globalization have allowed immigrants to sustain transnational networks that—in contrast to prior eras—allow them to participate simultaneously in the civic and economic life of the old country and the new host nation (Appadurai 1996; Bashi 2007; Liu 2005; Robert Smith 2005). These studies play an important role in updating and complicating earlier theories of integration by drawing attention to social dynamics that operate outside of the territorial boundaries of the nation-state.

My analysis in this chapter is informed by this body of research, but it draws some of its observations in a different direction. As these studies have pointed out, transnational migrant networks have been shaped by a climate of adversity created by anti-immigrant sentiments, get-tough immigration laws, and changing patterns in labor market stratification that push them into ethnically segmented employment sectors (among other things). So although these studies highlight the creativity and resilience of migrants they also, implicitly, acknowledge that migrants have had little option but to create transnational support networks. In this regard, cultural hybridity and transnational identities are not just a product of the new mobilities that have been opened up by globalization—they are also adaptations to an environment that has become more perilous for immigrants. The nation-state (and the United States in particular) has become a more exclusive and fortified entity, and one of the ways in which this has become most apparent is in the legal classifications currently being doled out to migrant populations.

This way of framing things pays more attention to the way that the state has shaped the climate to which migrants are adapting, rather than focusing on the adaptations of the migrants themselves (though it bears noting that all of the aforementioned research has explored the dynamic relationship between migrant networks and macrostructural dynamics, including state policy). Nevertheless, a distinguishing feature of my analysis in this chapter is that it focuses exclusively on the governing strategies and policy priorities of the state and explains how they have changed what immigration means today. Even though this analysis is relevant to research on the immigrant experience, it comes out of a somewhat different, and rather new, body of critical research on immigration enforcement and the state. These sorts of critical studies can be traced to the late 1980s and early 1990s—most notably to the work of Kitty Calavita (1992)—but they have become more prevalent in recent years. Many of the scholars who have contributed to this body of research are not people who have specialized in the study of immigrant settlement or integration. Some of the most important contributions have come from sociologists, criminologists, legal scholars, and investigative journalists whose trajectory of work has been more focused on the analysis of state power, racial disparities, and patterns in socioeconomic stratification (Dow 2005; Cole 2003; Kanstroom 2010; Massey, Durand, and Malone 2003; Welch 2002).

One of the unifying themes of this body of research is an interest in extending the analysis of structural inequality to the workings of the U.S. immigration system. This chapter extends these sorts of arguments to the policies and practices that have been used to regulate the nonimmigrant flow. It contributes to a relatively new body of critical research on immigrant visa holders (Banerjee 2010; Neumayer 2006; Rosenzweig 2006). It also engages issues that are relevant to a much larger body of critical research on unauthorized migrant populations (Bacon 2009; Chavez 1997; De Genova 2005; Ngai 2005; Rothenberg 2000; Willen 2007). Like the policy debate over immigration, this research has focused its attention on distinctions between legal and "illegal" migrant populations. But there are other kinds of legal distinctions that separate immigrants from nonimmigrants and that distinguish different classes of nonimmigrants from each other.

In the current era, for example, the social dynamics of migration (which have to do with how and why people migrate) have become increasingly abstracted from the legal categories that are being assigned to migrants. The migrant flow can be broadly described as a social process that structures the movement of people in and out of the United States. As some scholars have noted, migrant flows have always been constructed, in part, by the diplomatic and economic interests of state systems (Massey, Durand, and Malone 2003; Sassen 2000). The migrant flow is shaped by the culture, social networks, and resources of the migrants themselves, and also by a variety of institutional actors (multinational corporations, embassies, military bases, etc.). But whereas the migrant flow is partly structured by state and corporate actors, the immigrant/nonimmigrant distinction is a construct that is wholly created by the state.

In this regard, the immigrant should not be confused with the one-who-migrates. The term, "immigrant," is better understood as a legal status that the U.S. government confers on a very limited cross section of the noncitizen population. In recent years, the vast majority of people who have physically migrated to the United States have not been legally defined as immigrants. And conversely, the majority of people who are being classified as immigrants are not people who have just migrated to the United States; they are people who have already been living in the United States for sometime under a temporary legal status, who finally managed to have their status adjusted to that of a legal permanent resident.[2]

This is why it is important to take a closer look at the nonimmigrant population. In many respects, it has become the dark matter of the U.S. immigration system, a vast, amorphous flow that is exponentially larger than the immigrant or the "illegal" population but that is rarely addressed (as a distinct class of persons) in the public debate on immigration. Even so, the changing form of the nonimmigrant flow has been quietly shaping U.S. migration trends and has been factored into most of the state's strategies for regulating and policing migration flows.

I use the concept of statelessness to frame my analysis of the nonimmigrant flow. I use it to describe the precarious legal terrain that is being produced by the regulatory priorities of the state, which leads many non-immigrants to get caught up in a legal limbo of indefinite duration. I also describe the policy and enforcement trends that have been used to regulate and police these migrant flows. The final section examines racial-ethnic disparities and patterns of racial-ethnic concentration within the nonimmigrant flow. The aim of the closing discussion is not simply to show why race still matters for U.S. immigration policy but also to complicate the way that race matters. There are, for example, several different patterns of racial-ethnic segmentation at work within the nonimmigrant flow that are not entirely derivative of each other. These permutations complicate the stateless condition of the nonimmigrant—almost to the point of incoherency—but they are also a defining feature of this condition, allowing it to proliferate invisibly, without making an imprint on the public discourse on immigration.

ALMOST STATELESS: MIGRANT MARGINALITY IN AN ERA OF "NONIMMIGRATION"

Only a very small minority of noncitizens who enter the United States each year do so with the right to become citizens. Over the past two decades, this number has been a very small fraction of the total migrant flow (typically less than 5 percent).[3] The overwhelming majority of noncitizens are admitted as temporary arrivals, or nonimmigrants. One telling sign of this transformation is the current ratio of immigrant to nonimmigrant flows. In the early twentieth century, the flow of temporary arrivals was a small fraction of the immigration flow. Today, this relationship has been turned on its head. The nonimmigrant flow now outnumbers the annual growth of the immigrant population by a ratio of more than thirty to one (see figure 2.1).

The vast majority of nonimmigrants do not plan on becoming permanent settlers. Most of these persons (approximately 90 percent) are required to leave the United States within a matter of weeks or months.[4] On the other hand, there are a sizable number of nonimmigrants who enter with visas for a year or more. Many of these persons enter with dependents and with an intent to settle. Relative to the size of the total nonimmigrant flow, this group of hopeful settlers is fairly small (probably no more than 10 percent of the total nonimmigrant flow).[5] But when compared to the annual growth of the immigrant population, this inflow of hopeful settlers is quite large. The government does not release data on the number of applications for permanent residence that are declined each year. But if you read between the lines of the available data, clearly the population of noncitizens already residing in the United States who are seeking permanent resident status is much larger than the number of people who are actually awarded this status in any given year.[6] For the former group of persons, the nonimmigrant visa becomes a probationary

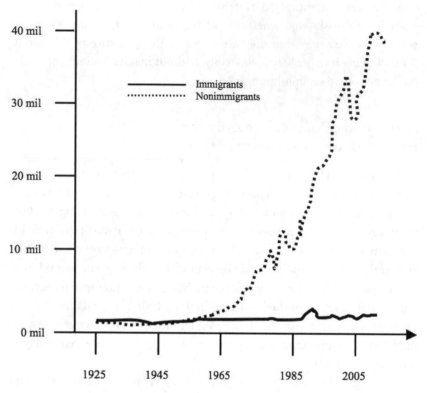

FIGURE 2.1   Immigration and Nonimmigrant Flows, 1925–2009.
Source: Data derived from DHS 2004c, 2009a, 2009d, and from *Historical Statistics of the United States* 2006, Table Ad1014–1022, "Nonimmigrants Admitted, by Class of Admission, 1925–1996."

legal status that must be continually renewed until permanent resident status can be secured. This process often requires visa holders to risk the hazards of illegality. It has been estimated that visa overstayers account for as much as 40 percent of the annual growth of the unauthorized migrant population (Passel 2006, 16).

The term "visa overstayers" provides an implicit explanation for this legal quandary that focuses on the culpability of the migrant (they are the people, after all, who have decided to overstay their visa). But the visa overstayer is also a product of the tenuous legal status through which they gained entry to the United States and the variety of informal pressures that lead them to remain here. Kitty Calavita's (45–47; 2005) observations about "institutionalized irregularity" provide an apt summary of this situation—whereby the laws and policies that have been put in place to regularize migrant workers actually contribute to their social and legal marginalization. Notably, Calavita focuses on the predicament of unauthorized migrant workers. But this situation also extends to nonimmigrant visa holders, despite the fact that they are protected from many of the coercions that are routinely experienced by unauthorized migrant workers. The main point, in this regard, is not that the labor market experience of unauthorized migrants is comparable to that of the visa holder but that there is a continuity in the policy priorities and (de)regulatory strategies that have been used to cultivate both of these migrant flows.

For example, most nonimmigrants who end up becoming long-term residents are high-skilled persons who are eligible to compete for jobs that offer "middle-class wages." If they entered the United States with a work visa, it is very likely they were also granted the opportunity to apply for legal permanent residence (although the outcome of their application is by no means guaranteed). And most of these nonimmigrants still have a nation to which they can return. Even so, the privileges of membership in this other nation have little bearing on the limited rights and vulnerability to deportation that are a direct consequence of the legal status they hold in the nation in which they live and work. This results in a kind of statelessness that is relatively unique to the nonimmigrant population. In order to understand the defining features of this condition, it is necessary to rethink the conventional definition of statelessness.

The example that comes to mind when we think of stateless people is usually that of noncitizens who are seeking legal status in the United States because their nation of birth no longer exists or no longer recognizes them as a citizen. In this case, the legal dilemma of the stateless person can be formally recognized as such under national and international law, and this, in turn, makes them eligible for protections and remedies that have been developed specifically to deal with the problem of statelessness.[7]

The recent literature on statelessness has made a deliberate effort at complicating the relationship between statelessness as a formal, legal-juridical status and statelessness as a sociopolitical condition. Linda Ker-

ber (2005) has argued that the U.S. legal system has a long history of ma-
neuvering white women and racial minorities, who are formally regarded
as citizens, into a condition of de facto statelessness. Margaret Somers
(2008) has also explained that new kinds of stateless conditions are being
created by political and economic dynamics that are eroding earlier para-
digms of citizenship and that this erosion of citizen rights has dire consequences for the most vulnerable segments of the immigrant and native-
born population. In this regard, statelessness is not merely the lack of
formal membership in a political community, it also includes people who
are not completely excluded from membership but who are subjected
to exclusionary laws and practices that make it very difficult to exercise
their claim to membership. These sorts of ambiguities can be found in the
earliest discussions of statelessness in the postwar era. Jane Carey (1946)
notes, for example, that the stateless person can be broadly defined as any
individual who is without the protection of a government. So, U.S. citizens
traveling abroad are testing the boundaries of statelessness insofar as they
can be sanctioned by foreign governments that may not afford them the
protections that would normally be extended to citizens.

In the Cold War-era, statelessness was treated as a rupture in the normal operation of national and international law (Samore 1951; Weis 1962).
It was presumed that the duty of the nation-state was to protect its citizenry from the dangers of statelessness and, moreover, that national belonging was an inalienable right that should be protected by international
law. In the current era, however, state policy routinely maneuvers migrants (and portions of the citizenry) into a situation of de facto statelessness. Studies have shown that this kind of legal marginality has become a
pervasive feature of the way that migrant labor markets are being regulated in many advanced, industrialized nations (Calavita 2005; Cornelius
et al. 2004). And if statelessness means being without the protection of a
government, then it is a condition that also applies (as Margaret Somers
has argued) to the victims of hurricane Katrina, U.S. citizens who have
been subjected to warrantless searches (and who have been stripped of
the right to sue the government for conducting unreasonably invasive investigations), and immigrants who have lost the right to raise legal questions about the reasons for their detention. This kind of de facto statelessness is a relative condition that can be measured in degrees and in ways

that slip around the legal remedies granted to those persons who are formally designated as stateless.[8] Effectively, these people are subject to the
law but not protected by the law.

This kind of statelessness does not always take the form of a stigma-
tizing marginality. A Foucauldian understanding of positive power is
perhaps the most appropriate way of describing this situation (wherein
power is not simply used to punish and restrict but to entice and facilitate).[9] Unlike unauthorized migrants, nonimmigrants are not treated as
an undesirable Other who "shouldn't be here." Instead they are treated
more like a useful Other who belongs to a massive, depersonalized migrant flow that can be expanded or restricted in response to any variety
of contingencies. It is not unusual for nonimmigrants to be treated as desirable assets by one branch of the immigration system and as potential
security threats by another.

The authority of the state is reflected not only in the way it regulates
the nonimmigrant flow but also in the very definition of the term "nonimmigrant." Through the strategic application of this term, it has become
possible for the federal government to dramatically expand migrant flows
in ways that do not register in the official tally of the immigrant population. It also becomes possible to create a class of noncitizens who are, in
actuality, long-term residents but who are classified in such a way that
they are unable to access the same legal rights and protections extended
to legal permanent residents (that is, the "official" immigrants).

It is also rather telling that there are no statistics that provide a definite
count of the number of individual nonimmigrants who enter the United
States each year. The statistics that are included in all the figures and tables for this chapter are based on nonimmigrants who entered the United
States after filing I-94 forms. Estimates of the nonimmigrant flow quin-
tuple when accounting for all temporary arrivals—which includes people
who cross the U.S.-Mexico and U.S.-Canada border without filing I-94
forms.[10] These are all soft estimates, however, because the unit of enumeration for the nonimmigrant flow is not the individual migrant but the
fractal, arrival event.

Statistical descriptions of the nonimmigrant flow can include multiple
entries by the same individual over the course of the year. The likelihood
of an individual making a large number of multiple entries is much more

likely for land-border entrants. This is why all of figures and tables in this chapter use I-94 estimates, because most of these arrival events involve individuals who entered the United States through the lengthier and more expensive process of international airline travel.[11] Hence, I-94 estimates of the nonimmigrant flow provide a closer approximation of the person-based enumeration standards that are used to assess the growth of the immigrant population. But, in a very real sense, the migrant is not regarded as a *person* until he becomes a legal permanent resident. Until such time, the migrant is enumerated within a flow of tourists, business visitors, and temporary workers (among others) who are valuable for a variety of economic and diplomatic reasons but are not as intrinsically valuable to the state as the formally defined citizen-subject.

This distinction is not unreasonable in and of itself. It is not unreasonable, for example, for the state to set limits on its obligations to migrant populations that are not expected to become permanent residents. The problem, however, is that the immigrant/nonimmigrant distinction obscures more than it reveals about the present-day dynamics of U.S. immigration. It gives the impression that permanent residents and temporary visitors are two distinct populations. But the immigrant population is closely tied to the amorphous mass of depersonalized, arrival events that constitute the nonimmigrant flow.

Pathways to Permanent Residence

Most of the people classified as immigrants by the state in recent years are not new arrivals; they are nonimmigrants who adjusted to permanent resident status. Figure 2.2 illustrates how these trends have unfolded over the past twenty-five years.

This is a fairly recent phenomenon. The first time in U.S. history when the number of adjustees eclipsed the number of new arrivals was shortly after the enactment of the 1986 Immigration Reform and Control Act (IRCA). This was primarily due to the amnesty provisions of IRCA that were implemented as part of a broader strategy for controlling unauthorized migrant labor. But from 1998 onward, a different trend has emerged.

Unlike the post-IRCA spike in adjustments to permanent resident status, most of the people who have adjusted to legal permanent resident status in recent years are not unauthorized migrant workers. Furthermore,

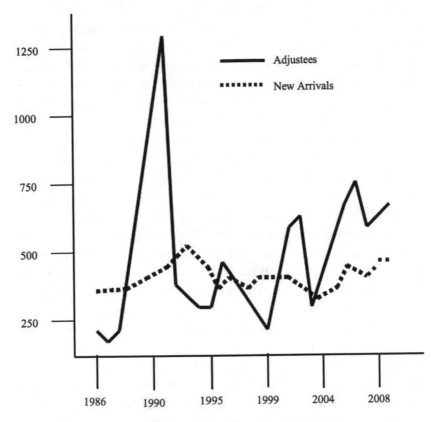

FIGURE 2.2   Adjustments to LPR Status vs. New Arrivals, 1986–2009.
Source: Data derived from DHS 2009c and 2004a.
Note: Quantities in thousands.
Note: LPR = lawful permanent resident.

most of these people have attained permanent resident status through channels that have become a standard feature of U.S. immigration law (as opposed to the IRCA amnesty program that was only intended to function for a limited period of time). The largest category of nonimmigrants who adjusted to permanent status over the past two decades are noncitizens who married U.S. citizens.[12] Employment-based adjustments and refugee adjustments are two other frequently used pathways to permanent resident status. Meanwhile, new arrivals have become a much less significant feature of the growing immigrant population.

In recent years (from 2000 onward), new arrivals account for little more than one-third of the annual growth of the immigrant population; the rest are nonimmigrant adjustees (see figure 2.2). Adjustments to legal permanent resident status seem to be how most noncitizens become immigrants, and this is now part of the normal functioning of the immigration system. Basically, the nonimmigrant visa has become the primary gateway for immigration to the United States.

These statistics provide a revealing insight into how immigration works today: most people who become immigrants today enter the United States with a legal status that offers them no guaranteed pathway to permanent residence. These people are not unauthorized migrants, but they could be described as migrants who have not been preauthorized to enter as permanent settlers. For these would-be immigrants, the task of becoming a permanent resident begins *after* they enter the United States. Until this status is secured, these people live in an indefinite legal limbo, in which the danger of illegality (or removability) always looms on the horizon—even if it is a more distant concern for some compared to others. Most of these people leave the United States; many others become permanent residents by marrying U.S. citizens; others gain permanent residence through provisions included in their work visas; and still others remain in the United States after their legal status has expired, joining the ranks of the undocumented. The nonimmigrant flow has become a conduit for all of these possibilities, which complicate the hard and fast distinctions often used to distinguish the "legal" and "illegal" immigrant.

The Rise of the Temporary-Worker Class

Another defining feature of the new immigration is the expanded recruitment of nonimmigrant workers. Although they are a small fraction of the total nonimmigrant flow,[13] this workforce has grown faster than any other category of nonimmigrants. Historically, tourists and business visitors have been the single largest segment of the nonimmigrant flow. Since the early 1980s, this portion of the nonimmigrant flow has tripled in size. The nonimmigrant worker population grew almost eightfold during the same period of time,[14] and by the late 1990s, the inflow of nonimmigrant workers began to outpace the growth of the immigrant population (see table 2.1).

TABLE 2.1   *Visitors, Temporary Workers, and Immigrants, 1981–2009*

YEAR	Tourists and business visitors	Temporary workers[a] and dependents (nonimmigrants)	Immigrants
2009	32,190,915	1,703,697	1,130,818
2008	35,045,836	1,949,695	1,107,126
2007	32,905,061	1,932,075	1,052,415
2006	29,928,567	1,709,268	1,266,129
2005	28,510,374	1,572,863	1,122,257
2004	27,395,921	1,507,769	957,883
2003	24,358,500	1,431,472	703,542
2002	24,333,016	1,468,421	1,059,356
2001	N/A	1,541,703	1,058,902
2000	N/A	1,414,256	841,002
1999	28,683,523	1,183,640	644,787
1998	27,641,742	1,010,636	653,206
1997	N/A	N/A	797,847
1996	22,880,330	701,619	915,560
1995	20,886,872	603,988	720,177
1994	20,318,933	583,023	803,993
1993	19,879,443	519,631	903,916
1992	19,299,007	511,939	973,445
1991	17,234,400	492,577	1,826,595
1990	16,079,666	444,504	1,535,872
1989	14,667,303	427,350	1,090,172
1988	N/A	N/A	641,346
1987	N/A	N/A	599,889
1986	N/A	N/A	600,027
1985	8,405,769	307,625	568,149
1984	N/A	N/A	541,811
1983	N/A	N/A	550,052
1982	N/A	N/A	533,624
1981	10,650,592	217,434	595,014

Source: Data derived from DHS 2009a, 2009d, and 2004c.

Note: N/A = no data available.

[a] Data for temporary workers prior to 1998 disaggregated intracompany transferees, treaty traders/investors, and representatives of foreign media from the total count of temporary workers. For the sake of consistency with the 1998–2007 data, these categories have been reincorporated into temporary worker totals for 1981–1996.

Nonimmigrant workers are allowed to enter the United States with dependents, and they comprise the majority of persons who are granted longer term residential visas.[15] As a result, nonimmigrant workers are more likely than other nonimmigrants to enter the United States in a manner similar to that of a "regular" immigrant. Work visas for professional-class workers often contain provisions that grant the visa holder (and their dependents) the option to apply for permanent residence. For example, the H1B visa program for high-skilled workers allows employers to recruit workers who may enter the United States with dual intent; to provide services as temporary workers but also with an interest in becoming permanent residents (Lowell 2000, 5–6). A similar dual intent clause has been included in the L1 visa for intracompany transferees, which was created in 1970 for high-level executives but is currently being used by a wide array of corporate employees (Wasem 2006).

Visa terms for professional workers contrast sharply with those for low-skilled workers. Recruitment levels for professional workers are also much higher than they are for low-skilled workers (see table 2.2). The H2 visa, for example, has been used to recruit a wide range of agricultural and seasonal workers. The H2B visa for nonagricultural workers (including construction workers, hotel staff, and other categories) has an annual cap of sixty-six thousand migrants, similar to the cap that was placed on H1 visas in 1990. The recently created H2R visa category for returning H2B workers allowed this category to be significantly expanded (USDS 2008).

There is no annual cap, however, on the recruitment of seasonal agricultural workers who can be recruited with H2A visas. So taken as a whole, there are fewer restrictions on recruitment levels for H2 nonimmigrant workers than there are for professional-class workers (which includes the H1 visa, along with several other visa categories, all of which have annual caps; Lowell 2000). Even so, recruitment levels for H2 visa holders are still half the size as recruitment levels for the professional-class visa population (see table 2.2). Furthermore, H2 visas last no longer than one year (compared to the three- to six-year term for visas typically granted to professional-class workers), and they do not allow the worker to enter the United States with dual intent.

These recruitment trends underscore the preference for professional-class workers that resonates throughout the work visa system. Profes-

TABLE 2.2   *Annual Growth of Guest Worker and Unauthorized Population, 2000–2009*

YEAR	Professional-class guest workers[a]	Seasonal and agricultural guest workers[b]	Annual growth of the unauthorized migrant population
2009	904,726	206,306	–1,100,000
2008	1,020,149	277,721	–600,000
2007	1,111,653	242,211	900,000
2006	972,616	180,503	500,000
2005	883,666	129,327	800,000
2004	857,348	109,099	500,000
2003	807,074	116,927	500,000
2002	844,213	102,615	–100,000
2001	896,542	100,082	1,000,000
2000	826,303	84,754	800,000

Source: Data for visa recruitment levels derived from DHS 2009d; data on the growth of the unauthorized immigrant population derived from Wasem 2009.

[a] H1, H3, L, O, P, and TN visa holders.

[b] H2 visa holders.

sional workers are recruited in higher numbers. They are also granted visas of longer duration that offer a pathway to permanent status than the visas granted to low-wage workers. Hence, socioeconomic disparities between higher and lower skilled migrant workers tend to correlate with legal status disparities. Visas for low-wage migrant workers are less flexible and of shorter duration, leaving them more vulnerable to the danger of "becoming illegal." These visa holders are also concentrated in the same employment sectors as unauthorized migrant workers.[16]

The unauthorized migrant population is also much larger than the low-wage guest worker population. It grew by several hundred thousand persons per year between 2000 and 2005 (see table 2.2).[17] This period of growth came to an abrupt end with onset of the U.S. recession. Even so, the number of unauthorized migrants living and working in the United States (which is hovering between 10 and 11 million persons according to recent estimates; Wasem 2009) is still much larger than the size of the

H2 worker population. Because H2 visas last for no more than one year, this population does not accumulate in size from year to year, like the unauthorized migrant population has over the past fifteen years. And even though the H2R visa (for returning H2 workers) has allowed the annual recruitment quota for these workers to expand, it is not widely used. In 2009, for example, only 162 migrant workers were granted H2R visas (DHS 2009d). Therefore, the size of the H2 visa worker population currently residing in the United States is probably no more than one-twentieth the size of the total unauthorized migrant population.[18]

This same disparity shows up in recruitment trends for H2 workers. Over the past ten years, the annual inflow of H2 visa workers was, at best, no more than one-fifth the annual growth of the unauthorized migrant population (see table 2.2). So whereas the recruitment of professional workers occurs within the formal channels of the work visa system, the recruitment of nonprofessional workers is much more informal, occurring largely outside of the work visa system. This is why several researchers have argued that the growth of the unauthorized migrant population has been guided by a more or less deliberate strategy for managing low-wage migrant labor markets (Calavita 2005; Ngai 2005, 127–166;Welch 2002, 58–82).

Putting Unauthorized Migration in Context

The nonimmigrant flow is partly responsible for the growth of the unauthorized migrant population (by way of the visa overstayer). But the growth of the low-skilled, unauthorized migrant workforce has been propelled by other factors that have very little to do with the nonimmigrant flow.

Despite all the attention that has been focused on controlling unauthorized migration, the annual growth of this population is a very small fraction of the annual flow of nonimmigrants Even when using the largest estimates, the annual growth of the unauthorized migrant population is no more than 3 percent the size of the nonimmigrant flow.[19] The same is true for Mexican nationals. The number of Mexican nationals who are admitted with visas greatly outnumbers the flow of unauthorized migrants. Over the past ten years, the Mexican portion of the unauthorized migrant population grew by almost 7 million persons, but during this same period of time more than 47 million Mexican nonimmigrants were lawfully admitted to the United States (using I-94 estimates only).[20] This is a very conservative estimate of the Mexican nonimmigrant flow. Because Mexican nonimmigrants enter the United States by land, the vast majority do not file I-94 forms. The size of the Mexican nonimmigrant flow easily quintuples (exceeding 200 million arrival events over the past decade) if accounting for Mexican nationals who were lawfully admitted without filing I-94 forms.[21]

When viewed in this context, it is apparent that the majority of Mexican nationals, like most nonimmigrants, abide by the terms of their temporary legal status. Given the size of the legal flow of Mexican nonimmigrants into the United States, it is also apparent that the size of the Mexican unauthorized population could easily be much larger than it already is if more Mexican nationals simply decided to become visa overstayers. So why hasn't this happened?

The simple answer to this question is that most unauthorized migrants are drawn into the United States by a combination of social networks and recruitment practices that operate completely outside of the nonimmigrant visa system. Ethnographic studies have shown that unauthorized migrant flows are shaped by social networks that connect specific townships in Mexico and Central and South America to employment sites in the United States (Adler 2008; Chavez 2007). Migrants who enter the United States without authorization usually have a very concrete idea of where they will look for employment, and the process of finding work will often be facilitated by friends or family members already living in the United States who are aware of the employers in their area who are open to hiring unauthorized migrants. Employers who hire unauthorized migrants often rely on the social networks of their unauthorized migrant employees to find these workers. As a result, it is not only common for unauthorized migrants to work in ethnically segmented employment sectors but also to live and work in the United States alongside the members of their hometown communities.

In addition to integrating new migrants into local labor markets, migrant social networks regulate the pace of migrant recruitment. Unauthorized migrants living in the United States sponsor the coyotes who

smuggle new migrants across the border, as well as supplying information to people back home about the condition of U.S. labor markets.
This is one reason why immigration scholars and policy analysts have
attributed the sharp decline in the growth of the unauthorized migrant
population that occurred between 2007 and 2008 to the recessionary
downturn in the U.S. economy (Cornelius 2008; Passel and Cohn 2008).
The capacity of unauthorized migrant flows to respond so quickly to
U.S. labor market trends is made possible by the constant communication between unauthorized migrants in the United States and their
home communities. In this manner, migrant social networks have been
a very effective form of laissez-faire labor market regulation, by helping
to tailor unauthorized migrant flows to employer needs (Hanson 2007).
Meanwhile, as Mae Ngai has pointed out, Mexican labor has been effectively illegalized by the extremely low quotas on Mexican immigration
imposed by U.S. law.[22]

It also bears noting that the illegality of Mexican workers is inextricably bound up with their geographic proximity. In other words, it has been
convenient to recruit Mexican nationals as "illegals," because they are *native* to the American continent. Although the effects of neoliberal restructuring on the Mexican economy are an important part of the story behind
the recent surge in unauthorized migration (see Bacon 2009), these push
factors do not explain, in and of themselves, why so many Mexican migrants are being incorporated into U.S. labor markets as "illegals." Mexican unauthorized migration is also facilitated by the preexisting socioeconomic ties between Mexican workers and Latino communities in the U.S.
These cross-border networks (which can be traced to a history of migration, trade, and community life that predates the present-day Mexican
border) have effectively subsidized the cost of labor migration for U.S.
employers, making it convenient for Mexican migrants to be used as illegal, disposable labor.

In contrast, employers have been willing to invest more resources
(in the way of processing fees, incentives, and benefits) to recruit high-
skilled, nonimmigrant workers that fly into the United States from other
continents, and the Congress has been willing to grant these migrants
legal options that are not extended to lower skilled migrant workers. In
this regard, recruitment practices for professional-class migrant workers

tend to protect them from the hazards of illegality. Meanwhile, the illegality of low-wage migrant workers keeps them trapped in their unenviable labor market position. It is a mistake to assume that these migrants have been recruited as low-wage labor *because* they are "illegal" (as if illegality were a preexisting condition that they bring with them into U.S. labor markets). Instead, illegality has become the organizing framework for recruiting and regulating this workforce.

POLICING PROFESSIONAL-CLASS MIGRANT WORKERS

Compared to unauthorized migrants, professional-class nonimmigrants are a privileged class of workers. Although the legal situation of the nonimmigrant is not entirely secure, it is nowhere near as dire as that of the unauthorized border crosser. This is most apparent in the way that unauthorized migrants have been targeted by the immigration enforcement apparatus. Under the Obama administration, for example, federal prosecutions of immigration violators (most of whom are unauthorized migrants) have reached historic highs (TRAC 2009). But it is also important to recognize how immigration enforcement has been used to regulate the entire migrant flow.

There is a close relationship between the expansion of immigration enforcement and the expansion of the nonimmigrant flow. These enforcement practices are no less pervasive than the ones used to apprehend unauthorized border crossers, but they are guided by a different set of priorities. Instead of being used to restrict the growth of an undesirable ("illegal") workforce, they have been used to monitor and police the ranks of a mostly desirable flow of legal migrant workers.

In many respects, this type of immigration enforcement is the direct corollary of a free market approach toward immigration. The interest of the state in creating a flexible, just-in-time migrant workforce leads it to liberalize recruitment channels for professional-class migrants who are admitted with temporary visas that are tailored to suit particular kinds of employment conditions. This, in turn, creates a growing population of nonimmigrant residents who are timing out of their legal status every year, which places new pressure on immigration enforcement to monitor this population. Hence, the dramatic increase in the issuance of nonimmigrant visas in the mid-1980s (see figure 2.1) can be viewed as a precursor to the expansion of immigration enforcement that began in the mid-1990s. The nonimmigrant visa allows a greater number of noncitizens to enter the United States under the condition that they are not to be treated as permanent settlers. The expansion of immigration enforcement from 1996 onward merely enhanced the capacity of the state to monitor this growing population, and remove nonimmigrants who do not abide by the terms of their temporary legal status.

These priorities are consistent with the goals of the electronic border system that became a popular framework for conceptualizing national security strategies in the aftermath of the attacks of September 11, 2001 (Carter 2001; James Edwards 2003; Sagarin 2003; J. Steinberg 2003; United States 9/11 Commission 2004). Unlike the build-a-wall perspective on border control, the electronic border system was premised on the idea that it was possible to improve the security of international trade and migration flows without restricting these flows.

The electronic border was conceived as a network of databases that would allow for an unprecedented degree of spatial dispersion while also being amenable to centralized, administrative oversight. At all points of entry into the United States (which could include sites located outside of U.S. territory) it would be possible to create a data file on each entrant that could be tracked and accessed by enforcement officers during several crucial points in each person's "visit," whether this was a matter of days or years. One of the goals of this system was to increase the responsiveness of enforcement agencies to visa violations. It also required a greater degree of joint planning and information sharing between government agencies, some of which—like FEMA or the EPA—were only marginally involved in federal enforcement operations. The guiding rationale for the system is that improved security requires a more expansive and integrated information database that will traverse all major government agencies.

Antiterrorism has been the overarching justification for the expansion of this security apparatus. But according to government statistics, persons deemed to be national security risks are a tiny fraction of the hundreds of thousands of persons removed from the United States on an annual basis (amounting to no more than fifteen people per year).[23] Nevertheless, the idea of national security has been expanded to include a variety of issues that are only tangentially related to terrorism. Unauthorized migration

TABLE 2.3   *Relationship Between Immigration Flows, Nonimmigrant Flows, and*
Expansion of Immigration Enforcement

	Annual growth of the immigrant population [a]	Annual growth of the nonimmigrant population [b]
	1925–2009	
Formal removals (deportations) (N=84)	.612 [a]	.856 [a]
	1986-2009	
Formal removals (deportations) (N=23)	.131	.907 [a]

Source: Data for immigration levels, enforcement actions, and recent trends in the nonimmigrant flow derived from DHS 2009a, 2009d, and 2009h. Data on the historic nonimmigrant flow (1925 onward) derived from *Historical Statistics of the United States* 2006.

Note: All statistics are for tests of association. Gamma was used due to the relatively small size (N=23/84). N represents paired cases of aggregate totals for each year

[a] $p < 000$

has become a security concern because of fears that these migrant networks could provide safe haven for terrorist cells (Deborah Meyers 2003). In a similar vein, global flows of trade and (legal) migration have become a security concern because of fears that the openness of these flows can also be exploited by terrorist organizations (Carter 2001).

There is nothing especially new about these anxieties. This dynamic relationship between the liberalization of migration flows and the intensification of immigration enforcement has been unfolding for the better part of the twentieth century. Evidence is provided by the steady growth in the number of people who have been deported from the United States over the past eighty-four years.[24] These trends are summarized by the statistics presented in Table 2.3.

From 1925 to 2009 there was a moderately strong association between the rising number of deportations and the growth of the immigrant population. There is a similar but stronger association between deportations and the expansion of the nonimmigrant flow. But when these same trends are viewed from the mid-1980s onward, a different picture emerges. Between 1986 and 2009, enforcement trends for the immigrant and nonimmigrant flow head in opposite directions. The association between immigration levels and deportations becomes extremely weak (and statistically insignificant). Meanwhile, the association between deportations and the growth of nonimmigrant flow becomes markedly stronger.

Deportations (or formal removals) have been the fastest-growing category of enforcement actions over the past two decades—making these enforcement actions the best indicator of the recent intensification of immigration enforcement. In terms of absolute numbers, the most frequently administered enforcement action is the voluntary departure, which is mainly connected to the actions of the U.S. border patrol. Voluntary departures are used to return immigration violators to their nation of origin without processing them through the immigration court system. Because they have been historically focused on returning unauthorized migrants who are apprehended near the U.S. border, the annual number of voluntary departures is closely tied to fluctuations in the growth (or decline) of unauthorized migration. So even though voluntary departures have always outnumbered formal removals, they have fluctuated erratically over the past several decades. Consider, for example, that the number of voluntary departures in 2009 was actually 30 percent *lower* than it was in 1989.[25] Meanwhile, the annual number of deportations has climbed steadily from year to year, growing eleven times in size during this same period of time.[26]

This steady increase in deportations, from the late 1980s onward, occurs during the same period of time when the federal government dramatically increased the use of visas as a means of cultivating new migrant flows (see figure 2.1). This is also the period of time when immigration becomes increasingly abstracted from the flow of new arrivals (see figure 2.2). So one reason why the nonimmigrant flow becomes more closely associated with deportations from the mid-1980s onward is because it has become the primary source of new arrivals to the United States—taking over from the role played by the immigration flow in the earlier part of the twentieth century. But once again, this is not just because there has been an absolute increase in the number of migrants entering the United States. It is also a product of the regulatory priorities that have allowed more migrants to enter the United States, but under the condition that they are classified as "nonimmigrants."

When viewed from a macrohistorical perspective, this appears to be a rather smooth process whereby the state liberalizes migrant flows, cultivates denationalized pools of nonimmigrant labor, and then creates a security-enforcement apparatus to monitor these flows.[27] But there are countervailing tendencies at work within this security apparatus. The imperative of security can give rise to enforcement practices that are more concerned about the "dangerousness" of particular national origin groups than with regulating the nonimmigrant flow as a useful asset. In this case, an interest in managing the flow of economically useful noncitizens is displaced by more panicked concerns about stemming the flow of alien Others.

In the late 1970s, the Iran hostage crisis generated demands among federal enforcement agencies to account for the flow of Iranian nationals in the United States. The Immigration and Naturalization Service was pressured to improve its enumeration and tracking methods for persons admitted to the United States with student visas, many of whom were Iranian nationals. In 1980 the INS produced a brief that acknowledged that it had no reliable method for estimating the flow and dispersion of the student visa population within the United States—and the agency developed a plan for accomplishing this task (GAO 1980). Prior to this time, Iranian students were inconspicuous members of a relatively privileged class of skilled nonimmigrants. They came under the scrutiny of the immigration system not because there was an interest in exploiting or regulating them as an economic resource but because they were regarded as a suspicious national origin group that might be harboring "enemy aliens."

This relatively benign concern for improving the INS' data collection strategies can be contrasted against the 2002–2003 Special Registration program that was also initiated by concerns about the domestic Arab Muslim population (Ifitikhar 2008). In this case, Arab Muslim nationality became an explicit criterion for gathering information on terrorist suspects. Persons who were required to participate in the program faced the immediate prospect of deportation and detention—contingent on the quality of their participation. The Special Registration program was accompanied by new reporting requirements and travel restrictions on persons admitted with student visas (including but not limited to Arab Muslim noncitizens) that still remain in effect. These are just two examples of how the pressure to intensify the surveillance of immigrant populations can be instigated by singular events that focus public attention on specific national origin groups.

There are other surveillance strategies that have not explicitly targeted noncitizens by national origin but that focus on visa categories that contain large concentrations of non-European nationals. A notable example is the monitoring practices used by the immigration system to assess the prevalence of fraud in the H1B visa program, which contains a large concentration of Indian nationals (USCIS 2008).[28] These kinds of enforcement programs are part of a much broader array of surveillance, enforcement, and data gathering strategies that the federal government has used to police the nonimmigrant flow. This includes, among other things, the development of new methodologies for assessing the number of visa overstayers who enter the United States via commercial airlines and the development of enforcement strategies that are better attuned to the changing composition of the nonimmigrant worker population and the conditions under which these workers may lose their status (GAO 2008, 1995, 1992).

These strategies can all be regarded as practical attempts to catch up with the complex array of legal channels through which noncitizens enter and exit the United States. Once again, this illustrates how the expansion of the nonimmigrant flow has set the stage for the emergence of a more expansive and intensive kind of immigration enforcement. The aim of these practices is to create a seamless web of interior surveillance and policing mechanisms that can track the nonimmigrant through the entirety of their stay in the United States (so that enforcement can more easily trace these people if or when their legal status expires). As a result, immigration enforcement has become increasingly focused on policing the movements of noncitizen bodies—and not just on policing the borders of a geographic territory. In this context, legal constructs of alienness cannot be easily disentangled from the national origin and racial profiles that are often associated with the idea of the foreigner.

RACIAL-ETHNIC DISPARITIES AND NONIMMIGRANT FLOWS

Within the critical literature on immigration there is little debate about the role that racial profiles play in shaping the likely targets of immigration enforcement (Dow 2005; Fernandes 2007; Hing 2003; Ndaula and

Satyal 2008). Coded discourses on race can be used to justify enforcement practices that seek to keep out (or kick out) particular kinds of national origin groups. On the other hand, racial disparities in migrant recruitment trends can reinforce patterns in racial stratification that coercively integrate migrants into the lower tiers of the U.S. economy. In this section, I take a look at racial disparities that are no less complex but that have more to do with the legal channels that bring noncitizens into the United States—and the implications this holds for who is most likely to become a citizen, remain an alien, or become "illegal."

From a broad historical perspective, there is a clear correlation between legal status and race. In the antebellum era, race *was* a legal status that played an instrumental role in reproducing the racial strata of that era. Vilna Bashi (2004) has explained how U.S. immigration law has historically been used to recruit black migrants, and other racialized populations, as disposable labor. Assigning a migrant a temporary legal status that offers no pathway to naturalization makes it much easier for local authorities to treat them in this manner. This is why, as several scholars have pointed out, the processes of illegalization and racialization are inextricably intertwined (Calavita 2005; Chavez 2008; Ngai 2005; Willen 2007).

If we extend these observations to the nonimmigrant flow, we might assume that legal distinctions between immigrants and nonimmigrants correspond with a new kind of racial hierarchy. So we should expect the more secure legal categories (the legal permanent resident and the citizen) to be dominated by historically preferred racial-ethnic groups and the least secure legal categories (the nonimmigrant and the unauthorized migrant) to be used as recruitment channels for a new, racialized underclass. But this is not exactly what is happening.

The nonimmigrant flow has become a conduit for several different patterns of migration, which correspond to the role this flow is now playing as the primary source of all new arrivals to the United States. It also appears that current patterns in racial-ethnic stratification have less to do with the immigrant/nonimmigrant distinction itself and more to do with the range of options that different populations have to enter the United States, the ease by which they can adjust to permanent status once they arrive, and their vulnerability to losing this status even after it has been attained.

In this regard, a migrant's legal status does not automatically determine whether, or to what extent, she is pushed into a condition of de facto statelessness. The migrant's legal status can be regarded as a mitigating condition that determines how vulnerable he is to these hazards, but it does not explain how this latent possibility (of being deported, of losing your legal status, of being forced to work under the condition of "illegality," etc.) is converted into an immanent reality. It is not the formal letter of the law that matters so much as the factors that determine how the letter of the law is interpreted (or ignored) in specific instances by specific social actors.

This situation is typical of the way that U.S. law has historically justified (and obscured) the dynamics of racial discrimination (see chapters 4 and 5). These discriminatory practices operate within a gray zone of discretionary authority that determines how laws and enforcement practices are applied to specific bodies at specific points in time. This is why there is quite a bit of slippage between the hierarchy of legal statuses that has recently been created by U.S. immigration law and existing patterns of racial-ethnic stratification. For some populations, legal permanent resident status does not guarantee immunity from the hazards of statelessness. For other populations, the nonimmigrant visa can function as a relatively privileged kind of legal status. Migration patterns for African, Caribbean, and European nationals provide a good introduction to these disparities.

Racial Disparities in Nonimmigrant Admissions

Over the past decade, the number of African and Caribbean nationals who became legal permanent residents has been slightly greater than the number of European nationals who became permanent residents (see table 2.4). This might seem surprising given the historic restrictions that the United States has imposed on the migration of black immigrants. Of course, the United States has done nothing to discourage migration from Europe. European migration flows have declined over the course of the twentieth century because there has been an overall decline of mass emigration from advanced industrialized European nations. Furthermore, U.S. immigration policy has incorporated some mechanisms, like the visa lottery program, that clearly privilege European nationals (Hing 2003, 93–114). These preferences seem to have been most successful in boosting the flow of European nonimmigrants. A major factor is the visa waiver program that allows noncitizens from designated nations to visit the

United States for up to ninety days without having to apply for a special visa. Notably, most of the designated nations included in this program are western European. The majority of nonimmigrants (who file I-94 forms) that enter the United States each year, do so by way of this program. But European nationals also figure prominently in every class of nonimmigrants, especially among professional-class nonimmigrant workers (see table 2.4). So although European nationals account for 14 percent of the annual growth of the permanent resident population, they comprise almost 40 percent of the total nonimmigrant flow.

For African and Caribbean nationals this pattern is completely reversed. These migrants are best represented in the annual growth of the permanent resident population (at 15 percent) but they are only 5 percent of the total nonimmigrant flow and are an even smaller minority of nonimmigrant workers. Recall that the nonimmigrant flow overshadows the annual growth of the immigrant population by a ratio of more than thirty to one. So the only place where black immigrants have achieved parity with European nationals is in a rather tiny sliver of the U.S. migration flow (which becomes even tinier, when considering that new arrivals account for no more than a third of the annual growth of the legal permanent resident population).

These statistics illustrate how nonimmigrant visas can be used to facilitate historic preferences in migrant recruitment.[29] Foreign nationals of European heritage have become an increasingly small share of the U.S. immigrant population. But they remain the single largest national origin group within a nonimmigrant flow that dwarfs the annual growth of the immigrant population.[30]

Connecting Admissions Disparities to Labor Market Disparities

There are other kinds of racial-ethnic disparities within the nonimmigrant flow that are more closely tied to selection processes that favor professional workers. For example, over 75 percent of all unauthorized migrants who entered the United States between 1998 and 2008 were Latin American nationals. In contrast, Latin American nationals account for only 34 percent of all persons who were granted legal permanent residence during this same period of time, and they are an even smaller share (20 percent) of the professional work visa population (see table 2.4).

TABLE 2.4 *Immigrants, Nonimmigrants, and Unauthorized Migrants by National Origin*

	Asian	Latin American	European	African & Caribbean
U.S. resident population[a]	13,549,064 (4.5%)	46,943,613 (15%)	199,491,458 (66%)	37,171,750 (12.2%)
Immigrants[b]	3,934,282 (34%)	3,953,114 (34%)	1,644,546 (14%)	1,727,833 (15%)
Nonimmigrants[c]	98,363,670 (25%)	102,654,494 (26%)	155,507,755 (39%)	19,762,175 (5%)
Unauthorized migrants[d]	1,300,000 (11%)	9,125,000 (77%)	525,000 (4.4%)	800,000 (6.7%)
Professional-class visa holders[e]	2,339,518 (29%)	1,633,148 (20%)	2,569,672 (29%)	335,608 (3.6%)

Source: U.S. resident population: *U.S. Census Population Estimates* 2008. Numbers for the European and African/Caribbean population are for the total non-Hispanic white and black populations respectively (without disaggregating recent immigrants from the native born). Immigrants: DHS 2009b, 1999a. Total for Latin American nations includes data for Mexico, Cuba, Central America, and South America. Estimates for the Caribbean exclude Cuba. Nonimmigrants: DHS 2009e, 1999c. Total for Latin American nations derived from data for Argentina, Belize, Bolivia, Brazil, Chile, Colombia, Costa Rica, Cuba, Ecuador, El Salvador, Guatemala, Honduras, Mexico, Nicaragua, Panama, Peru, and Venezuela. Estimates for the Caribbean exclude Cuba. Unauthorized migrants: Passel and Cohn 2009. Estimates of the European and African/Caribbean unauthorized population are inflated because this report treats European and Canadian unauthorized migrants as a single category. Also, all African unauthorized migrants were aggregated as part of an "other nations" category (300,000 persons). Professional class: DHS 1998, 1999b, 2000, 2001a, 2002, 2003, and 2004b. Total for Latin American nations derived from data for Argentina, Belize, Bolivia, Brazil, Chile, Colombia, Costa Rica, Cuba, Ecuador, El Salvador, Guatemala, Honduras, Mexico, Nicaragua, Panama, Peru, and Venezuela. Estimates for the Caribbean exclude Cuba.

[a] As of July 1, 2008; 2008 is the most current year in which national population has been made available (prior to the results of the 2010 census).

[b] H2 visa holders.

[c] Temporary visa holders, I-94 only, 1998–2009.

[d] As of 2008; 2008 is the most current year in which comprehensive national-origin data by region is available.

[e] For 1998–2004; this is the only period for which DHS provided data on specific visa categories cross-tabulated with national origin. Estimates include data for H1, L1, O, and P visas.

It is very telling that more Latin American nationals entered the United States as unauthorized migrants during this period than as legal immigrants. For immigration restrictionists this statistic would seem to offer a case for stronger border control, but it also draws attention to a historic reluctance to encourage legal migration from Latin America, and from Mexico in particular. The U.S.-Canada border has not been policed as intensively as the U.S.-Mexico border, despite the fact that it is more than three times the size of the U.S.-Mexico border.[31] U.S. policies on Mexican immigration have also been much more restrictive than those of other liberal, democratic societies that share a common border. For example, the transferable political, social, and civil rights that are extended to the citizens of all European Union member states would be unthinkable at the present time as a framework for U.S.-Mexico relations (Gelatt 2005). All of this underscores the defensive posture that the United States has taken toward Latin American immigration.

This defensive posture also becomes apparent when comparing migration trends for the two largest racial-ethnic segments of the U.S. migration flow; Latin Americans and Asians. Given the geographic proximity of North and South America, the emphasis of U.S. immigration policy on family reunification and the fact that the U.S. Latino population is three times larger than the U.S. Asian population, one might expect that Latin American nationals would have a natural advantage over Asian nationals in attaining legal permanent residence. However, this "advantage" only seems to have been realized in unauthorized migrant flows from Latin America, which are seven times larger than the Asian unauthorized migrant flow. In contrast, the number of Asian nationals who became legal permanent residents between 2000 and 2008 was equivalent to the growth of the Latin American legal permanent resident population (see table 2.4).

So although the U.S. Asian population is much smaller than the Latino population, it is made up of a much larger proportion of legal residents. And the number of Asian nationals who enter the United States as professional-class migrant workers is almost 50 percent higher than for Latin American nationals (see table 2.4). This disparity is an important part of the explanation for the relatively fast growth of the Asian legal permanent resident population. Professional-class visas holders are granted options to adjust to permanent resident status (and to migrate with dependents) that are denied to other nonimmigrants. It is still possible for racial constructions of Asians to inform the way they are treated by employers and the U.S. security apparatus (Banerjee 2010; Ibrahim 2005; Sheikh 2008). Even so, the concentration of Asian migrants in the skilled guestworker population offers some protection from the kinds of legal hazards that are experienced more routinely by unauthorized Latino migrants.

It would be difficult to explain this disparity as being influenced by a racial preference for Asian nationals, given the long history of anti-Asian bias in U.S. immigration policy. It does illustrate, however, that the current demand for professional-class workers is more powerful than the historic tendency of U.S. immigration policy to reserve its most severe exclusions for Asian migrants. Conversely, the slow growth of the Latino permanent resident population should be viewed in light of the reasons why this population has become a convenient source of illegalized, low-wage labor for many U.S. employers.

Criminalization as a Route to Statelessness

African and Caribbean nationals are in a distinctly different position than Asian or Latin American nationals. Instead of being overrepresented in the upper or lower tiers of the migrant labor market, they are conspicuously underrepresented in the entire of pool of temporary migrant workers (including professional-class guests workers and "illegals"). These migrants are also more concentrated in the ranks of the legal permanent resident population than any other national origin group. Even so, it does not appear that black immigrants are privileged by their concentration in the permanent resident population but that their migration flows are mostly restricted to this population. By comparison, Asian and European nationals have more options to enter the United States—as immigrants or nonimmigrants.

If these disparities are indicative of a systemic bias against black migrants, it is of a very different order from the process whereby Latin American nationals are incorporated into the United States as a stigmatized, low-wage workforce. It would appear that black migrants are not being granted the same "opportunity" to enter into the stateless dilemma of the low-wage guest worker or the professional-class visa overstayer. However, black migrants *are* deported for criminal reasons at a rate that is unsurpassed by any other racial-ethnic group.[32] These kinds of deportation proceedings can target legal permanent residents—which is the segment of the noncitizen population in which black migrants are the most concentrated. It is even possible for deportation proceedings to be carried out against naturalized citizens.

In 2004 Lionel Jean-Baptiste, a Haitian American, became the first naturalized citizen in several decades to be deported for criminal reasons.[33] Although a rarity, Jean-Baptiste's trial was important because federal prosecutors thought it could be used as a test case that would prepare the way for future deportation proceedings involving naturalized citizens. In this regard, the Jean-Baptiste case sent a signal that the threshold of deportability could be extended deeper into the black foreign-born population.

Jean-Baptiste's predicament illustrates a kind of statelessness that immigrant rights activists have described as "delegalization"; the use of criminal convictions to strip migrants of their legal status for the purpose of deportation (Kateel and Shahani 2008). The end goal of this process is removal as an end in and of itself. This is a very different kind of statelessness than that of the nonimmigrant who can be treated as a desirable but disposable asset. It is also different from unauthorized migrants who remain deportable, even as they are coercively integrated into the bottom tiers of the labor market. The statelessness of those persons is defined by their inability to secure a permanent legal status. Criminalized noncitizens can become stateless even after they acquire (what they thought was) a secure legal status.

The irony of Jean-Baptiste's situation is that he was formally recognized as a stateless person after he was ordered to be deported because the Haitian state objected to his repatriation.[34] Jean-Baptiste truly became a man without a country. But this condition of de jure statelessness was prefigured by a condition of de facto statelessness that placed Jean-Baptiste at greater risk of losing his legal status than most foreign-born persons.

PERMUTATIONS OF STATELESSNESS

It is possible to view statelessness as a transitional phase in the evolution of citizenship. From this optimistic perspective, it could be argued that the hazards of statelessness will eventually be eliminated as the inequities and inconsistencies of national law are supplemented by an emerging system of postnational legal statuses and global human rights (see Bosniak 2000; Soysal 1998). In this chapter, however, I describe a kind of statelessness that calls attention to the limits of this postnational vision. Some populations are, indeed, benefiting from a privileged kind of migrant mobility that allows them to travel freely across national borders and claim multiple nationalities. But for migrants who are most vulnerable to the hazards of statelessness, global migration is a much more precarious venture that reinscribes the importance of national citizenship (see Koopmans and Statham 1999)—even though this safeguard has been placed further out of reach by policies that have made the nonimmigrant visa the primary gateway for entry to the United States.

This kind of statelessness is not isomorphic with the nonimmigrant visa. Noncitizens do not become stateless simply by virtue of being granted a visa. They enter into a condition of de facto statelessness when they attempt to use this visa as a probationary legal status that could pave the way to legal permanent residence. If this labyrinth of legal statuses is poorly navigated (or if the nonimmigrant simply has a stroke of bad luck in dealing with a difficult administrator) the nonimmigrant enters into a condition of "illegality"—a more dire kind of statelessness.

There is no available data that comprehensively describes how many nonimmigrants have their visa renewal applications, applications for permanent status, or applications for another kind of visa status rejected each year. But the ratio of nonimmigrant arrivals to nonimmigrant adjustees (which is on the order of fifty to one) indicates that this is probably a sizable figure.[35] And assuming that visa overstayers comprise up to 40 percent of the growth of the undocumented population, then it is likely that, over the past decade, at least one hundred thousand nonimmigrants "became illegal" each year.[36] To get a truly comprehensive picture of the number of nonimmigrants who are in legal limbo, it would be necessary to count the number of nonimmigrants who entered the United States with the intent to settle and are still living with a temporary visa *and* the number of nonimmigrants who have lost their status and joined the ranks of the undocumented population.

Not surprisingly government statistics cannot provide an accurate count of this population. In many respects, the purpose of these statistics is not simply to describe an objective reality but to validate the discursive

categories of the state and the governing stratagem in which these categories are embedded. Nevertheless, these statistics can be used to examine
the changes in the legal-administrative categories that the state uses to
represent the wider world to itself. This is largely what I have attempted
to do in this chapter. For example, my comparison of immigrant and nonimmigrant flows (figure 2.1) and adjustees versus new arrivals (figure 2.2)
documents changes in the way that the state is categorizing migrant flows.
The statistics in table 2.1 (which show the inflow of temporary workers
eclipsing the growth of the immigrant population) also shed light on the
relationship between the state's immigration policies and labor market
practices.

The main goal of this chapter is to outline some of these trends and
permutations, in the way that the government has been classifying and
regulating the nonimmigrant flow. In this regard, it focuses on the outcomes of the state's regulatory strategies. The next chapter takes a closer
look at the paradigm of governance that has guided these practices. The
goal of this discussion is to examine a form of state power that shapes the
law but also operates outside the confines of the law. This form of power
is related to the kind of statelessness described in this chapter. Consider,
once again, the case of Lionel Jean-Baptiste.

The legal context for Jean-Baptiste's detainment was established by
federal laws that expanded the range of criminal violations that could
trigger deportation proceedings. But the ability of the courts to strip a
foreign-born person of his citizenship was not stipulated in any of these
laws. In fact, current legal precedent protects naturalized citizens from
deportation. Nevertheless, Jean-Baptiste's deportation was made possible
by the discretionary authority of an immigration court judge who—in ac-
cordance with the arguments of federal prosecutors—reasoned that the
crime for which Jean-Baptiste was being deported had been committed
prior to his obtaining citizenship. According to the judge, Jean-Baptiste's
oath of citizenship was invalid because when he took this oath he falsely
claimed that he had no outstanding criminal charges against him (despite
the fact that Jean-Baptiste was not charged with drug trafficking until
after his naturalization hearing).[37]

The aggressiveness of the prosecution against Jean-Baptiste should
also be viewed in light of the U.S. government's longstanding concern
for discouraging Haitian asylum seekers. (Jean-Baptiste originally en-

tered the United States as a political asylum seeker, fleeing the Duvalier regime.) Throughout the 1980s, the United States used more restrictive standards for processing Haitian asylum seekers than for Cuban asylum seekers (Lennox 2003; Loescher and Scanlan 1984). The Clinton and Bush administrations (1992–2008) both developed special protocols that were designed to prevent a further mass exodus of Haitian refugees. These programs were part of a broader continuity of Haitian-focused interdiction and deportation practices that began in the early 1970s.[38]

The common thread connecting these practices is that they were guided by the discretionary authority of the executive office that, at the time, was occupied by the 2000–2008 Bush administration. Because the U.S. immigration system is managed by executive appointees, the deportation proceedings against Lionel Jean-Baptiste were subject to the oversight of the executive office. The judge who heard Jean-Baptiste's case was a Bush appointee, and it is likely that he was influenced by the interest that federal enforcement took in the case.[39] So even though Jean-Baptiste was a naturalized citizen on paper, he was effectively treated as a noncitizen who had never been naturalized. As such, he assumed the status of a person who had lost the right to have rights. This kind of reasoning is characteristic of how sovereign authority has been used to reshape the law.

3

THE SECRET LIFE
OF THE STATE

In 1905 Theodore Roosevelt issued a series of policy statements that were designed to resolve a heated debate over Asian immigration (Beale 1956, 192–199). Although immigration debates are often influenced, at some level, by concerns about the cultural or racial difference of newcomers, this debate was squarely focused on the question of race. In particular, it was focused on the future of the Asian exclusions that had been introduced to U.S. immigration policy in the late 1800s that were due to expire in 1904.[1] Given Roosevelt's many public statements on the danger of "race suicide,"[2] it is likely that the coalition of immigration restrictionists and eugenicists who were seeking to extend the Asian exclusions felt that they had an ally in the president. They would be disappointed.

Roosevelt was remarkably pragmatic in his efforts to appease both pro- and anti-immigration interests. His policy solution streamlined the flow of Asian students and professional-class persons into the United States but upheld race-based exclusions that would effect less-educated laborers. Roosevelt's decision affirmed the legitimacy of enforcement practices such as those authorized by the Supreme Court's 1893 *Fong Yue Ting* decision, which allowed U.S. citizens to assist in the identification and deportation of Asian nationals who were suspected of residing in the United States without authorization.[3] But on the other hand, it exempted Asian

professionals from all immigration exclusions and even encouraged federal agencies to be more expeditious in processing the legal paperwork
for these persons, even if there were suspicions about the legitimacy of
these documents.

Despite Roosevelt's efforts at liberalizing admission procedures for
(some) Asian migrants, U.S. relations with China and Japan continued to
sour. Meanwhile, the political winds driving immigration policy were still
dominated by restrictionist sentiments, culminating in the 1921 and 1924
Immigration Acts. Nevertheless, Roosevelt's solution to the "Asian controversy" was remarkable in the way that it foreshadowed the direction U.S.
immigration policy would take over the course of the twentieth century.

Roosevelt's 1905 policy decisions can be viewed as a rough sketch of
the priorities that would come to shape a bifurcated immigration policy
regime; one that is more or less welcoming to immigrants who are recruited into the more privileged employment sectors of the U.S. economy,
while reserving its most severe exclusions for migrants who are tracked
into low-wage employment sectors. This system is more nuanced than it
first appears. One of its most obvious effects is the way that it reinforces
class stratification, by recruiting migrants under conditions in which low-
wage workers have much weaker social, political, and civil rights than migrants who are recruited as professional-class workers.

But if one looks closer at U.S. immigration policy, it is apparent that the
systemic disparities in the way it has treated "laborers" versus "professionals" have also been accompanied by a great many exceptions. In some
cases, professional-class migrants are treated much worse than (or no different than) unauthorized migrants. Japanese professionals who entered
the United States as a relatively privileged class of immigrants in the early
1900s could still be rounded into detention camps a few decades later
after the bombing of Pearl Harbor. Arab-Muslim civic organizations composed of middle- and upper-class professionals who had been courted by
presidential candidates were shunned as possible terrorist sympathizers
and heavily scrutinized by immigration enforcement after the attacks of
September 11, 2001.[4]

These incidents can be viewed through the lens of racialized anxieties
that are specific to the way that the Asian/Easterner has been constructed
in the Western imagination. But they are also products of a legal-adminis-

trative system that is capable of reshaping its policies toward any migrant group within a fairly short period of time. So the flexibility that makes it possible for the immigration system to develop different practices for managing lower skilled and higher skilled migrant workers is the very same capacity that makes it possible for the immigration system to treat professional-class migrants as dangerous Others when this treatment seems to be warranted by emergency conditions.

This flexibility is not unique to the immigration system. It should be situated in light of political developments that, from the nineteenth century onward, have steadily increased the discretionary authority of the executive office. From this vantage point, the most significant feature of Roosevelt's 1905 policy decisions is that they were issued as presidential executive orders that were used to circumvent the Congress—precisely because Roosevelt knew that his exemptions for Asian professionals would not survive a public vote.[5] Theodore Roosevelt has been described as the first modern president because of his extensive use of executive orders as a governing stratagem, setting a precedent that has been followed by subsequent administrations (Barber 1998; Burton 1997).

In the remainder of the chapter I briefly review the expansion of executive authority within the U.S. presidency and explain how this expanded authority has been used to craft immigration policy. One goal of this discussion is to shed more light on the political and institutional dynamics that have shaped the policy priorities described in chapter 2. Free market principles have had a significant influence on immigration policy. This influence is especially apparent when looking at the policy preferences of the executive office. However, the imperatives of neoclassical or neoliberal economics do not, in and of themselves, explain the process whereby political authority becomes increasingly centralized in the executive office. In many respects, classical liberal theory is stridently opposed to the expansion of government authority. Nevertheless, over the course of the twentieth century, the process of market expansion has been orchestrated by an executive office that has been able to deregulate, precisely because of the power it is able to wield over the law—and over other branches of government. This political process has a rather curious history. It has been fueled by several different ideological orientations, some of which can be traced to discourses on sovereign rule that gave rise to the modern nation state, and others that have been credited with (or accused of) dismantling and transcending the nation-state. The one strategic orientation that all of these agendas have in common is the creation of an authority that is capable of transforming the law and making exceptions to the law, so that it can better realize the "spirit" of the law.

ON NECESSITY, REVOLUTION, AND THE MODERN STATE

The law of the state, as ideally conceived, is a self-referential and internally consistent body of rulings. It is an ordered space wherein the actions of all persons—regardless of title or rank—are subject to the oversight of the law, and every decree is justified by prior legal precedent. The special powers of the executive office, on the other hand, are supposed to regulate those unpredictable circumstances that have not been adequately anticipated by the law. Like the foreigner/newcomer, these are phenomena that are alien to the law, things that hail from a wider unknown. When faced with these sorts of challenges, the law does not preserve itself by looking to its own precedent. To handle the exceptional circumstance, the executive office develops strategies that do not have to conform to the normal rule of law.

In his discussion of the recent political history of executive authority, Giorgio Agamben explains how the authority to make exceptions to the law is often grounded in a discourse on necessity. Citing the Italian jurist Romano, Agamben observes that "necessity" can be regarded as a "state of affairs that, at least as a rule and in a complete and practical effective way, cannot be regulated by previously established norms" (Agamben 2005, 27). This formulation leads Romano to observe that actions carried out under conditions of dire necessity cannot be bound by the law. But Agamben also notes that this sets the stage for an alternative paradigm for interpreting the law that becomes integrated within the practice of the law (Agamben 2005, 1–31). These exceptions to the law are guided by their own particular kind of ordering logic. They might appear to be alien from the perspective of conventional jurisprudence, but from the perspective of the executive office, they are guided by their own norms and precedents.

This is the point where the rationale for the exertion of executive authority over the law turns to the revolutionary movement for its inspiration. As Agamben explains, "the state of exception . . . appears (alongside revolution and the de facto establishment of a constitutional system) as an 'illegal' but perfectly 'juridical and constitutional' measure that is realized in the production of new norms" (Agamben 2005, 28).[6] The French Revolution and its aftermath serve as an apt example of this process.[7] The Revolution is not simply distinguished by its opposition to the legal-juridical structures of the state. It also represents a qualitatively different paradigm-of-law, which subordinates legal continuity to a concern for adapting the law to a new vision of society . Instead of viewing the law as something that must be preserved, the Revolution treats it as a transformative instrument that must be evaluated according to the effects it produces. Although this may appear to be a rather instrumentalist view of the law, it is also highly ideological since the desired effects, and the necessity of producing these effects, are defined by the revolutionary agenda.

Under these conditions, the revolutionary ideology becomes the sole measure of the law. Because the law has been decomposed into a fluid array of revisable guidelines, it is not possible for the law to justify itself. The transformation of the law must be justified according to a value system that is viewed as the only true source of the legitimacy of the law. Of course, it is always possible to interpret the revolutionary ideology in any number of ways—as evidenced by the bitter factionalism that has marked all modern political movements. This problem is resolved by allowing the interpretation of the revolutionary ideology to become the exclusive preserve of a single leader or central committee, which for all practical purposes serves as the executive office of the movement.[8] Hence the transformative agenda of the movement requires a constant restructuring of the law to new conditions, and this process is guided by the underlying principles of the movement as interpreted by the executive.

This is just one interpretation of the relationship between revolution and necessity. Michel Foucault has provided another significantly different account that is connected to his analysis of the rise of the neoliberal state. In his discussion on the birth of biopolitics, Foucault associates the imperative of necessity with raison d'etat,[9] which he traces to a form of governance that originates in the feudal era and is a direct expression of the monarch's sovereign authority. In contrast to Agamben, Foucault argues that revolutionary movements attempted to strengthen the rule of law. Instead of rewriting the law, Foucault notes that they often tried to improve the enforcement of existing laws and juridical norms in order to check the discretionary authority of the sovereign (Foucault 2008, 27–50).

These differences between Agamben and Foucault are not as insurmountable as they first appear.[10] They also shed light on what is most distinctive about Agamben's discussion and what it contributes to the analysis of state power. Foucault has admitted that he was not concerned with examining the way that "governor's really governed" but with analyzing "government's consciousness of itself" (Foucault 2008, 2). As such, his analyses explored the discourses that were used to make the art of governing intelligible to those who practiced it, which leads Foucault to examine the government's idealized conception of itself.

Agamben, in contrast, uses the rationale of necessity to examine those features of modern governance that fall outside of this idealized conception. According to Foucault, the use of discretionary authority stems from a paradigm of sovereign rule that precedes the disciplinary orientation of modern governance (Foucault 2007, 333–362; 2008, 27–50). Agamben, on the other hand, observes that the use of this discretionary authority (by way of emergency measures and the "state of exception") persists under the modern state, regardless. The main difference is that under the Ancien Regime this discretionary authority was explicitly understood to be a legitimate exercise of state power. For the modern state, this kind of power becomes a kind of repressed knowledge that the government has of itself. It is a form of power that the state continually resorts to using, even though it is not supposed to be a principal feature of modern governance—which explains why these governing practices must be rationalized as exceptions to "normal governance."

It is also very telling that, in Agamben's account, the jurists of the early modern nation-state want to discover the imperative of necessity within the revolutionary movement. This "discovery" helps to legitimate the discourse on necessity as an extralegal principle that is born alongside the eruption of modern nationalism. So, despite the difficult questions it raises about due process, democracy, and state power, the discourse on necessity can at least be portrayed as something that is more or less unique to modern governance. The more troubling possibility (which Agamben explores in *Homer Sacer* [1995]) is that this discourse on necessity has a political lineage that is much older than this, which complicates many of the myths that the modern nation-state, and liberal democracy in particular, has spun about itself.

To the extent that this is acknowledged, it becomes apparent that there is a forbidden continuity that connects the power practices of modern governments to those of the feudal monarchy. This could mean that modern governments are not quite as modern as we have imagined, or (as Foucault has suggested) that the foundations of modern governance can actually be traced to the feudal era. In any event, the analysis of this form of state power requires the government to be interrogated from the vantage point of its actual practices and not its idealized conception of itself.

Continuity, however, does not mean isomorphism. The state of exception may not be unique to present-day, liberal democracies, but this does not mean that, through an act of vulgar reductionism, the governing strategies of these state systems should be understood as being derivative of a feudal-era paradigm of state power. An argument can certainly be made that the modern liberal state has left its own distinct imprimatur on the state of exception. As Agamben has observed, the state of exception has been routinized by liberal democracies in ways that have made it almost indistinguishable from the normal practice of government. Hence, it could be argued that the state of exception—and the sovereignty to which it refers—has been subjected to the same techniques of normalization that Foucault has associated with the exercise of biopower. And the U.S. government has used this form of power in ways that are very different from that of the feudal monarch. It is not just a form of power that is exerted by a sovereign power over its subjects, but an array of techniques that government uses to act on itself.

THE EXPANSION OF EXECUTIVE AUTHORITY UNDER THE MODERN PRESIDENCY

Agamben observes that the Civil War is the first occasion when the state of emergency sets the tone for the governing paradigm of the U.S. executive office (Agamben 2005, .20–21). A primary example is the Emancipation Proclamation. The proclamation was issued by President Lincoln in his capacity as commander in chief and, as such, did not require ratification by Congress. These circumstances have led historians to interpret Lincoln's motives in a rather cynical manner, especially since the proclamation did not free slave populations in states that were loyal to the Union. It is possible to interpret the Emancipation Proclamation entirely through the lens of a military strategy that is used to deprive the Confederate states of a key segment of their labor force, as well as making it possible to enlist freed slaves in the Union Army (McPherson 2002, 108–109).

If it is argued too strongly, this interpretation runs the risk of creating a false divide between the strategic utility of the Emancipation Proclamation and Lincoln's abolitionist ideals.[11] The military-strategic context certainly constrained the scope of Lincoln's decision.[12] Nevertheless, it is possible to see how the abolitionist agenda was radically expedited by the strategic goals of the proclamation. Only under the conditions of a wartime presidency was Congress willing to grant Lincoln free rein to make unilateral decisions of this magnitude. Through his role as commander in chief, Lincoln was able to circumvent the political influence of southern planters in the halls of Congress. These same conditions made it possible for abolitionists to influence U.S. policy by capturing the ear of a single decider.

This dynamic, where emergency conditions set the stage for an ambitious reformist agenda, resurfaces in subsequent presidencies. Theodore Roosevelt has been hailed as the first modern president for precisely these reasons. One of the most important features of the paradigm shift initiated by Roosevelt is that the executive office begins to use its discretionary authority in an active, creative way, and not merely to manage temporal crises. Roosevelt frequently issued executive orders in the absence of a formally declared state of emergency (Dodds 2003). In these situations, the executive office is no longer reacting to unforeseen, calamitous events. It begins to craft the definition of "emergency conditions" in ways that complement its ideology, strategic interests, and specific policy objectives.

One counterintuitive result of this process is that it allows executive discretionary authority to become more invisible even as it becomes more expansive. The executive order is a rather crude expression of executive authority. The advantage of the executive order is that it allows the president to act swiftly, creating special commissions and making ad hoc policy decisions that do not require ratification from any other branch of government. But this is also a rather conspicuous use of power in which executive authority appears as something that is clearly distinct from the formal body of law. As a result, these sorts of executive decisions are often viewed as being supplemental to the law. They are pragmatic responses to unforeseen circumstances that should be largely consistent with existing legal precedent or, at least, should only take the form of a temporary interruption of prior legal precedent. The classic form of this kind of authority is the state of emergency that introduces special measures that take effect under the suspension of the law and expire once the rule of law is reestablished.

But this is not always what occurs. Policy decisions made during a state of emergency can be used to introduce changes that become a permanent feature of the law. The Emancipation Proclamation is a primary case in point. Franklin Delano Roosevelt's New Deal programs provide an even better illustration. In that case, executive discretionary authority, operating under a wartime, state of emergency, was used to develop an entirely new structure of governance, new social programs, and a legal-fiscal infrastructure of funding streams, taxation strategies, and public laws—laying the groundwork for the postwar liberal welfare state that lasted until the 1970s (Agamben 2005, .21–22; Reagan 2000). The due process exceptions and surveillance powers authorized by the USA PATRIOT Act provide a radically different example of a similar dynamic.[13] In this case, legislation enacted by the Congress acted in consort with executive decisions that were being used to expand the enforcement powers of the state during a formally declared state of emergency. So instead of merely suspending the law, executive authority sets priorities that are imitated and reinforced by the law. For example, many of the special surveillance powers expanded by the PATRIOT Act were initially intended as temporary measures that could be renewed at the discretion of the Congress (Etzioni 2004). In this regard, the law begins to operate in a manner that is not very different from a state of emergency, except in this case, the law interrupts itself. The "temporary" weakening of civil and legal rights is imposed by the law—rather than by an executive order that imposes itself on the law—which allows these interruptions to become routinized within the law, establishing a legal precedent that can be used to justify other kinds of interruptions. It also bears noting that this process is still amenable to the discretionary authority of the executive office. In its first year in office, for example, the Obama administration used its executive powers to renew the surveillance powers authorized by the PATRIOT Act and actually extended these powers in new directions (by exempting the federal government from being sued by U.S. residents for breaches of civil liberties that were connected to the use of its surveillance powers).[14]

Through these sorts of maneuvers it is possible for executive power to shape the law instead of merely interrupting the law. These sorts of maneuvers do not necessarily take shape as secret conspiracies that are hatched by the executive office to manipulate or circumvent other branches of government. The legislature is often willing to grant these discretionary powers to the executive office, even though it may later question the way those powers were used. Whether it is the Civil War–era Lincoln administration, the World War II–era Roosevelt administration, or the post-9/11-era Bush administration, the Congress has typically ceded authority to the executive office when the executive office demands it. Moreover, presidents who claim these special powers often do so with popular support, even though the public is never called on to formally ratify the expanded authority granted to the executive office. Theodore Roosevelt demonstrated a keen understanding of this process when observing that the American people were in need of a "benevolent czar," and as some historians have argued, this is a very revealing insight into how Roosevelt crafted his public persona and conducted himself as president (Genovese 2001, 11).

In this respect, Roosevelt was a classic example of a charismatic leader. But these expanded executive powers have become an institutional feature of the office itself rather than being a kind of authority that can only be wielded by especially gifted politicians. This process has also produced a subtle but very significant change within the national political culture. Classical liberal theories of the public sphere root the conscience of the nation in the civic sphere, which must continually check the authority of the government (Almond and Verba 1989; J. Cohen and Arato 1994). In contrast, the modern presidency bears witness to the rise of an executive office that plays an increasingly decisive role in defining the national identity for an awaiting public. The "nation" becomes a discourse on collective identity that is represented to the general public by the state, even as the workings of the state become more abstracted from the popular view of the nation.[15] On one hand, the executive office begins to play a more decisive role, as architect of the national identity, and on the other hand, it plays a leading role in orchestrating the restructuring of the global economy and plugging the "national idea" into this globalized terrain—both of these objectives being facilitated by its expanded discretionary authority. A very good illustration of this process is the program of neoliberal restructuring that has been advanced by the executive office from the 1980s onward.

"POPULIST REBELLION" AND THE NEOLIBERAL STATE

The social programs initiated under the administration of Franklin Delano Roosevelt took shape in an era in which the strong state was the rule. FDR's New Deal programs operated within the framework of the liberal welfare model that has historically defined U.S. social policy, but relative to what existed before, they were a decisive step toward a larger welfare state.[16]

The postwar liberal welfare state was "revolutionary" in the way that it converted the national idea into an economic development project guided by the firm hand of the executive office. In contrast, the governing agenda of recent administrations has been defined by economic neoliberalism.[17] Thus far, I have used the terms neoliberal, laissez-faire, and free market interchangeably, because they describe a similar set of market-oriented, policy priorities. But for the purpose of this discussion, neoliberalism is better understood as a particular, historical manifestation of these priorities.

It is important to note that the liberal welfare state of the mid-twentieth century was not orchestrated in opposition to free market principles. One of the explicit goals of its public welfare programs was to strengthen the social legitimacy of the market-based economy by granting most U.S. residents a minimum degree of protection from the economic downturns that could be produced by these forces (Piven and Cloward 1971, .80–112). By the late 1970s this imperative of shoring up the legitimacy of the market economy was displaced by a new emphasis on improving the competitiveness of the United States in the global market place. As a consequence, federal policy focused on producing a more productive working population and scaling back regulations that were blamed for restricting the wealth-producing capacity of investors and corporations.

But despite its rhetoric of scaling back government, this new paradigm of government did not literally reduce the size of the state. As some scholars have pointed out, the neoliberal state deepened its connections with the corporate sector, continued to expand its own federal bureaucracy, created a new legal-policy infrastructure that has guided the process of market expansion, and subsidized this process with tax dollars.[18] In this regard, the neoliberal state has been no less interventionist than the liberal welfare state of the Cold War-era, even though it has channeled its interventions in a different direction. Notably, many of these interventions have been focused on dismantling the policies and programs of the postwar liberal welfare state.

Under neoliberalism, the state enters into a cold war of sorts with its own institutional structures. The executive office uses its authority to weaken and restructure government agencies whose legacy mandates are antithetical to its policy agenda.[19] The downsizing of welfare programs and spending cuts for education and health services (among others) are framed as efforts to reduce the size of government in the interest of the tax-paying citizens (Segal and Kilty 2006; Kretsedemas and Aparicio 2004). The casualization of labor markets (including the softening of wage standards and worker rights) and the deregulation of trade and investment flows are also framed as efforts to roll back government control in order to stimulate a more robust kind of economic growth (Harvey 2005).

In this context, the executive office can position itself, curiously enough, as a force that is alien to the government. Although the executive office clearly has a commanding role within the government, recent administrations (from the 1980s onward) have tended to portray themselves as outsiders that seek to transform the government in the interest of the average citizen. Ronald Reagan, who is widely regarded as the first president of the neoliberal era, was very adept at cultivating this persona—of the populist reformer. The Reagan tax revolt, which he presided over as governor of California, helped to solidify this persona and set the stage for the maverick demeanor that Reagan skillfully adopted as president (Rogin 1988).

This sort of symbolic politics sets the stage for a very different way of legitimizing the use of extralegal, executive authority. Instead of behaving like a benevolent czar—in the vein of Theodore Roosevelt (and, arguably, FDR)—the executive office establishes a surreptitious fraternal bond with the voting populace.[20] The executive relates to the electorate as a co-conspirator in its war against big government, which is often portrayed as an overbearing maternal figure (i.e., the "nanny state"). This war against big government has been accompanied by a coded racial and gendered discourse that equates government spending on social programs with an undeserving black underclass (Gilens 2000; Neubeck and Cazenave 2001; Kelley 1998). One of the most powerful messages sent by this coded discourse is that the downsizing of social programs and entitlements will not effect the average person. These social programs are depicted as a corrupt patronage system that benefits minorities, whose use of these programs actually depletes the rights and resources of the average voter. This sets the stage for an ambitious restructuring project that seeks to dismantle these programs in the interest of fiscal and social responsibility. And in order to do this, it is necessary for the executive to be given free rein to craft and reshape the law. Hence, the expansion of executive power over the legislative and judicial branches of government is portrayed as an exercise in reducing the size of government—not as the further consolidation of the very form of centralized control that the executive office appears to be railing against.

Because of its emphasis on decentralization, privatization, and deregulation, the neoliberal discourse on governance has, arguably, been the most effective in distracting attention from this "forbidden continuity" that runs through the governing practices of all recent, U.S. administrations. The size of the federal bureaucracy and the expansion of executive authority have grown in tandem with each other throughout the course of the twentieth century—and the past thirty years of neoliberal governance have been no exception to this trend.[21] So although neoliberalism has facilitated this process, it does not suffice as an explanation of it. The argument that this expansion of executive authority is unique to liberal, capitalist economies is also not entirely convincing, though economists have observed that societies with market-based economies tend to have bigger state systems (Rodrik 1998).

One of the most compelling (and controversial) aspects of Agamben's argument about executive authority is how it traverses governments with radically different ideological orientations. In this regard, Agamben treats the expansion of executive authority as a political process that has become inextricably bound up with modern governance—and not to a particular ideological articulation of these governing practices. Agamben points out, for example, that the entire reign of the German Nazi party took place under the auspices of a "state of exception." Even so, the Third Reich merely expanded on precedents concerning the use of executive author- ity that had been established by prior liberal democratic administrations (Agamben 2005, 14–16). The lesson to learn from this sequence of events is not that expanded executive authority necessarily leads to fascism, but rather that it is not unique to fascism. Executive authority can continue to expand, in a linear direction, even as the ideologies of governing admin- istrations swing back and forth between liberal welfarism, neoliberalism, national socialism, democratic socialism, or even communism.[22]

Nevertheless, it can be argued that neoliberalism has left its own dis- tinct mark on the ongoing transformation of executive authority. The ex- pansion of executive authority under recent U.S. administrations has not only been characterized by a different kind of symbolic politics but also by real changes in the way this authority has been deployed. The execu- tive order is still an important part of the arsenal of these administrations. Even so, many aspects of neoliberal restructuring have been channeled through the law rather than through executive orders. Notable examples include the legislative acts that deregulated the telecommunications in- dustry, the financial sector, and the social service sector.[23] This legislation was also guided by other more fluid negotiations—between the executive office, the legislature, and multinational corporations—which took place outside of a formal deliberative process that was open to public oversight.

Just as the judicial system relies on informal plea bargains to expedite the formal sentencing process, the legislative system has always relied on backroom negotiations to expedite its deliberations. It is significant, however, that from the 1980s onward, these kinds of deliberations were pushed further outside the bounds of government. One of the primary vehicles for doing this is expanding the role of private corporations in shaping and implementing public policy. As Saskia Sassen has explained, these strategies do not literally transfer decision making authority from the public to the private sphere. Instead, they allow the government to privatize specific aspects of its own decision making—further removing these decisions from public oversight (Sassen 2007, 45–96). For example, government services may be contracted out to private corporations. But these corporations may be headed by individuals who formerly held government posts and who are involved in public-private sector planning projects that have been initiated by the executive office or by nongovernment agencies. As a result, the line between the public and private sector begins to blur. Furthermore, the network of bureaucrats, corporate heads, intellectuals, pundits, and others who craft neoliberal policies are partly embedded in the public sphere and are still capable of influencing public policy while remaining relatively independent of the regulations and authority structures of the public sector.

This situation draws attention to another distinguishing feature of the expansion of executive authority under neoliberalism. Although neoliberal policies tend to expand the discretionary authority of the executive office, they do not expand only the authority of the executive office, and this process is not always centrally controlled by the executive office. The executive office is just one node within a chain of influence that extends into the corporate sector. Furthermore, the effect of deregulation and federal devolution is to create spaces of decision-making authority—which free the individual from binding legalities—that can be granted to a variety of private and public actors. Private corporations are given more freedom to relocate their manufacturing centers and recruit (and terminate) workers as needed; financial institutions are given more freedom to develop speculative investment strategies; state legislators and frontline case workers are given more discretion in interpreting and implementing welfare policy; and so forth.

Quite often, the expansion of discretionary authority and the weakening of regulatory controls have been supported by acts of Congress. The net effect, however, is to grant more actors the ability to make decisions that are conditioned by the imperative of necessity—adapting one's decisions to unfolding contingencies rather than predefined rules and regulations.

In this regard, neoliberalism can be said to convert the exceptional powers of the executive office into a normal feature of the law and disburses these powers to an unprecedented array of actors. Within the context of the government, the president remains the ultimate decider. But the expanded power of the presidency is also parceled out to others who have a share in the discretionary authority that the executive office wields over the law.

EXECUTIVE AUTHORITY, GLOBALIZATION, AND IMMIGRATION POLICY

The political process I describe extends to immigration policy. It also bears noting that there has always been a special relationship between immigration policy and the discretionary authority of the executive office. Because the immigration system falls under the direct oversight of the executive office it is amenable to the prerogatives of executive authority. Although the immigration system is accountable to the immigration laws enacted by Congress, the interpretation of these laws is often carried out by judges and administrators directly appointed by the executive office. As a result, important policy decisions can be routinely shaped by negotiations that take place outside of the legislative process.

Consider U.S. policy on refugee resettlement, which has been shaped as much by the diplomacy of the U.S. executive office as by the legislative acts of Congress. Examples include the arrangements that the Clinton administration made with the Jamaican government to process Haitian asylum seekers in Jamaican waters (Subcommittee on International Law, Immigration, and Refugees 1994), the Bush administration's subsequent executive orders aimed specifically at deterring a mass exodus of Haitian refugees to the shores of South Florida (Wasem 2005), and the multifarious reasons that have led the U.S. government to award temporary protected status to foreign nationals fleeing political persecution and natural disasters (Wasem and Ester 2008).

In all of these cases, the executive office is not merely defining the rights that particular categories of noncitizens have under the law, it is also making decisions about whether particular categories of noncitizens have the right to have rights. At what point—or to what extent—can these persons be said to fall under the jurisdiction of U.S. law? Post-9/11 anti-terrorist investigations show just how indeterminate this process can be. Suspects can be removed from the normal protections of law and held for

secret reasons in secret locations, and these same individuals can be returned to the law, sometimes without being charged with a single criminal or civil violation (Cole 2000a; Ifitikhar 2008).

Researchers sometimes make the assumption that these sorts of practices always result in the curtailment of rights. Hence, recent debates
about the use of executive authority have tended to focus on the conflict
between national security versus civil liberties (Darner, Baird, and Rosenblum 2004). But executive authority does not act in just one direction. Executive decisions can also be used to strategically expand legal rights (in
the case of the Emancipation Proclamation) or to minimize restrictions
on immigrant rights that are being introduced through the legislature (as
illustrated by Roosevelt's executive orders on Asian immigration). And
national security is not the only reason for which the rights of noncitizens
have been restricted.

The expansion of migrant flows over the last three decades has created
a new population of nonimmigrant residents who enter the United States
with an impermanent legal status. During this period of time, the nonimmigrant workforce grew faster than at any other time in U.S. history. This
process was guided by federal laws, some of which attempted to cap the
flow of nonimmigrant workers into the United States. But despite these
efforts, it would be more accurate to say that these laws functioned in a
deregulatory manner. The introduction of new visa categories, changes
to the terms of existing visa categories, and exceptions that the Congress
granted to recruitment caps for H1 workers allowed for a major expansion
of migrant flows that operated outside of annual immigration quotas. The
trade-off is that migrant workers are being granted a very flexible kind of
legal status that renders them more easily removable than legal permanent residents. The end result is that limitations on noncitizen rights have
been determined by the conditions under which migrants are being recruited as workers—and in many cases, the right of these persons to lawfully reside in the United States is largely contingent on their productivity
and exclusivity with a particular employer (Papademetriou et al. 2009).

These labor market recruitment strategies can still be influenced by
concerns about security even if they are not completely determined by
them. For example, counterterrorism strategies have become interwoven
with concerns about safeguarding the process of economic globalization.

But popular ideas about "national security" can also conflict with the corporate-economic priorities that have guided the most recent phase of globalization. The Dubai port authority controversy provides an interesting point of reference.

For the Bush administration, there was nothing inherently contradictory about contracting security services for U.S. ports to a corporation based in the Middle East. Valid points were raised about how effective this Dubai-based company had been in handling security breaches at ports in its home city.[24] But these complaints merely raised questions about the competence of the Dubai-based security firm—which could have been assessed (and compared against other contractors) independently of concerns about the national origins of the people who owned the firm. In a similar vein, concerns about contracting port security services to private corporations could apply just as easily to U.S.-based private security corporations. In this regard, criticism of the decision that focused on the Bush administration's subservience to corporate interests rang hollow. This criticism was certainly not misplaced, but it obscured the underlying contradiction that had made this incident newsworthy to begin with: that the Bush administration was willing to contract a major feature of U.S. security services to a corporation that was owned and operated by people of the same national origins who had orchestrated the attacks of 9/11. It also bears noting that this controversy vanished from the news headlines shortly after the Dubai-based corporation decided to cancel its contract with the U.S. government. No complaints about the corporate control of U.S. port security were raised when this foreign-owned company sold its U.S. security assets to a much larger multinational corporation, the American-owned AIG Global Investment group.[25] AIG would make headlines two years later for its own financial troubles, which presaged the Wall Street–,mortgage industry meltdown and the ensuing global economic crisis.

One of the most remarkable things about this scandal is the way it managed to focus public outrage on a kind of transaction that has become fairly routine for U.S. administrations and that pales in comparison to the government's level of involvement in negotiating global trade agreements. Many of these transactions have been guided by executive decisions and executive orders. The use of executive discretion in these matters allows the government to act swiftly, to respond to emergent conditions and unexpected contingencies—and it also removes these decisions from the sphere of public debate. A primary case in point is the North American Free Trade Agreement (NAFTA), which was enacted by international agreements and executive orders that were initiated by the 1989–1992 Bush administration and the Clinton administration.[26] It is also notable that NAFTA contains statements about immigrant and worker rights that can be applied to nonimmigrant workers and unauthorized migrants (Sassen 2006b). These rights exist at the level of international law but they can be used, with varying degrees of success, in cases that are tried in the U.S. court system. One of the most effective means of enforcing these rights is through the diplomatic pressure that the executive office of one nation is able to exert on the corporations and executive office of other nations. This sort of diplomacy underscores the pivotal role that the executive branch has played in crafting international trade agreements.

During the same time that the Clinton administration was liberalizing trade relations and labor flows with Mexico, it was also facing pressures from the Congress to impose new restrictions on the social and legal rights of immigrants. This process culminated in the 1996 Welfare Reform Act, which imposed unprecedented restrictions on immigrant access to federal means-tested social programs. Although the law was signed by President Clinton, he later expressed misgivings about the welfare restrictions and used his executive discretion to exclude some categories of immigrants from the welfare restrictions (Singer 2004, 21–34). Despite its political differences with the Clinton administration, the 2000–2008 Bush administration found itself in a similar situation when it attempted to introduce a new guest worker program that offered a path to legalization for some unauthorized migrant workers.[27]

What all of these scenarios share in common is a clash between congressional representatives pressured by the restrictionist demands of their constituents (and by national lobby groups) and an executive office facing pressures from immigrant rights constituencies (which can include foreign governments, employers who rely on migrant labor, and the advocacy networks of immigrant communities). In these situations, neoliberal administrations have tended to make decisions that do not impede the free flow of migration but that also contain overtures to both pro- and anti-immigration constituencies.

Once again, the 2000–2008 Bush administration is a good example. The Bush administration has been credited with shifting neoliberal priorities toward a strategic model that placed more emphasis on the use of the military to pursue narrow geopolitical interests—as opposed to the Clintonian diplomatic model that placed more emphasis on creating global markets and building international consensus around its key policy objectives (Bello 2005, 1–31). This is a fair description of the foreign policy stance of the Bush administration, but on the matter of immigration a very different picture emerges. The Bush administration's approach to immigration was much more derivative of a classic laissez-faire model of labor market regulation than was that of the Clinton administration.

Despite the fact that Democratic administrations are often viewed as being more proimmigrant than Republican administrations, recent Democrat administrations have actually been tougher on border control and immigration enforcement. The peak years for border patrol apprehensions (in all of U.S. history) occurred between 1996 and 2000, during the last term of the Clinton presidency.[28] The 1996 immigration and antiterrorism laws, which laid the foundations for the recent expansion of immigration enforcement, were also enacted under the Clinton administration.

By contrast, border enforcement under the Bush administration fell by an average of five hundred thousand apprehensions per year, compared to the peak years that occurred under the second term of the Clinton administration.[29] Ironically, the Bush administration continued to enact laws and approve budgetary proposals that expanded the size of the border patrol (Deborah Meyers 2005). The peak years in the annual growth and absolute size of the unauthorized migrant population also occurred under the tenure of the Bush administration[30]—so these low enforcement levels cannot be explained by a decline in the number of unauthorized border crossings (even though this does begin to occur in 2007 with the onset of the global recession). The Bush administration's initial proposal for a new guest worker program also contained no new enforcement provisions, making it the "least militarized" of all of the proposals that were initially put forward by Republicans and Democrats in the Senate.[31]

From all appearances, the Bush administration's stance on unauthorized migration and border control was a faithful replication of the wink-and-nod attitude that the U.S. government has historically adopted toward

unauthorized Mexican migrant labor in the Southwest.[32] Meanwhile, over
the last several decades the political climate surrounding immigration has
forced the government to adopt a much tougher stance on all kinds of immigration violations. As a result, the position of the U.S. government on
unauthorized migration has become much more complex. For example,
the Bush administration criticized the vigilante enforcement efforts of
the Minutemen movement and became bitter enemies with immigration restrictionists in the House of Representatives, increased spending
on border patrol, and touted its efforts to control unauthorized migration
(efforts that were not very effective), advocated for the legalization of unauthorized migrants and the expansion of the guest worker program, affirmed the U.S. government's commitment to protecting immigrant rights,
and affirmed the inherent right of local authorities to enforce federal immigration laws (Kretsedemas 2008a).

One of the most remarkable things about this assortment of policy positions is not its incoherency, but the fact that it is not markedly different
from that of other contemporary administrations (from the Reagan-Bush
era to the Obama presidency). There have been some notable differences in the way different administrations have weighted these priorities,
but the general tendency has been to move forward on all these fronts—
strengthening enforcement, facilitating the expansion of migration flows,
fending off the more hard-line proposals of the immigration control
movement, and advancing laws that generally weaken immigrant rights
(while attempting to protect immigrant rights in some narrow areas).
This orientation toward immigration policy is largely responsible for the
enforcement trends and the changing relationship between immigrant
and nonimmigrant flows (see chapter 2).

The priorities that underlie these decisions are similar to the logic of
executive discretion, and many of these policy decisions have been facilitated by the use of this discretion. Nothing is set in stone. The goal is to
be able to adapt existing policy to an array of unexpected contingencies.
Hence, support for immigrant rights—including the rights of unauthorized migrants—does not translate into support for the uniform reinstate-
ment of social, civil, and labor rights that have been eroded by the past
several decades of neoliberal restructuring. Even when the executive office uses its authority to selectively strengthen immigrant rights, this does

not necessarily result in the creation of a formal, legal precedent (that could be referenced by immigrant rights advocates in the legal arguments they are using in local and federal courts). Instead these decisions tend to function as an affirmation of executive discretion over the expansion or protection of immigrant rights.[33]

In a similar vein, executive support for immigration enforcement tends to translate into support for the discretionary use of these expanded enforcement powers (which fall under the authority of the executive office). In contrast to immigration restrictionists, recent administrations have shown no signs that they are interested in effecting a long-term decline in immigration levels. Nevertheless, there are situations in which an intensification of immigration enforcement—including strategies that resemble the mass deportation proposals of immigration restrictionists—could be deemed "necessary" for a variety of political and economic reasons. A good example is 1954's Operation Wetback, which was used to terminate the Bracero program initiated almost a decade earlier. Under Operation Wetback, the U.S. immigration system deported almost 1 million Mexican nationals (Ngai 2005, 127–166).

APPLYING EXECUTIVE DISCRETION TO IMMIGRATION ENFORCEMENT

In recent years, Operation Wetback has been championed by immigration restrictionists as a model to which immigration enforcement should aspire.[34] As Kitty Calavita (1992) has explained, however, Operation Wetback is better explained as a labor market regulation strategy and not as an immigration control strategy. It was not used to effect a permanent decrease in unauthorized migration but to carry out a crackdown during a time when there was a perceived oversupply of migrant labor. Just as important, the Bracero program and Operation Wetback were both creatures of discretionary executive authority.

The Bracero program was the product of an executive agreement between the United States and the Mexican government that expanded the recruitment of Mexican migrant labor throughout the Southwest. The Bracero program was justified as a temporary solution to the decline in available native-born males because of the U.S. involvement in World War

II. In a similar vein, Operation Wetback was conceived as a joint operation between immigration enforcement and the U.S. military, and the entire operation fell under the command of high-ranking military officials. As such, the operation was convened by the president through his capacity as commander in chief and not merely through the administrative oversight that he already exercised over the immigration system.

From one perspective, mass deportation strategies like Operation Wetback may appear to be an anachronistic (not to mention politically controversial) way of regulating migration flows. Today, most immigration policy analysts, and even some immigration control advocates, agree that mass deportation strategies are logistically impractical (Capetillo-Ponce 2008). In addition, the expanded deportation powers of the immigration system are increasingly rendering these sorts of mass deportation strategies unnecessary. The present immigration system routinely removes more noncitizens on an annual basis than it did during the peak years of Operation Wetback, without the help of the military.[35]

This is another illustration of how policies and practices that are initiated under the special powers of the executive office can foreshadow the future direction of normal, institutional practice. Like a typical state of emergency, Operation Wetback was made possible by an executive decision that temporarily suspended normal legal-administrative procedure to allow for a special partnership between the military and immigration enforcement. The emergency conditions that justified the operation were both political and economic in nature, but they were far removed from the sorts of unforeseen, calamitous events that typify a "classic" state of emergency. In this regard, Operation Wetback foreshadowed the expanded definition of national security that has informed the enforcement strategies of recent administrations.

These expanded definitions of national security have been accompanied by a more expansive and creative use of executive discretion. Instead of merely interrupting the law, executive authority becomes a guiding force that establishes priorities for lawmaking. It is also possible for executive decisions to change the course of the law by introducing new interpretations of legal precedent (see table 3.1). In this case, the executive office circumvents the legislature in order to create an entirely new terrain of lawmaking.

In 2002, for example, the Department of Justice and the Bush administration issued a internal memo that reinterpreted prior legal precedent on the authority of local governments to enforce federal immigration laws (Appleseed Foundation 2008, 24–27).[36] The 1996 Immigration Reform Act had already granted local police and local governments the ability to receive training from the immigration system to enforce immigration laws and to establish working partnerships with federal enforcement officers (Appleseed 2008, 17–20). However, the enforcement powers that were authorized by the Bush administration allowed local governments to enact immigration laws and implement enforcement practices independently of the federal immigration system. Although the internal memos claimed that these local enforcement powers were consistent with existing interpretations of immigration law, they marked a major shift in the development of legal precedent. The arguments about prior legal precedent that were included in these memos were never vetted within the judicial system. As a result, many counties and townships throughout the United States have begun to enact laws whose legality and constitutionality remain in doubt. Since 2004 the number of local immigration laws enacted by state and local governments has increased at a rate of more than two hundred per year.[37]

The secretive process that opened the door for these laws was unorthodox, even when compared to the ad hoc rationales that have historically been used to justify the exercise of executive authority. But the unprecedented nature of this process can be situated within a broader continuity wherein the exercise of executive discretion over the law has been progressively expanded over the course of the past two centuries.

Kitty Calavita's (1992) explanation of Operation Wetback has drawn attention to the role it played as a form of labor market regulation—being focused on reducing the size of the unauthorized migrant workforce in the Southwest. By comparison, the Bush administration's memos on immigration enforcement seem to have been a response to political pressure from the immigration control movement (which was creating rifts within the Republican party).[38] Unlike Operation Wetback, the recent expansion of local enforcement began occurring at a time when unauthorized migrant flows were still expanding and when employers were petitioning the state to have freer access to migrant labor. It is also rather telling

TABLE 3.1   *A Typology of Strategic Uses of Executive Authority Over the Law*

"Classic" state of emergency	The executive introduces security measures that require the suspension of some legal rights and procedures, which are restored after the cessation of the emergency.
	EXAMPLE: 2001–2003 Special Registration program[a] Established by executive appointees. Introduced special reporting requirements for Arab Muslim males residing in the United States.
Laws that act in consort with executive discretion	Legal rights and procedures are temporarily suspended or permanently revoked by other laws, creating an effect that is similar to a "classic" state of emergency but that can last for an indefinite period of time.
	EXAMPLES: 1996 Antiterrorism and Effective Death Penalty Act Introduced secret evidence to deportation proceedings. 2002 USA PATRIOT Act Temporarily suspended warrant and due process requirements for a broad range of security-related surveillance and enforcement actions. 2005 REAL ID Act Revoked the writ of habeas corpus for most noncitizens in deportation proceedings.
Executive decisions that create new terrains of lawmaking	Executive discretion is used to reinterpret prior legal precedent in order to clear the way for an entirely new terrain of lawmaking.
	EXAMPLE: 2002 policy statements by White House and Department of Justice Endorsed "inherent authority" of local governments to enact laws concerning immigration enforcement.

[a] Special Registration was just one feature of the broader National Security Entry-Exit Registration System (NSEERS), which is still in existence. Special Registration was established immediately after the 9/11 attacks by the immigration system. Most of the domestic interview requirements of the Special Registration program were phased out in 2003. However, the restructured NSEERS program (including a revised version of Special Registration) was incorporated into the new U.S.-VISIT program, which has been conceptualized as a comprehensive biometric security and tracking system for all temporary arrivals to the United States (Department of Homeland Security. U.S.-VISIT, www.dhs.gov/xtrvlsec/programs/content_multi_image_0006.shtm [accessed January 10, 2009]).

that Bush administration officials did not begin to speak in favor of local enforcement until their plans for expanding the guest worker program met stiff resistance from Republicans in the House who were demanding tougher controls on immigration (Kretsedemas 2008, 566).

It is still too early to tell what the national-level impact of these local enforcement practices will be. It is possible that local enforcement can be expanded in ways that are generally consistent with neoliberal priorities for immigration enforcement. In that case, local enforcement would contain the ambitions of the immigration control movement within a patchwork array of local policies and practices that can be used to police migrant labor flows (and secure political consent for the continuing expansion of these flows) but that are ineffective as a strategy for restricting immigration. But it is also possible that the expansion of local enforcement could pave the way for a new kind of federal-local consensus that manages to incorporate the free market position on immigration within an economic nationalist agenda. In either case, the outcome will have been made possible by the expanded sphere of executive discretion over immigration policy that has been produced by the last several administrations.

Neoliberal governing strategies have left an indelible mark on this process, but they represent just one phase in the expansion of executive authority. Like the revolutionary movements of the late eighteenth century, neoliberalism has attempted to restructure the state—and the global economy—after its own image. The common thread that connects these two extremely different governing ideologies is an interest in cultivating a kind of authority that is greater than the law, which can be used to guide an ambitious, transformative agenda. In the next chapter, I take a closer look at this process by examining the recent expansion of local enforcement laws.

4

CONCERNED CITIZENS, LOCAL EXCLUSIONS

LOCAL IMMIGRATION LAWS AND THE LEGACY OF JIM CROW

The last chapter examined immigration policy from the vantage point of the executive office. This chapter engages a very different political terrain, but one that is no less complex: immigration laws that have been enacted by state and local governments. On one hand, local immigration laws seem to be an apt example of the expansion of executive authority under neoliberalism (see chapter 3). Similar to recent experiments with deregulation and federal devolution, local immigration laws have allowed the authority of the federal government to be parceled out to a variety of state and nonstate actors. This has produced a situation in which police officers, landlords, election booth workers, and health care workers have been given more freedom to participate in enforcement practices that used to be regarded as the exclusive preserve of the federal immigration system.

But this expanded discretionary authority is not always used in ways that are consistent with the federal government's priorities for immigration. Furthermore, this kind of discretionary authority is connected to a legal history, and to ideas about popular sovereignty, that predate neoliberalism. The push to get more local governments involved in immigration enforcement has also been a major objective of the immigration control movement, and many of these laws are informed by an economic nationalist agenda that is directly opposed to the idea that employers should have access to a free flow of migrant labor. So even though some of these laws may have further extended the "long arm" of the federal government into the realm of state and local affairs, they have also become a heated battleground that has the potential to undermine the federal government's policy priorities and enforcement objectives.

Irrespective of how this struggle is resolved, these laws are clearly a matter of concern for immigrant populations. Although local immigration laws deploy race-neutral language, it is hard to deny that there is a racial undertone to the popular discourse on illegal immigration, which is one reason local enforcement practices have been criticized for encouraging a new kind of Latino profiling (Appleseed 2008; Muchetti 2005; Shahani and Greene 2009). These concerns are pertinent to the issues I explore in this chapter, but the scope of my analysis is much broader than this. The primary aim of this chapter is to explain how local immigration laws connect to a history of legal rationales and political dynamics that have been used to justify the discriminatory treatment of minority populations in the United States. In making these connections, my discussion draws parallels with the Jim Crow laws enacted by hundreds of state and municipal governments in the late nineteenth and early twentieth century.

I must note from the outset that there is nothing especially original about the idea that get-tough immigration laws bear a family resemblance to the race-based exclusions of the Jim Crow era. Journalists and immigrant rights activists have drawn attention to the parallels between the racialized policing of legal status in the current era (sometimes referred to as Juan Crow) and the explicitly racial legal categories of Jim Crow (Kateel and Shahani 2008).[1] Local immigration laws have also been criticized for encouraging a new kind of racial profiling—making implicit comparisons with the racial profiles that have been used to target black populations.[2] But these references to the problem of institutional racism may also pose a problem for the mainstream immigrant rights movement. In coming to grips with this problem, we must be prepared to engage the biases and inequities that have blocked the social mobility of racialized populations in the United States. This history of structural inequality and racial marginality runs against the grain of the optimistic narratives on immigrant integration that are often used to frame the immigration debate for the American public.

One lesson that the black experience holds for immigrants (and low-income immigrants of color, in particular) is that the process of becoming "integrated" into the U.S. economy may also be bound up with structural dynamics that will lead some immigrants to become members of a racialized underclass. A number of researchers have been exploring this problem (Bashi 2007, 36–75; Calavita 2005; Chang 2000; Massey 2007, 113–210; Portes 1994). There is compelling evidence that immigrants are still, on average, more productive than native-born workers and help to sustain higher wage levels for all U.S. workers (Hanson 2005; Peri 2009). But there is also evidence that changes in the U.S. wage structure, which are correlated with the new patterns in the gendered and racial-ethnic segmentation of the U.S. workforce, have widened the immigrant–native born wage gap, making it much more difficult for immigrants to achieve parity with native-born workers (compared to pre-1965 immigrant cohorts; see Butcher and Dinardo 2002). For Latino migrants, in particular, there is a close relationship between poverty, spatial segregation (from the white, English-speaking population), and employment in ethnically segmented job sectors. Notably, the concentration of Latinos in these low-wage, "ethnic job sectors" has increased in tandem with the growth of the Latino immigrant population (Catanzarite 2002; Marchevsky and Theoharis 2006, 33–67).

Keeping these trends in mind, the problem posed by local immigration laws is not simply the way they are being used by anti-immigrant activists to target unauthorized migrants (and to depress the growth of the broader, immigrant population). It is also important to consider how these laws are operating alongside other policies and practices that are incorporating immigrants into local economies. In this regard, local immigration laws should not simply be viewed as a strategy that is being used to "keep immigrants out" but as one feature within a broad array of recruitment mechanisms, policies, and social dynamics that are being used to coercively integrate some immigrant populations into U.S. society (and in a way that underscores the significance of legal status as a marker of social status). The process I have just described extends beyond the debate over local immigration laws. But local immigration laws can still provide a very insightful window into this process.

The comparison with Jim Crow is instructive because it sheds light on a similar process that was used to segregate and to coercively integrate

African Americans into a modernizing economy. Like local immigration laws, Jim Crow laws spread in a patchwork manner, as an assemblage of state, county, and municipal ordinances. I am not going to argue that the impact of these laws for immigrant populations is comparable to the marginalization that has been historically experienced by African Americans. Even though local immigration laws are creating new hardships for noncitizens, they are not producing the same kind of segregation as Jim Crow. Nevertheless, it is possible to see how Jim Crow and local immigration laws connect to a more abstract continuity of practices that have been used to justify the discriminatory treatment of racial minorities in the United States. But before entering into this analysis, it will help to review the recent history of local enforcement and local immigration laws.

LOCAL ENFORCEMENT AND LOCAL IMMIGRATION LAWS: THE POLICY CONTEXT

There is no need for local enforcement to be compared to Jim Crow for the sake of stirring up controversy. Local enforcement laws have stirred up enough controversy in their own right. Perhaps the biggest controversy surrounding these laws is whether they are legal to begin with. One reason for this controversy has to do with the methods used by the executive office to open the door for local governments to enact these laws. Because the Bush administration issued its legal rationale for local enforcement through an internal memo that circumvented the federal court system, hundreds of local immigration laws were enacted before the courts could evaluate their continuity with prior legal precedent (see chapter 3). Hence, the legal debate over local immigration laws is occurring in the wake of the massive expansion of these laws that has occurred from 2005 onward. As table 4.1 illustrates, the number of immigration laws enacted by state and local governments increased more than fivefold between 2005 and 2009.

The most vexing legal question posed by these laws has to do with the way they redefine the scope of local authority on immigration matters, and how this relates to prior interpretations of the supremacy of federal law. The 2002 memos issued by the Bush administration pushed the interpretation of immigration decisively in favor of local governments. But

TABLE 4.1   *Local Immigration Laws Enacted, 2005–2009*

	2005	2006	2007	2008	2009	No. of laws (% of total)
Law enforcement	3	8	16	12	16	55 (8)
Education	3	3	22	12	27	67 (10)
Employment	5	14	29	19	21	88 (13)
Health	0	0	14	11	28	53 (8)
Human trafficking	9	13	18	5	16	61 (9)
ID (driver's licenses & other licenses)	9	6	40	32	46	133 (20)
Legal services	2	5	3	2	0	12 (2)
Miscellaneous	3	6	14	36	46	105 (16)
Omnibus/multi-issue measures	0	1	1	3	3	8 (1)
Public benefits	5	10	33	9	15	72 (11)
Voting	0	6	0	1	4	11 (2)
No. of laws	39	72	190	142	222	665 (100)

Source: Data derived from NCSL 2005, 2006, 2007, 2008, 2009a.

Note: Resolutions are not included in data.

even prior to these memos, federal court opinion on this matter was rather ambiguous. This situation is further complicated by the fact that two bodies of legal argument are woven through the debate over these laws. One argument concerns the inherent authority of local governments to enact their own immigration laws. The other argument concerns the role of state and local police in enforcing *federal* immigration laws. This latter argument intersects with the debate over local immigration laws, but it is more accurately described as a debate over "local enforcement"—which focuses on the relationship between state and local police and the federal immigration system. Throughout this chapter I often (but not always) use the terms "local immigration laws" and "local enforcement" in tandem with each other. Even though, in practice, these fields of debate are closely related, they cannot be reduced to one another, which is why I have resisted the urge to reduce them to a single catchphrase.

Although local immigration laws can include special measures that authorize police to become more involved in immigration enforcement, they can also be used to enact immigration-related measures that extend far beyond the role of the police. And even though local immigration laws can be used to give police a green light to become more involved in immigration enforcement, there are many ways that state and local police can become involved in immigration enforcement that do not require the enactment of local immigration laws. It also bears noting that the federal orientation of the local enforcement debate sidesteps much of the debate over local immigration laws (since it has to do with the authority that local police have to enforce federal immigration laws). Nevertheless, some of the biggest controversies surrounding local immigration laws have stemmed from enforcement measures that allow police to screen people for legal status.

As several researchers have explained, these enforcement practices lead, inevitably, in the direction of racial profiling (Goldsmith et al. 2009; Muchetti 2005; Shahani and Greene 2009). The problem is that there is no way of being absolutely sure that someone is undocumented until police officers check them for their legal status. As a result, officers are likely to screen individuals whom they already suspect of being unauthorized migrants. Even if race is not an explicit feature of the criteria used by police officers to identify likely suspects, it can still influence the criteria that are used to determine these suspects (such as manner of dress, manner of speech, the part of town that one lives in, etc.). An alternative approach would be to develop a strategy that would make it possible for local governments to screen all residents for their legal status on a routine basis. Proposals for this more intensive kind of local enforcement—which would probably entail the issuing of national identification cards and the incorporation of local police into a federally coordinated, nationwide enforcement strategy—have been challenged by citizen and immigrant rights groups who fear the creation of a national police force (and also by many police departments). These are some of the reasons why the 2002–2005 Congress failed to enact a federally mandated local enforcement law (Kretsedemas 2008b). This resistance to local enforcement via federal legislation provides more insight into why these enforcement practices evolved into a localized process of selective screenings informed by the discretion of police, public servants, and private citizens.

So the resistance to local enforcement as national legislation played a role, ironically, in pushing the debate over this issue toward the domain of state and local policy. Local immigration laws make it possible for police involvement in immigration enforcement to be more finely tailored to local conditions. But the federal courts have also tended to be more critical of local immigration laws than they have been of police involvement in enforcing federal immigration laws. Meanwhile, the position of the Obama administration on these matters appears to be moving in polar opposite directions. As it concerns the debate over local immigration laws, the federal government has sent signals that it wants to limit the inherent authority of state and local governments (counteracting the signals sent by the internal memos of the Bush administration). But as it concerns the debate over local enforcement, the Obama administration has been more proactive about providing opportunities for state and local police to become involved in enforcing federal immigration laws.

Prior to the 2002 Bush administration memos, the most widely accepted legal precedent concerning local police and immigration enforcement had been established by the 1983 Gonzalez v. City of Peoria decision.[3] This legal precedent was generally consistent with language in the 1952 Immigration and Nationality Act (under section 1252) that specified the criteria under which it was lawful for state or local police to arrest civil immigration violators (Appleseed 2008, 13–17). The Gonzalez precedent asserted that police did not have the authority to enforce federal immigration laws unless these actions were relevant to an ongoing criminal investigation or had been explicitly authorized by the federal government. Hence, it was assumed that police had no inherent authority to inquire into the legal status of U.S. residents or to arrest noncitizens for civil immigration violations if they had not, first, committed a criminal violation. This interpretation of the role of police in enforcing civil immigration laws was upheld by the Department of Justice prior to the 2002 memos, and it is still held by many police departments across the United States (Major Cities Chiefs 2006).

Prior to the memos, there were already signs that the influence of the Gonzalez precedent was beginning to weaken. The 1999 United States v. Vasquez-Alvarez and 2001 United States v. Santana-Garcia decisions both involved immigrant defendants who believed that police officers had overstepped the bounds of their authority by arresting them for civil im-

migration violations when there was no evidence that they had committed a criminal violation (Appleseed 2008, 21–23).[4] In both cases, the Tenth
Circuit Court supported the discretionary authority of the police—sending the signal that the federal courts were willing to broadly interpret the
role of local police on matters relating to immigration enforcement.

The 2002 Bush administration memos shifted legal opinion even further in this direction. In addition to the statement concerning the inherent authority of local governments, these memos reversed a longstanding Department of Justice (DoJ) opinion that was consistent with the
language of the Gonzalez precedent. As a result, the "inherent authority"
principle was extended to the enforcement powers of the police. Instead
of presuming that the police had limited authority to enforce immigration
laws (conditioned by exceptions provided under federal law), it was now
presumed that civil immigration enforcement was a legitimate and normal feature of criminal law enforcement (Appleseed 2008, 24–25).

In this regard, the 2002 Bush administration memos voided the restrictions that the Gonzalez precedent had imposed on the immigration
enforcement powers of police. But putting this aside, the inherent authority principle also allows local governments to become involved in immigration enforcement in ways that sidestep the Gonzalez precedent. That
precedent focuses specifically on the role of local police, but the inherent
authority argument addresses the broader discretionary authority of local
government—and it so happens that the majority of local immigration
laws do not concern the role of local police.

As table 4.1 demonstrates only 8 percent of local immigration laws
enacted between 2005 and 2009 have had to do with law enforcement[5]
Many of these local immigration laws are not focused on screening immigrants for legal status and some have attempted to protect immigrant
rights.[6] Even so, the most popular categories (including laws concerning
drivers licenses, employment, and public benefits, which account for 54
percent of all laws enacted) have overwhelmingly been focused on screening noncitizens for legal status. There are other miscellaneous laws that
have introduced screening requirements for a wide variety of transactions
such as gun purchases, land purchases, and rental agreements among
other things.[7]

So although police involvement is an important feature of the enforcement powers that have been expanded by local immigration laws, it is just

one element within a broad array of screening practices that are being used to expand the network of actors who are becoming involved in verifying the legal status of local residents. It also bears noting that this enforcement strategy shares some features in common with the electronic border system that became popular with federal lawmakers after 9/11 (see chapter 2). Recall that the goal of this system was to create an integrated web of screening practices that could be used to track people of temporary legal status for the entirety of their stay in the United States. Local immigration laws are distinguished by their focus on restricting the movement of unauthorized migrants within a particular state or municipality—as opposed to tracking the movements of noncitizens who have been legally admitted with temporary visas across a national territory. Even so, it is not difficult to see how the screening practices authorized by these local laws could be plugged into the national surveillance networks that are being developed under the auspices of the electronic border system.

So although local immigration laws have become a source of controversy among federal lawmakers they are also, in some ways, consistent with many of the same enforcement priorities that have been supported by most federal lawmakers. Federal lawmakers have also created new avenues for police to become more involved in immigration enforcement in ways that do not require the enactment of local immigration laws. For example, the 1996 immigration reform law created a new program that was geared toward enhancing federal-local partnerships on immigration enforcement. The 287(g) clause of this law allows local governments to request training from federal agents on how to participate in immigration enforcement activities. The 287(g) clause was reformed by the Obama administration to increase the involvement of local police in this program (Cristina Rodríguez et al. 2010). The 1996 immigration reform law also allowed governors to draft memorandums of understanding (MOU) that can be used to involve state police in enforcement partnerships with federal immigration authorities.[8] These agreements are initiated with the presumption that state and local police are acting under the guidance of federal enforcement. Nevertheless, some of these agreements can be very fluid, like the Florida MOU that gave all state police the authority to partner with federal enforcement on an as-needed basis (as opposed to being limited to participating in sting operations initiated by federal enforcement; Appleseed 2008, 19).

Another avenue for local enforcement is the National Crime Information Center (NCIC) database that was expanded to include data on immigration violators and persons deemed to be national security risks (Appleseed 2008, 17; Gladstein et al. 2005). As a result, local police can now screen individuals for immigration violations on a fairly routine basis, which can include suspects for which the police have probable cause, as well as person's who are detained for questioning or during traffic stops. It bears emphasizing that the NCIC database does not verify the legal status of the individual in question and since most unauthorized migrants have not been cited with immigration violations, they will not show up in the database. Nonetheless the NCIC database stretches the boundaries of the Gonzalez precedent by expanding police involvement in immigration enforcement beyond the questioning of suspects who are relevant to criminal investigations.

Another important factor to consider is federal legal precedent concerning the search, seizure, and interrogation powers of the police. In this case, we must look beyond the immigration debate and toward court decisions that have been focused, more generally, on criminal enforcement. Many of these cases have raised questions about the racial profiling of black populations. Within this body of legal opinion, the federal courts have a long history of giving law enforcement officers the benefit of the doubt when routine questioning and search and seizure practices appear to violate constitutional rights. These rulings have been justified by arguments that view the benefits of aggressive criminal enforcement as a reasonable trade-off for what are presumed to be moderate curtailments in Fourth Amendment or due process rights (Cole 2000b). There is a similarity between these sorts of arguments and the arguments that have been used to expand the extralegal powers of the executive office. Exceptions to the letter of the law can be justified as long as they appear to serve the "spirit" of the law.

This is one reason why debates over legal precedent offer only limited insight into the future of local enforcement practices. The law is one of the principal terrains on which the battle over local enforcement will be waged. But the law does not in and of itself explain the various (and warring) constructions of necessity that are being imposed on the law. It is important to consider how ideas about race and class have shaped these constructions of necessity, determining how the protections of the law have been interpreted and meted out to different segments of the U.S. population. The comparison with Jim Crow is one way of drawing the analysis of local enforcement outside the confines of the law—into this broader terrain where national imaginaries, racial identities, economic development strategies, enforcement practices, state policies, and legal decisions converge and reflexively shape each other. The comparison with Jim Crow also protects against the hazards of presentism by illustrating that the issues at stake in local enforcement are not unique to the current era or even, for that matter, to the realm of immigration policy.

SEGREGATION OR COERCIVE INTEGRATION?
THE POLITICAL DYNAMICS AND OUTCOMES OF
LOCAL EXCLUSIONARY LAWS

There are many obvious differences between local enforcement laws and Jim Crow. The exclusion of the black person under Jim Crow was justified by their so-called racial difference. The exclusion of the undocumented migrant, on the other hand, is justified by the fact of their unauthorized entry. It is also apparent that public space is not being segregated in quite the same way as it was in the Jim Crow era (for example, there are no "citizens only" signs installed on public washrooms), and even though the discourse on illegal immigration is racialized, unauthorized migrants are not understood to be a distinct race (in the way that African Americans have historically been racialized as a separate racial group). But putting these differences aside, the things that Jim Crow and local enforcement laws have in common have less to do with the characteristics and treatment of their target populations and more to do with the way that these laws have been used to police and regulate these populations. In the case of Jim Crow, these practices were used to keep blacks disenfranchised while, at the same time, incorporating them into the lower tiers of southern society. As some scholars have explained, this process was bound up with the drive to modernize the South.

Richard Chesteen (1971) has observed that state-sanctioned racial segregation was at a more advanced stage in northern states in the early postbellum era because of the structural damage caused by the civil war (segregated facilities would have been too expensive for most southern states) and because of the political climate of the Reconstruction era South. This analysis complements Howard Rabinowitz's explanation of the relationship between Jim Crow laws, urbanization, and industrialization. Rabinowitz (1978) argues that Jim Crow laws were used to maintain social distances under labor market conditions that required workers of different races to work in close proximity to each other. Hence, the purpose of these laws was not simply to separate but also to allow for greater flexibility of interaction between individuals of different racial castes without compromising these racial distinctions.

According to C. Vann Woodward (1955), this is why Jim Crow laws only began to take root in the South with the drive toward industrialization, led by the architects of the New South. Woodward also insists that the defining features of Jim Crow did not take shape until the late 1890s. His thesis instigated a long debate between historians who have argued, along with Woodward, that Jim Crow was created by elite interests in the postbellum era and other critics who insist that Jim Crow emerged from a more deeply rooted continuity of racist attitudes that preceded the Civil War (Cell 1982, 82–102) . William Julius Wilson (1976) advances an argument that is sympathetic to Woodward's thesis but draws more attention to the racist sentiments of the white working class. Wilson concludes that Jim Crow laws emerged from a devil's bargain between the southern planter class, northern politicians and industrialists, and working-class populists who decided that it was in their mutual interest to arrange for the political disenfranchisement of the southern black population (as opposed to competing for their loyalties). This analysis complicates aspects of Woodward's argument. However, Wilson still observes that the push toward southern industrialization was an important factor in the creation of racially stratified labor markets.

A common theme underlying all of these arguments is that Jim Crow segregation was used to coercively incorporate black populations into the economy and public life of the industrializing South. Following a similar pattern, local immigration laws have expanded during the same time that low wage employment sectors throughout the United States have become increasingly reliant on immigrant labor (and especially on Latino immigrant labor). It is also rather telling that punitive local immigration laws (which are geared toward apprehending unauthorized migrants) have grown the fastest in southern states with small but growing Latino migrant populations (Laglaron et al. 2008; Shahani and Greene 2009). Hence, it can be argued that local immigration laws add a new twist on the way that immigration enforcement can function as a form of labor market discipline that is oriented toward policing and controlling the migrant workforce (as opposed to restricting the growth of this workforce; see Parenti 2000, 139–162). This tendency is even more apparent in northeastern and West Coast states that have enacted a more balanced combination of local immigration laws, that have selectively expanded immigrant access to some services and authorized new screening practices for others (Laglaron et al. 2008). In these states, it is more apparent that the new enforcement provisions, authorized by local immigration laws, are part of a broader strategy for incorporating migrant populations into the local economy.

Jim Crow functioned more transparently as a process of institutionally structured, downward mobility for black populations. Local immigration laws, in contrast, reserve their most severe exclusions for unauthorized migrants, but they also have the potential to reinforce the social marginalization of all noncitizen populations that might be confused with unauthorized migrants. It is in this sense that local immigration laws—and local enforcement practices more generally—carry implications for the patterns of segmented assimilation that have been used to explain the downward mobility of second-generation immigrant youth (Portes and Zhou 1993). Like Jim Crow, these laws may be viewed as an exercise in coercive integration that secures a place for most noncitizens in the U.S. socioeconomic order, but in a way that underlines the inferior legal and social status of unauthorized and low wage migrant populations.

This process is not just being driven by structural economic factors. Once again, this is where a comparison with the history of Jim Crow can be helpful. Explanations of the rise of Jim Crow have drawn attention to the political process that shaped these laws. Jim Crow was shaped by a political consensus that emerged from an array of formerly warring interests.[9] This does not belie the fact that economic elites benefited from the new forms of labor market stratification produced by Jim Crow or that black populations were also being displaced by the structural transformation of the Old South's plantation system (akin to the skills mismatch theories that have been used to explain black joblessness after deindustrialization).[10]

Even so, these structural-economic factors do not, in and of themselves, explain why blacks became the primary target of popular racism, as opposed to other marginalized populations (like new immigrants),[11] or why the consensus that shaped the ruling coalition of the New South did not take the form of an alliance between black leaders, radical Republicans, southern planters, and northern liberals and industrialists in opposition to the most disaffected segments of the white working class.[12] Anyone familiar with racial politics of the South would understand why this would have been a very unlikely development. Even so, the hypothetical coalition that I just described could have sufficed to advance the class interests of northern and southern elites, and it is not very different from the alliance network that briefly dominated southern society in the Reconstruction era.

In any event, the main point is that the white majority identity of the Jim Crow era was shaped by a political process that cannot be explained solely in terms of structural-economic factors (Cell 1982, 131–170). So although neofunctionalist arguments (in the vein of the segmented assimilation thesis) and neoMarxist arguments (which focus on labor market competition between different segments of the working class) provide important insights into how this process unfolded, they are not entirely sufficient.[13]

It is also important to consider the role that Jim Crow laws played in securing the legitimacy of a social order that was undergoing a series of dramatic transformations. Jim Crow laws helped to crystallize the majority group identity that would define this emergent social order. In this regard, Jim Crow laws played an important role in reconsolidating white racial identity in the postbellum era. White exclusivity was an integral feature of the political consensus between the dominant political factions of that era, which transcended class, culture, and political ideology. This is one reason why racial exclusivity was such a prevalent feature of the working-class movements of the nineteenth and early twentieth century and why these demands for racially exclusive employment sectors (and residential communities and migrant flows) were usually respected by governing elites (Cell 1982; Hing 2003; Ngai 2005; Roediger 2008).

There is evidence that the contemporary anti-immigrant movement is still steeped in the racial ideologies of the Jim Crow era and that this has carried over into the movement to expand local enforcement laws. For example, there are connections between many of the same immigration control groups that have supported local enforcement and white supremacist organizations (and notably, the Ku Klux Klan has tried to use local complaints about illegal immigration as a recruitment tool).[14] But there are other features of local immigration laws, and of the public discourse on immigration, that do not conform to the racial common sense of the Jim Crow era (see Jacobson 2008). For example, it does not appear that Latino migrants are being treated like a separate racial caste, as was the case for black populations during Jim Crow. Recent changes to the U.S. census have fragmented the racial identifications of the Latino population instead of consolidating them into a homogenous racial bloc. According to the 2000 census, approximately 48 percent of the U.S. Latino population currently identifies as "white," a slightly lower number identify as "some other race," and little more than 2 percent identify as "black."[15] Although there are openly racist forms of anti-immigrant discourse that target blacks and Latinos, the public discourse of the anti-immigrant movement has adopted a colorblind stance, and immigration control activists have tried to drive this point home by forming alliances with blacks and other minorities.[16] There is also a sizable literature on racial tensions between Latinos and non-Latino blacks that illustrates how antiblack racism and anti-immigrant nativism have taken root in both populations (Mindiola, Niemann, and Rodriguez 2003; Portes and Stepick 1993; Vaca 2004).

All of this draws attention to the contested nature of the majority group identity that is taking shape in the United States today. This emergent identity cannot be cleanly separated from the legacy of Jim Crow, but it would be a mistake to assume that it is strictly derivative of the racial ideologies of that era. The idea that the United States is a postracial nation is popular among many U.S. citizens. In this case, it is assumed that there is no longer a U.S. majority group, or that the majority group is now defined by a colorblind value system. As critical race scholars have pointed out, whiteness still remains the default reference point for this colorblind value system—especially considering that its most vocal proponents are cultural conservatives who have helped orchestrate the white racial formations of the post–Jim Crow era (Bonilla-Silva 2009; Omi and Winant 1994, 113–136). But there is also evidence that this white racial formation is undergoing a period of crisis that has been spurred on by anxieties about the growth of the nonwhite population and about its coherence as a dominant political bloc (which was further underscored by the multiracial coalition of voters that supported Barack Obama's successful bid for the presidency; R. Smith and King 2009).

There is no question that race still matters, but race can matter in many different ways. This is one reason why the focus on the illegal alien as a target for social exclusion may be attractive to some populations, because it appears to cut through all of the antagonisms and ambiguities of race in the United States today. Consistent with a colorblind discourse on race, illegal aliens are not defined by what they "are" but according to something they have done (the act of unauthorized entry). Hence, outrage against the illegal alien appears to offer a legitimate—that is, nonracist—way of redefining the scope and limits of an increasingly complex society. One of the most important things that this field of discourse does is channel public outrage in ways that reconsolidate the definition of the American majority (We Americans are law-abiding citizens, native-born persons, legal residents, etc.). At the same time, it remains stubbornly blind to the history of racist sentiments and institutional practices that have produced the overwhelming concentration of Latinos within the unauthorized migrant population. One of the most powerful features of this field of discourse is its commonsense moralism, which can even resonate with people who employ unauthorized migrants. Consider the following excerpt.

> "People have no idea how essential these guys are to the economy," said the business owner. . . . When asked if he would support a hiring site for the men, he answered emphatically. "No. I don't think tax dollars should go to this. . . . So how can I [complain] about a hiring hall when these guys just built my driveway?" He did not answer his own question.[17]

This quote is taken from a report on the controversies surrounding the growth of the unauthorized migrant workforce in Farmingville, New York. It captures the ambivalent attitudes that set the tone for the way unauthorized migrant workers were incorporated into the local economy.

The presence of the unauthorized migrant was tolerable so long as their relationship with their citizen employer was hidden from public view. But this relationship became problematic when an attempt was made to formally recognize the existence of this workforce and to use tax dollars to pay for a hiring hall that could be used to regulate transactions between local employers and these migrant workers. The ambivalent attitudes of the business owner mirror those of Farmingville's city council members. The city council initially supported the idea of the hiring hall, assuming that it was the most practical way to meet the needs of local employers and to address complaints about the public nuisance created by the unregulated nature of the hiring process (Sandoval 2003). However, this employer-friendly solution to the day laborer controversy was shelved once city council members became aware of the intensity of public disapproval of the hiring hall plan. A vocal segment of the local citizenry did not simply want the unauthorized migrant workers to be better regulated or discretely hidden from public view—they wanted them removed from the local community. So after being persistently lobbied by immigration control activists, the council members began to see unauthorized migration as a law enforcement problem.

This scenario provides an apt illustration of how anti-immigrant sentiments have been able to influence local authorities. It also draws attention to the political function of law enforcement solutions for unauthorized migration, the aim being to convince local constituents that the government is restoring order to what appears to be an "out of control" situation. Complaints about unauthorized migration, however, tend to focus on public nuisance issues (overcrowded apartment buildings, loitering, and so forth) and not on the institutional dynamics that produce illegal migrant populations. In the case of Farmingville, it is likely that the controversy over unauthorized migration would not have mushroomed as quickly as it did if it were not for the proposal to establish a government-funded hiring hall. Even though the local city council initially supported the idea, it found that the public outrage generated by the proposed hiring hall threatened to do more harm to its political legitimacy than the economic problems that would be caused by restricting employer access to unauthorized migrant labor This scenario provides one example of how the desire to control unauthorized migration can become an exercise in appearance management. So the goal of restoring a compromised social order gravitates in the direction of creating public spaces that are free of unassimilated bodies or introducing get-tough laws that affirm the importance of nativity and legal status as a marker of community belonging.

This is why the public spectacle produced by immigration enforcement actions is often of equal, if not greater, importance than the practical effects of these enforcement practices. For example, the 2000–2008 Bush administration was softer on border control than the Clinton administration, but it orchestrated a series of high-profile workplace raids that gave the distinct impression that the government was cracking down on unauthorized migration.[18] There is evidence that the Bush administration took a similar approach in the counterterrorism strategies it pursued after 9/11. Programs like Operation TIPS, which encouraged U.S. residents to report suspicious people to federal authorities, did not turn up a single lead to terrorist operatives, but they tapped into the public desire to become more involved in the business of homeland security. There is also evidence that federal agencies conducted high profile arrests of Arab Muslim persons for suspicion of involvement in terrorism, and continued to give the impression that the deportation of these persons was important for national security, even though the actual charges brought against them had nothing to do with terrorism. (Most of these "terrorist suspects" were deported for civil immigration violations [Sheikh 2008].)[19]

Much more could be written about the way immigration enforcement is used as a public spectacle to manage moral panics about immigration (see, for example, Welch 2006). For the purpose of this discussion, however, it is most important to consider how these practices are used to distinguish the mainstream society from its margins. In this regard, the desire to crack down on unauthorized migrants can function as a way of redefining the inner and outer spaces of a society that is organized around the legal/illegal distinction. Illegality becomes something that is policed in ever more intensive ways but is never eliminated—indeed, it cannot be completely eliminated, because it has become the organizing framework for defining who "we" are (and what we are not) as a society.[20]

The situation that I have just described does not suffice as a comprehensive account of present-day U.S. society. However, it does reflect a set of ideas and institutional tendencies that have had varying degrees of success in shaping local law enforcement priorities across the United States. Lawmakers have attempted to craft immigration policies that address the concerns of immigrant communities, the native-born working population, and employers—and the position that they take usually reflects their sense of the emerging balance of power between these conflicting sets of interests. In a similar vein, the contents of local immigration laws provide insights into the local balance of power between pro- and anti-immigrant constituencies. In communities that have become especially anxious about immigration, these laws provide some degree of assurance that the government will protect the interests of the citizenry.

These sorts of concerns are not radically different from the anxieties about free black populations that fueled the rise of Jim Crow. Jim Crow laws gave white citizens some assurance that the social order would be maintained in the midst of a time of radical transformation. Local immigration laws can be used to assure nervous citizens the government is committed to preserving a different kind of social order, one that is organized around the illegal/legal distinction. And anxieties about immigration can vary widely from one locality to the next. Cities and states that are historic destination points for U.S. migrant flows have larger immigrant communities and a more developed set of immigrant advocacy networks. In these areas, there has been a greater emphasis on using local laws and services to integrate newcomers and to limit the immigration enforcement responsibilities of local police.[21]

The patchwork spread of local immigration laws has made it possible for them to be adapted to these variations in the balance of interests that are shaping the immigration debate. This is why the spread of local immigration laws cannot be explained simply in terms of the growing influence of the immigration control movement, even though this movement has certainly played a role in the expansion of these laws (James Edwards 2003; Numbers USA 2010). Local immigration laws have not been used, uniformly, as a mechanism for excluding immigrants. Instead, they are best understood as an expansion of local sovereignty over immigration matters, which can be deployed in any number of directions (by either strengthening or restricting immigrant rights). But regardless of the direction in which it moves, this process can still play a role in reinforcing status and power differentials between immigrant and native-born populations.

In a nutshell, local enforcement laws allow one segment of the local population (which includes all legal residents but is largely composed of the native-born citizenry) to make decisions about policies and practices that will be applied to the noncitizen population. As a result, the enactment of these laws, even when they are beneficial for immigrants, also reinforces distinctions within the local body politic between those who are deciders of the law and those who are subjects of the law. Most important, these laws foster a field of discourse and institutional practice in which legal status becomes the primary terrain through which these distinctions are realized. Meanwhile, the localization of immigration policy decentralizes the interpretation and implementation of immigration law, which creates more room for slippage between federal law and local practices.

The federal government has a long history of turning a blind eye to this slippage, allowing it to lay the groundwork for patterns in institutional discrimination. In this case, the most pervasive forms of racial inequality are not justified by the letter of the law but by the exceptions and (in)discretions that allow these disparities to be concealed within the margins of the law. Once again, the history of Jim Crow provides an important point of comparison.

INTERPRETING THE LAW: EGALITARIAN NORMS/INEGALITARIAN PRACTICES

An important similarity between Jim Crow and local enforcement laws is their shared connection to a discourse on local sovereignty. Like executive power, this kind of sovereignty can be understood as a discretionary authority that is loosely informed by existing legal precedent but does not strictly conform to the law. This is one reason why states' rights (or inherent authority) arguments have served as a convenient rationale for both Jim Crow and local enforcement.

States' rights arguments are rarely used, in an explicit manner, to justify inegalitarian norms. Instead, they allow for a flexible interpretation of egalitarian norms that leaves their final determination up to the discretion of local authorities. In the case of Jim Crow, this meant that the racial segregation of public facilities, schools, and residential areas were tailored to local preferences, with the caveat that the facilities and services made available to each race were, ostensibly, roughly equivalent. Similar to local enforcement, Jim Crow allowed the white political establishment of each city, township, and state to define its relationship with the black population on its own terms. Some towns and cities used Jim Crow laws to segregate public transportation, but left other parts of the public and social service sector essentially unregulated. Other towns went as far as segregating facilities for the blind and handicapped.[22]

The legal rationales that facilitated the spread of these exclusionary laws were not unique to Jim Crow. As David Cole (2000b, 101–131) has explained, the U.S. court system tolerated the widespread use of all-white juries despite the fact that as early as 1860 the Supreme Court ruled that all-white juries violated the Sixth Amendment rights of black defendants. This contradiction was allowed to persist because the courts adopted extremely narrow criteria for determining whether the jury selection process had truly been discriminatory. Absent proof of a clear intent to exclude black jurors on the basis of race, the courts were not willing to rule that discrimination had taken place. The federal courts also gave trial judges and prosecutors broad leeway to develop after-the-fact explanations for striking black persons from the trial jury.

Jim Crow laws were justified by the legal fiction of separate but equal. In contrast, the all-white jury was justified by a legal fiction concerning the colorblind nature of the jury selection process. Despite their differences, they both rationalized racial inequality by opening up an ambiguous space between the egalitarian norms affirmed by the federal courts and inegalitarian local practices that were also protected by the discretion that the federal courts were willing to grant to local courts and policy makers. In this manner, the authority that white citizenries wielded over nonwhites was allowed to operate within a state of exception that was tacitly protected by the law (and as a legal principle, whiteness itself could be described as a state of exception that is woven through U.S. jurisprudence). This is what made it possible for the racial inequality (and racial violence) of the Jim Crow era to be contained in a space that existed outside of the framework of the law—instead of using the law to overtly justify these practices.

These sorts of (extra)legal rationales proliferated under Jim Crow, but it is important to emphasize that they outlasted Jim Crow. Throughout the twentieth century, variations on these legal rationales were used to affirm the nondiscriminatory nature of racial disparities that pervaded the criminal justice system—including street-level enforcement practices, incarceration rates, and sentencing practices. Even when the evidence of racial disparities in enforcement and sentencing practices was impossible to deny, the federal courts consistently argued that statistical documentation of these disparities did not, in and of itself, constitute proof of racial discrimination (Cole 2000b, 132–168). Unless clear evidence of *intent* to discriminate was provided, the courts were generally willing to assume that enforcement and sentencing practices were being carried out in a race-neutral manner (Ashfaq 2008; Cole 2000b; Dow 2005).

This legal history carries important implications for the way that the federal court system is likely to handle cases involving enforcement practices that appear to be guided by racialized immigrant profiles. The only national study of local enforcement practices has shown that Mexican nationals constitute over 70 percent of all immigration violators apprehended by local police between 2002–2004, despite the fact Mexicans comprise only 56 percent of the unauthorized migrant population (Gladstein et al. 2005).[23] Apprehension rates for Caribbean and African immigration violators were even more skewed. Members of this population were apprehended at a rate that was more than five times the size of their presence in the unauthorized migrant population. In contrast, European and Asian immigration violators were apprehended at rates that were much lower than their presence in the unauthorized migrant population.

There is also evidence that the federal courts are likely to protect the discretionary authority of the police in cases where this authority is challenged by immigrants who believe they have been unfairly profiled (and screened for legal status). The *U.S. v. Vasquez-Alvarez* and *U.S. v. Santana-Garcia* are two examples. An even more compelling example is the case of *Mena v. City of Simi Valley* that was appealed to the Ninth Circuit Court (and was later appealed to the Supreme Court in *Muehler e .al. v. Mena*).[24]

Iris Mena is a legal permanent resident of Mexican heritage who was interrogated by police during the course of a raid that targeted a boarding house in which she was living. The police entered the boarding house with a warrant to search the premises and arrest one of the tenants who was a member of an organized crime ring made up of unauthorized Latino migrants. Mena's room was forcibly entered and she was detained for several hours until it was finally determined that Mena was a legal resident with no connection to the crime ring. The 9th Circuit Court, corroborating the ruling of a lower court, found that the police officers had violated Mena's Fourth Amendment rights. This ruling, however, was overturned when the police officers involved in the raid appealed the case to the Supreme Court. The Supreme Court overturned the circuit court decision, ruling that Mena's detainment—though perhaps more aggressive than necessary—operated within the scope of existing law.[25]

The issue of racial profiling was never explicitly addressed in this case, either by the lower court decisions that ruled for Mena or the Supreme Court decision that ruled against her. Even so, the officers' testimony in the case indicated that Mena's ethnic appearance and the fact that she was living in a house with known members of an undocumented migrant crime ring were some of the criteria that led them to suspect she might have been undocumented. The Court's decision on the legality of this aspect of the police interrogation was consistent with its other decisions on police searches and seizures (Cole 2000b, 16–62: 101–131). It ruled that Mena's detainment was justified by an overriding government interest in securing the safety of the investigating officers, Mena herself, and the general public. The Court also ruled that the police did not need reasonable suspicion to question Mena about her legal status, negating any questions about the possibility that racial profiling had biased the officers' actions.

It is significant that the wording of the Court opinion on this matter was very broad. The Court did not limit the questioning powers of the police to criminal investigations. The justices made an explicit comparison between the right of police officers to inquire about a person's legal status and their right ask other kinds of routine questions that may not be directly pertinent to a criminal investigation. Drawing on the earlier precedent of *Florida v. Bostick*, the Court stated that "when officers have no basis for suspecting a particular individual, they may generally ask questions of that individual" and concluded that "the officers did not need reasonable suspicion to ask Mena for name, date and place of birth or immigration status."[26]

The connection to the Bostick case is significant because of the role this case played in justifying search and seizure practices that targeted black populations (the defendant in the Bostick case was an African American male). In this regard, the *Muehler et al. v. Mena* decision demonstrated that the Supreme Court was prepared to apply the same arguments that had been used to defend the aggressive policing of black populations to other cases that raised questions about the aggressive policing and racial profiling of Latina/os.

RACIAL DISPARITIES, LOCAL ENFORCEMENT, AND THE SILENCE OF THE LAW

The Mena decision carries important implications for search and seizure practices that target Latina/os. But its relevance to the current debate over local immigration laws is much more ambiguous. The Simi Valley police who were involved in the raid were acting in partnership with federal immigration agents as part of an arrangement that had been authorized by the 287(g) clause of the 1996 immigration reform act. Their actions also operated within the conventional view of the role of local police in immigration enforcement that dates to the 1983 *Gonzalez v. City of Peoria* decision. So one lesson that can be drawn from the Mena decision is that the federal courts are willing to grant local police the broad authority to question people about their legal status, so long as these enforcement powers are explicitly authorized by federal law. This guiding framework seems to have been reinforced by the recent debate over the Arizona immigration law (senate bill 1070), which was proposed in April 2010 and enacted in late July of the same year.

Soon after it was drafted, this law became one of the most notorious local immigration laws in recent history. In its original form, it was widely regarded to be the most aggressive local immigration law ever drafted (although other local immigration laws have introduced similar measures).[27] Among other things, the law authorized local police to detain people whom they suspected to be undocumented and mandated all Arizona residents (regardless of legal status) to carry proof of legal status in public—or be charged with a misdemeanor offense. The wording of the law explains that officers are only expected to screen people for legal status in the course of routine police work (similar to the way that many police departments have incorporated the NCIC database into their routine activities). Nevertheless, it is clear that the law gives the local police the authority to initiate legal screenings with anyone whom they suspect to be "illegal," irrespective of whether the individual has committed a prior violation or is the subject of an ongoing investigation. This is a broader interpretation of police authority than has been advanced by other local immigration laws.

In some important respects, the law's interpretation of the immigration enforcement powers of police is not very different from the language of the Mena decision. In both cases, the police appear to have been given wide discretion to enact legal screenings that are not directly relevant to criminal investigations. The big difference is that the Mena decision was addressing a case in which local police were carrying out their immigration enforcement duties in partnership with federal agents. The Arizona law authorized police to carry out legal screenings completely outside of the provisions provided under federal law. This distinction underscores the argument that the federal courts (and the federal government more generally) is willing to protect the immigration enforcement powers of local police, so long as these actions fall under the auspices of federal law.

The federal government has taken steps to oppose the Arizona law, on the grounds that it violates the supremacy of federal law.[28] President Obama has criticized the bill,[29] and a lawsuit against the bill was filed by the DoJ in the spring of 2010, accompanied by lawsuits from a number of civil rights and immigration rights coalitions. Federal supremacy arguments are a prominent feature of most of these challenges (and are central to all of the arguments against the law that have been developed by federal officials).[30] For example, when an Arizona District Court judge struck down some of the most controversial features of the Arizona law, she argued that these provisions were unlawful because they duplicated enforcement practices and sanctions that were already included in federal law.[31] Similar arguments are included in the DoJ lawsuit against the bill.[32]

Federal supremacy arguments have played a role in the dismantling of other controversial local immigration laws, such as the anti-illegal immigration law that was enacted by the City of Hazleton, Pennsylvania, in 2006 (which was, arguably, the most infamous local immigration law prior to the 2010 Arizona law).[33] The Hazleton law contained a number of measures that have been championed by immigration control advocates, including aggressive sanctions for private citizens who contract with unauthorized migrants, new procedures for involving local police in immigration enforcement, and an English-only town ordinance.

As with the Arizona law, complaints about racial profiling were a prominent feature of the public debate over the Hazleton law, but they were not a prominent feature of the legal debate over these laws.[34] Surprisingly, the legal arguments crafted by the opponents of the Hazleton immigration laws only obliquely addressed the matter of racial profiling (observing how the laws drove Latino customers away from local businesses).[35] Furthermore, the Pennsylvania district court that struck down the laws did so on the grounds that they violated the supremacy of federal law.[36] This decision was eventually affirmed by the Third Circuit Court (after a very long delay—the circuit court took almost two years to arrive at a final decision).[37]

The federal law that was referenced in the original District Court ruling was the 1986 Immigration Reform and Control Act (IRCA). The court argued that, because IRCA had already introduced sanctions for employers (and other private citizens) who contracted with unauthorized migrants the Hazleton laws were unnecessary (and unlawful). The irony of this decision is that IRCA has been roundly criticized for the ineffectiveness of its employer sanctions. The senators who drafted the bill have acknowledged that there never was a serious interest in enforcing sanctions against employers.[38] Several researchers have observed how employers evaded IRCA's sanctions by turning to "middle man" contractors (Martin and Taylor 1991; Phillips and Massey 1999; J. Taylor, Martin, and Fix 1997). One of the most prominent examples came to light in 2004, when it was discovered that Walmart had been subcontracting most of its janitorial services to employment agencies that recruited unauthorized migrant labor.[39]

When viewed in this light, the objection of the federal courts to the Hazleton laws seems to be focused on protecting employers from excessive scrutiny from state and local governments. There is a continuity between these interests and the double standard that the federal government has historically tolerated on unauthorized migration (enacting strict quotas on Latin American immigration, enforcing immigration laws against unauthorized migrants, but exempting employers who hire unauthorized migrants from being severely sanctioned; Ngai 2005).

The debate over the Arizona law has not been as focused on the question of employer sanctions (even though the Supreme Court has agreed to hear a case involving an Arizona law that imposes new sanctions on employers who hire unauthorized migrants).[40] Nonetheless, the opposition to this law has gravitated toward similar kinds of federal supremacy arguments. These supremacy arguments could prove to be an effective means of protecting immigrant rights, if they are able to prevent a shift toward an even more aggressive kind of local enforcement. (Several states looking to enact local immigration laws similar to Arizona's are awaiting the outcome of the legal debate over this law.)[41] But even if these arguments are successful, they will not establish legal precedents that strengthen the legal and civil rights of U.S. residents. Once again, this is because they are oriented toward limiting the legislative powers of local lawmakers—not toward strengthening Fourth Amendment rights (and other rights that could be used to challenge arbitrary and overly aggressive enforcement practices). Any limitation that these challenges effect on the discretionary authority of law enforcement will remain specific to the debate over local immigration laws. But they will be of virtually no consequence for the broader debate over racial profiling and the struggle to end selective enforcement practices that target racial minority populations.

This is why the Supreme Court's decision in the case of Iris Mena is very significant. It draws attention to a trajectory of legal opinion that is moving a in a very different direction from the federal supremacy arguments that are being used to challenge local immigration laws. The Mena decision demonstrates that when you look beyond the debate over local immigration laws federal lawmakers are willing to grant police the power to question people about their legal status (and are also willing to give the police the benefit of the doubt in cases where there is some question over whether they engaged in racial profiling that violated a suspect's Fourth Amendment rights).

So the debate over the Arizona immigration law obscures much more than it reveals about the federal opinion on the role of police in immigration enforcement. It can still be argued that the opposition to the Arizona law is an important milestone in immigrant rights activism. But the opposition to the Arizona law does little to change the situation of people in Iris Mena's situation. This includes noncitizens (and citizens who "look like" immigrants) who are subjected to legal status screenings that have nothing to do with local immigration laws In these cases, the discretionary authority that the federal courts have been willing to grant to police also allows room for racial profiling.

In effect, these court decisions make it possible for discriminatory acts to operate within spaces of discretionary authority that have been created by the law. As a result, they create a slippage between egalitarian norms (i.e., constitutional rights) and inegalitarian practices (that require the use of racial profiles) that are not very different from the kinds of slippages produced by the legal rationales that were historically used to justify racial disparities in the United States—dating back to the era of Jim Crow.

The significance of the Mena decision becomes even more apparent when looking comparatively at incarceration rates for first-generation immigrants and their second-generation offspring. The opposition to local immigration laws is, in large part, an attempt to protect unauthorized migrants from aggressive screening practices. One of the aims of this movement is to solve the problem of unauthorized migration by creating new paths to legalization for these migrants (which could be provided by a new federal immigration law) instead of criminalizing this population. One fact that has given more weight to these arguments is that the crime rates of first-generation immigrants (legal or unauthorized) are significantly lower than crime rates for native-born populations (Butcher and Piehl 2005; Rumbaut and Ewing 2007). There also appears to be a correspondence between rising levels of immigration and reductions in crime—which is tied to the lower proclivity for criminal activity among first-generation immigrants (Rumbaut and Ewing 2007; Sampson 2008; Sampson, Raudenbush, and Earls 1997). But there is also evidence that the second-generation offspring of immigrants have a very different experience with law enforcement than their parents. One unfortunate outcome of socioeconomic "integration" is that incarceration rates for the second generation begin to approximate those of other native-born populations. For Latinos this change is especially dramatic, shifting from lower than average incarceration rates for first-generation migrants (compared to native-born whites), to higher than average incarceration rates for second-generation offspring of these migrants (Pew Hispanic Center 2008).

Incarceration rates for Latino populations are being conditioned by many of the same factors that have contributed toward the overincarceration of black youth. This includes, among other things, racial ideologies that have constructed Latino/as as a "crime threat," the concentration of crime control spending on poor neighborhoods, socioeconomic stressors that weaken family ties, limited opportunities for higher education and secure, full-time employment, and the growth of the informal economy in response to the blocked opportunities for social mobility produced by the aforementioned trends (Brotherton and Barrios 2004; Oboler 2009; Rumbaut 2008). So it would appear that the African American experience of racialization, resource deprivation, and incarceration is the future that awaits many second-generation children of today's immigrants.

What is most important—for the purpose of this discussion—is that the challenges facing the second generation have been largely ignored by the mainstream immigration debate. Unfortunately, the concern for protecting the rights of first-generation immigrants has not translated into a concern for addressing the structural inequalities and forms of institutional discrimination that may effect the life chances of their children. In part, this is because the sympathetic image of the hardworking immigrant reproduces many of the narrative themes (of personal responsibility and moral integrity) that have been used to rationalize race and class inequality in the United States—conveying the implicit message that people who have less than others (and who are more likely to be incarcerated than others) have simply made poorer choices about what to do with their lives.

This distinction between the deserving and the undeserving (or between noncriminals and criminal suspects) has left its mark on the debate over local immigration laws. Opposition to police involvement in immigration enforcement has been the strongest when these enforcement practices are used to target noncitizens on the basis of nothing more than the suspicion of illegality (and, notably, the screening practices that have been authorized by local immigration laws have mainly targeted this population). These are also the sorts of screening practices that are most likely to be struck down by the federal courts. The federal courts have been much less inclined to challenge the legality of similar kinds of screening practices if they are deployed in the context of criminal investigations or in the context of other local enforcement initiatives that are authorized by federal law. Even if it turns out (as it did in the case of Iris Mena) that the persons subjected to these legal-status screenings are innocent of the criminal infractions of which they are suspected, there is still a presumption that the interrogation was warranted by the fact that it was connected to the investigation of criminal activity. This line of reasoning is typical of the way U.S. legal opinion has focused on determinations of individual culpability within specific cases that are abstracted from the broader social and historical context. There is very little room, within this interpretative framework, for making connections between race, class. and the social construction of criminal activity. As a result, it is difficult to see that low-income minority youth are more likely to be interrogated for crimes connected to the illegal drug trade simply because of where they live (and what they look like)—even though they may be no more likely to use illegal drugs than youth in affluent, upper middle–class communities.[42] It is also difficult to see how the distribution networks for illegal contraband that are concentrated in poor minority communities are intertwined with consumption networks for this contraband that are woven throughout the U.S. class structure. (In this regard, the focus of antidrug enforcement on low-income racial minority populations reproduces the same kind of race and class bias that has led immigration enforcement to focus most of its attention on unauthorized migrant workers and not their employers.)

There is substantial evidence that the racial profiling of black youth has been shaped by these kinds of inequalities and biases, which lead some populations to be more closely scrutinized and aggressively policed than others (Alexander 2010; Arditti, Lambert-Shute, and Joest 2003; Boothe 2010; Petit and Western 2004; Tonry 1996). And there is a kind of immigrant profiling—that is not being addressed by the recent debate over local immigration laws—that appears to be connected to the same kinds of biases and enforcement strategies.

The curious thing about the debate over local immigration laws is that it has produced a critical discourse about immigrant profiling that exposes some of these biases, while turning a blind eye to others. From a proimmigration perspective, it would seem obvious that laws that allow for the indiscriminate targeting of "foreign-looking" people are racist. In this case, the goal of cracking down on unauthorized migration can easily become an exercise in policing the national identity (raising the question "who looks like an American?").

This is another reason why the history of Jim Crow is pertinent to the debate over local immigration laws: it offers another example of a local policy regime that was bound up with the symbolic politics of the majority group identity. But other kinds of problematic distinctions can crop up in the discourse of the proimmigration position. This position can, at times, be drawn into making distinctions between "good" and "bad" immigrants (which are used to emphasize that the immigration reform movement is only advocating on behalf of the "good" immigrants; see Kateel and Shahani 2008). In this case, the terms of exclusion do not revolve around the legal/illegal distinction but around a law-abiding/criminal distinction (which makes an exception for people who have only committed civil immigration violations). This distinction does not overtly appeal to racial stereotypes but it *does* normalize the forms of institutional discrimination that have allowed the goal of crime control to become connected to the policing of a racialized underclass.

The shift toward a more enforcement-heavy immigration policy—at both the local and national level—can be connected to the persisting influence of these discourses on race and crime. As I have tried to explain, the problem is not simply that these ideas are being resuscitated and used to aggressively police the boundaries of political membership in the United States. There is also a disinclination to examine the ways they have defined the normal functioning of major institutions (such as the immigration system, law enforcement, and national labor markets) and the apparently race-neutral concerns that have shaped immigration policy (such as concerns about national security, border control, and the problem of immigrant crime). I explore this dilemma in more depth in the next chapter.

5

RACE, NATION, IMMIGRATION

STRANDED AT THE CROSSROADS OF
LIBERAL THOUGHT

The Supreme Court's 1923 decision in the case of Bhagat Singh Thind is one of the best-known rulings on the matter of race and citizenship. It reinforced the message sent by the 1921 Takao Ozawa decision that Asian nationals were not eligible for naturalization on the grounds that they were not white persons.[1] Both decisions were informed by the racial common sense of their day. The Thind decision, in particular, was justified on the grounds that Asian immigrants did not meet the criteria that defined what was "popularly known as the Caucasian race."[2]

The irony of the Supreme Court's decision is that it preserved the integrity of white citizenship by undermining social Darwinist arguments that had been used to justify the racial exclusions of the Jim Crow era. Bhagat Singh Thind built the argument about his racial status around the idea that he was a genetic descendent of the original Aryans. This led Thind to argue that even though he was nonwhite in appearance his biological lineage was Caucasian. Thind's unusual argument has been corroborated by present-day geneticists who have demonstrated that it is possible for non-European people to share more genetic markers in common with European whites than they do with others of their same ethnicity and racial appearance.[3] These observations have been used to challenge the idea that humans belong to distinct biogenetic populations that share the same racial traits.

Thind, on the other hand, was attempting to prove that he was indeed a member of a "superior race." What he learned, however, is that his racial identity could not be strictly derived from his biological lineage, because the interpretation that he was trying to advance threatened to undermine the racial common sense of the Jim Crow era. This is why the Supreme Court did not merely attempt to falsify Thind's argument about his racial origins;[4] it insisted that these details were irrelevant to the fundamental question of his racial status under the law. The Court made it very clear that the race that Thind appeared to be in the eyes of the average American citizen was of greater significance than any evidence he could produce about his biological lineage.[5]

The Supreme Court did not go so far as to claim that race is a necessary fiction, but it did acknowledge that race was not simply a matter of biology. It insisted that the meaning of race also had to be interpreted in light of popular sentiments that had been shaped by the history and culture of a nation. In this regard, the Court treated race as a social construct rather than as a biological fact. And in a rather unlikely way, it used this constructionist interpretation to preserve the idea of white citizenship, not to dismantle it.

BEYOND THE LIMITS OF THE LAW

The Thind decision illustrates how perceptions of the racial difference of noncitizens can determine their right to have rights under the law. Today, this connection between race and rights is much more abstruse. Even so, perceptions of the cultural and racial difference of immigrants can still influence the general tone of immigration policy. In this light, it is worth considering that the "browning" of U.S. migration flows; the general weakening of civil, legal, and social rights; and the shift toward a more enforcement-heavy immigration policy agenda have occurred in conjunction with each other.

The 1965 Immigration Act removed the racial quotas that had been in effect for the better part of the twentieth century, and these changes, in turn, opened the door for a new flow of Asian and Latin American migration. By the 1980s the nonwhite migration flow had become the dominant source of new immigrants to the United States. This is the same period of time that the policy discourse on immigration became more enforcement

oriented (see chapters 2 and 3). And from the mid-1990s onward, the federal government imposed a series of new restrictions on immigrant social
and legal rights, along with other laws that curtailed privacy and social
rights for all U.S. citizens.[6]

Although the sphere of national law has become more inclusive in
some ways, it has, in many other ways, become less inclusive and more
fragmentary. The troubled relationship between race and nation is a part
of this problem—which concerns the willingness of a national citizenry
(and the institutions acting on behalf of this citizenry) to allow people
who are regarded as racial Others to be admitted without qualification to
their political community. In this regard, one of the most compelling features of the sphere of national law is not the law itself, but the ideas about
race and cultural difference that move through it—influencing the law, but
without always leaving an imprint on the law. In this chapter I explore
some of these ideas.

Unlike the previous chapters, this one does not focus on trends in
state and federal policy. Instead, it maps several currents of intellectual
thought that have been used to conceptualize the relationship between
the immigrant and mainstream society over the course of the twentieth
century. Much of this discussion focuses on the ideas of liberal thinkers
because of the defining influence they have had on American sociology,
United States jurisprudence, and the mainstream argument in favor of immigration. I also engage ideas that were influential at different stages of
the twentieth century. I use the historic sweep of the discussion to draw
attention to important turning points in the discourse on race, ethnicity,
and immigration—but my primary aim is to show how the antagonisms
that characterized early twentieth-century thought on these issues are
still a part of the contemporary discourse. Some of the ideas that I discuss
are rooted in assumptions that are not very different from the racial common sense that was articulated by the Thind decision, while others have
attempted to chart a new direction away from these ideas about race and
nation. Despite these differences, however, most of the bodies of thought
I discuss have shied away from critiquing the kinds of distinctions that
have defined the meaning of race in the United States. In this regard, they
have tended to acquiesce to these distinctions—even though, in most
cases, they have not actively defended them.

I must emphasize that this is, primarily, a critical discussion. I do not offer a definitive solution but a map of the various dead-ends that have characterized the intellectual discourse on race and immigration, At best, what I offer is a more compelling way of conceptualizing immigrant marginality that could point the way to a new solution for this problem. But perhaps the most important theme of this discussion is that this solution cannot simply be a "policy solution." The kind of solution that I am reaching for in this essay requires something more than the demand for equality under the law. It requires the resuscitation of lines of critical inquiry that can operate in the space that exists beyond the law; in order to excavate and rethink the assumptions and priorities that have influenced the interpretation of the law.

CULTURAL PLURALISM, ETHNICITY THEORY, AND THE PROBLEM OF LAISSEZ-FAIRE RACISM

Liberal thinkers have faced a great deal of criticism for evading the problem of racial inequality, and as some scholars have argued this limitation stems from antagonisms that run through the heart of liberal thought (Mills 1997; Parekh 1995; S. Steinberg 2007). On one hand, there is an aversion to openly defending race-based exclusions because they violate the meritocratic ideals of liberal individualism. Even though racial inequality may exist "in fact," in principle, all individuals should have the opportunity to rise to their own potential. But there is also an aversion to reforming the institutional practices that perpetuate racial inequalities—because these sorts of interventions are viewed as illiberal impositions on the individual rights and freedoms of others. Lawrence Bobo (1999) has used the term laissez-faire racism to describe this worldview, which begrudgingly acknowledges that racism is wrong but insists that the legal system (and the government in general) should not get involved in sanctioning individuals or institutions for their racist actions.[7]

This is not just a matter of criticizing a particular social formation within the United States that adheres to liberal ideals. It is also important to consider how liberal ideas have defined the policy and legal discourse of mainstream institutions and how they have been used to negotiate governing arrangements that have met with the approval of a broad cross section of the U.S. population—irrespective of their politics. For example, federal rulings of the Jim Crow era did not always endorse racial exclusions outright, but they protected the discretion of local authorities to interpret the law in the way they saw fit. In a similar vein, the Supreme Court's rationale for the Thind decision did not openly defend the ideas about racial inferiority that had shaped the anti-Asian racism of the times. It took these sentiments as given and defended the right of the citizenry to have their racial preferences respected. In each case, racial inequalities and racial preferences were justified by appeals to personal or collective freedoms—similar to the way that liberal arguments have historically been used to rationalize race, gender, and class inequities (Fraser and Gordon 1998).

This pattern of social exclusion changed with the rise of the liberal discourse on cultural pluralism. The shift toward cultural pluralism was shaped, in part, by an intellectual movement in the early part of the twentieth century that displaced biological theories of race with the concept of ethnicity. Ethnicity was regarded as a more scientifically sound concept than race, because it was not bogged down by erroneous assumptions of a biological inheritance that was presumably shared by all group members (Li 1999; Rees 2007). Furthermore, ethnicity theory provided intellectual ammunition for liberal scholars and policy makers who wanted to dismantle the racial caste system of the Jim Crow era. For liberal intellectuals (which included a great many sociologists), racial barriers to social mobility were an inexcusable contradiction for a modern society like the United States.[8]

It is telling, however, that the dismantling of scientific racism did not pave the way for a more stridently, antiracist liberal assimilation theory. Instead, the intellectual currents of the social science community drifted in the direction of cultural pluralism. The origins of cultural pluralist theory can be traced to the writing of Horace Kallen in the early 1900s (Ratner 1984). But it is Glazer and Moynihan's *Beyond the Melting Pot* that is widely regarded as shifting the mainstream academic discourse away from assimilation theory (Glazer and Moynihan [1963] 1970). *Beyond the Melting Pot* introduced the social science community to an idea of U.S. society that was characterized by a healthy degree of structural and civic integration but also by persisting, "unmeltable" ethnic differences.

Beyond the Melting Pot played a pivotal role in changing the way sociologists treated race and ethnicity (Omi and Winant 1994, 14–23). After *Beyond the Melting Pot,* it became increasingly common for sociologists to emphasize ethnicity over race. Sociologists used ethnicity theory to examine the agency of minority populations by looking at how ethnic identities and solidarities were used to overcome barriers to integration. These analyses were often used to illustrate how each ethnic minority created its own distinct pathway to integration (Fuchs 1990; Greeley 1974). As a result, there was no guaranteed end point at which all minorities and new immigrant populations become indistinguishable from the mainstream culture.

This emphasis on ethnicity built upon the qualified tolerance of cultural difference that was already part of liberal assimilation theory. In the context of liberal assimilation theory, however, cultural differences were tolerated only if they were subordinated to a national-civic identity that transcended parochial and ethnic-cultural differences (Almond and Verba 1989; J. Cohen and Arato 1994; Salins 1997; Walzer 1984). In contrast, postwar liberal pluralism opened up more room for ethnic identities to enter the public sphere. As Richard Rees (2007) has observed, "ethnicity" was exclusive to white, European immigrants when it was introduced into North American popular and scholarly discourse in the late nineteenth century. But from the mid-twentieth century onward, it was appropriated by racial minority populations and became a supplementary feature of almost every articulation of racial identity; giving rise to the concept of the racial-ethnic population. One of the advantages of this discourse on ethnicity for non-European immigrants is that it became more acceptable for them to integrate into the mainstream as ethnic minorities. Or in other words, it was possible for them to acculturate without necessarily becoming "white." In this regard, ethnicity appeared to offer new immigrants a way to transcend race without having to let go of their inherited culture. But the rise of this new discourse on ethnicity and cultural pluralism was also accompanied by continuing trends in racial stratification, especially for the native-born black population.

This is the fundamental ambiguity of liberal cultural pluralism. On one hand, it is possible to view this body of theory as a progressive step forward because of the role it played in delegitimizing biological notions of race difference. On the other hand, as its critics have argued, this desire to move beyond the legacy of scientific racism led it to deemphasize the continuing significance of race (Omi and Winant 1994; S. Steinberg 2007; Takaki 1994). The earliest forms of ethnicity theory and cultural pluralism focused exclusively on European migrant populations (Day 2000; Ratner 1984). Later applications of pluralist theory examined the situation of black populations but they were criticized for catering to discourses that pathologized the black poor. For example, the pluralist theory of Moynihan and Glazer has been criticized for connecting its treatment of ethnicity to a "by your bootstraps" model of social mobility that influenced later research on immigrants and ethnicity.[9]

According to their critics, Moynihan and Glazer advanced an argument that suggested that immigrants who used their ethnic networks wisely were capable of overcoming the barriers of racism, nativism, and class prejudice. As a result, the analysis of inequality focuses on comparisons between immigrant populations that have overcome barriers to integration and other minority populations that always seem to wind up on the bottom rungs of society. These arguments were part of a broader shift in the discourse on race and poverty, which moved away from structural explanations and began to focus more attention on cultural-behavioral dynamics within racial minority populations that were, presumably, reproducing the cycle of poverty. The concept of laissez-faire racism can be viewed as an attempt to explain the body of ideas that was produced by this transformation in the U.S. discourse on race—which made it possible to acknowledge that racism was unacceptable but also that the causes of present-day inequality had little to do with the ways in which the mainstream society viewed and treated these populations.

The critique of ethnicity theory and cultural pluralism has focused on the kinds of issues outlined above concerning the way it tends to excuse or avoid the problem of antiblack racism. However, there is another, less explored aspect of cultural pluralism that has quietly affirmed discourses on white exclusivity. This aspect of cultural pluralism turns the openness to the cultural difference of immigrants and minorities on its head. If immigrants have the right to preserve their culture and social networks, it follows that the white majority has the right to do the same.

UNLIKELY CONVERGENCES: LIBERAL
MULTICULTURALISM AND CULTURAL CONSERVATISM

Australia is the only nation in the world that transitioned from an era of explicit national origin (and racial) restrictions on immigrant admissions to an era of official multiculturalism. On one hand, this would appear to signal a radical transition from the racial identity politics that shaped Australian nationalism for the better part of the twentieth century. But as some scholars have observed, there is a submerged continuity that runs through the era of Australian white nationalism and the current era of multicultural postnationalism. The white Australia policy produced a national culture that was more or less exclusive to whites of European descent. In the current era this is no longer the case, but there is evidence that Australian multiculturalism has functioned as a rather innovative way of preserving the cultural dominance of the white majority (Jayasuriya and Gothard 2003; Povinelli 2001). So, although Australian multiculturalism has created more room for non-European Others within the public sphere, it has carried over some of the same cultural and racial hierarchies that defined the national culture of decades past.

Canada has followed a similar path (Fleras and Elliot 2002, 352–354). Canadian multiculturalism has been infused with neoliberal principles that are geared toward recruiting high-skilled migrant workers and increasing the competitiveness of the Canadian workforce in the global marketplace (Mitchell 2003). But alongside this openness to high-skilled immigrants, Canadian multiculturalism has institutionalized the right of the traditional, native-born population to preserve its cultural heritage. Treatises on Canadian multiculturalism assert that some native-born populations (including French Canadians, British Canadians, and Aboriginals) are entitled to have their inherited culture protected by state-subsidized institutional mechanisms that should not be extended to more recent migrant groups (Fleras and Elliot 2002, 168–170: 218–220; Kymlicka 1996).

These sorts of arrangements have proved to be an effective political solution for the present-day complexities of cultural diversity and mass immigration. From a liberal perspective, they certainly mark a step forward from the racially exclusive majority formations of the early twen-

tieth century. But they also evade a question that was central to liberal
assimilation theory concerning the matter of structural integration. Despite its shortcomings, liberal assimilation theory was more forthright
in arguing that the social mobility of minority populations cannot occur
without eradicating the prejudices and other kinds of barriers that separate the social networks of these populations from the majority group. In
contrast, liberal theories of cultural pluralism have placed more emphasis
on pathways to integration that can be pursued within ethnically exclusive networks. In this regard, liberal pluralist theory has tended to place
most of the responsibility for overcoming social barriers to integration in
the hands of immigrants themselves. Meanwhile, the society into which
new immigrants are integrating has become more stratified along lines of
race and class—which includes a growing socioeconomic divide between
immigrants and the native born.

Despite its shortcomings, the multiculturalism of Australia and Canada
is still a rather sophisticated response to the cultural complexities and
socioeconomic inequities of the present era that, at least officially, recognizes the cultural identities of minority populations. Meanwhile, the
United States has not reached the point of officially declaring itself a multicultural society. Instead ,it has gravitated toward a colorblind discourse
on assimilation that stands in stark contrast to the existing cultural pluralism, ethnic segmentation, and race and class stratification of U.S. society. It could be argued that the political culture of the United States is
not "liberal" enough to officially recognize the white, European American
population as a distinct cultural formation.[10] Nevertheless, discourses on
whiteness are still capable of exerting a powerful influence on U.S. political culture and national identity.

Even though whiteness has been dismantled as a state-administered
legal category, it has persisted as a diffuse array of solidarities and identities that have taken root within many segments of the native-born population. This type of racial formation is not very different from the white
national identity that was defended by the Thind decision. It describes
a people who see themselves as sharing a common bloodline, culture,
and history. In many respects, this popular discourse on whiteness has
become the collective identity that "dare not speak its name" within the
public sphere of the post–Jim Crow United States. It rarely uses the explicit language of race to express its grievances—resorting instead to in-

terpretations of national identity, a shared morality, or a middle-class sensibility that distinguishes itself from a racialized lower class and "liberal elites." As several scholars have noted, this coded discourse on racial identity has taken many forms over the past several decades, ranging from Jerry Falwell's moral majority to the flesh and blood nationalism of the anti-immigrant movement and, most recently, the populist rhetoric of the Tea Party movement (Chavez 2008; Omi and Winant 1994).[11]

On one hand, these kinds of identities are usually defined in opposition to liberalism. For example, anti-immigrant pundits tend to blame liberal elites for compromising the cultural integrity of the nation. But on the other hand, these constituencies have also fought to preserve status differences between minority and majority populations that had been tolerated for many decades by liberal thought (Cell 1982, 171–191). There are also some unlikely similarities between this kind of identity politics and the liberal discourse on cultural pluralism. In coming to terms with these similarities, it is important to keep in mind that primordialism (a perspective on ethnicity that is very similar to the flesh and blood nationalism of anti-immigrant populists) is a variant of pluralist theory (Kivisto 2005, 16). In this case, cultural pluralism evokes a field of racial-ethnic dividing lines that must not be transgressed. The primary concern of the primordialist is cultural preservation, not cross-cultural communication. Pluralism is not viewed as an ideal model of society but as an agonistic fact of existence, and because of the danger of being "contaminated" by other cultural formations, there is always an uneasy tension between primordial cultural identities and their various Others.

Samuel Huntington's writing on immigration and U.S. national culture is a good case in point. Like other leading voices in the immigration control movement, Huntington views the Latino population—and Mexican nationals in particular—as an unassimilable demographic threat (Huntington 2005, 221–256). According to Huntington, the only effective solution for Latino migration is to dramatically reduce the inflow of all Latinos into the United States. It is telling that Huntington's complaints target the entire Latino population and not merely an underclass of undocumented migrants.

Huntington's discussion drifts in the direction of a colorblind conservatism when he discusses African Americans, which he describes as a suitably assimilated minority population. Ironically, African Americans have been long been the target of conservative (and liberal) critics for many of the same reasons that Huntington has targeted Latinos. But according to Huntington, African Americans are desirable minorities, relative to Latinos, because of their English fluency, Protestant value base, and lower fertility rates (which are closer to white American levels; Huntington 2005, 146–151; 2004, 30). But despite Huntington's attempt at making his Anglo-Saxon cultural norms inclusive of racial minorities, his discussion still drifts in the direction of white racial identity. Huntington does not endorse a white nationalist identity politics. Nevertheless, he does argue that if there is not a concerted effort to preserve an exclusively Anglo-Saxon national culture, the native-born population will gravitate toward a white identity politics to define who they are as a national people (Huntington 2005, 295–316).

The most significant thing about Huntington's evocation of a white racial identity is that it takes the form of a begrudging acceptance of cultural pluralism. According to Huntington, this new kind of white identity politics is the sign of a majority formation in retreat. This is not quite the same thing as the desire to safeguard a national territory from unassimilable Others. Instead, it is a pluralist, postnational phenomena. It occurs once the majority group has resigned itself to the fact that its culture no longer defines the universal norms of the nation-state and becomes exclusively concerned for its own self-preservation. As a result, the idea of a national people becomes detached from the idea of the nation-state. The nation is no longer a place occupied by a sovereign people but is, instead, a sovereign people of shared cultural and "racial" heritage who remain a nation irrespective of the place they happen to occupy. At this point, Huntington's discussion of white identity politics also begins to approximate the deterritorialized diaspora identities that have been popularized by immigration and postcolonial scholars. It bears noting that the theme of exile has been a common feature of the far and new right, white identity politics of the post Civil Rights era (which describes a population that feels it has been betrayed by the nation-state; Omi and Winant 1994, 117–128). In this case, the concept of "exile" is best understood as a metaphor for the changing political circumstances of white populations (For example, Margaret Somers has observed how the mostly white popular-nationalist movements of the current era can be understood as a confused political response to the steady erosion of citizenship rights under neoliberalism; 2008, 140–143). Nevertheless, it evokes an identity in which one's primary loyalty lies with a race or a culture and not necessarily with the nation-state in which one happens to reside. Even though Huntington seems a little ambivalent about this kind of identity politics, his explanations of global politics evoke a similar kind of social formation. And once again, this leads Huntington toward a pluralist worldview that is oriented around the themes of cultural conflict and preservation.

One the best examples of these ideas is Huntington's controversial thesis on the clash of civilizations. According to Huntington's argument, civilizational loyalties—rooted in traditional ethnic cultures—are the main fault lines of the current era of global politics (Huntington 1998). Hence, a Korean American and a Nigerian American should still be viewed as members of foreign civilizations despite the fact that they can legally claim to be U.S. citizens. In contrast, an American of Anglo-Saxon origin, a white German national, and a white English national all share ties to the same western European civilization, irrespective of their legal status or where they happen to reside.

Huntington's civilizational thesis is not as porous as the theories that have been used to conceptualize the immigrant diaspora. The literature on transnational immigrant communities emphasizes the multiplicity of these identities—the capacity to belong to many different cultural and political worlds at once (Angelo 1997; Appadurai 1996; Arthur 2000). Huntington, on the other hand, seeks to narrow these identities down to a primary loyalty. Even so, his writing evokes a similar kind of sociocultural formation that has become abstracted from the territorial schema of the Cold War–era interstate system. Civilizational loyalties override the legal status that is granted to the individual by the state, and it is this ancestral culture—not one's legal status—that fundamentally defines one's loyalties. Once again, the nation is not a place but a people who remain a sovereign entity even if they happen to be dispersed across many different territories governed by various state systems.

LOOKING BEYOND THE CULTURAL PRIMORDIALIST VS. SOCIAL CONSTRUCTIONIST DIVIDE

The cultural primordialism evoked by the writing of scholars like Samuel Huntington and the social constructionist view of ethnicity that has influenced liberal pluralist theory are assumed to belong in two very different intellectual camps (Fenton 2003; Ichijo and Uzelac 2005). As the term implies, primordialism refers to an identity that remains unchanged for long stretches of time and that tends to overdetermine the loyalties of social actors. In contrast, social constructionism has paid more attention to the way that ethnic-cultural identities can be strategically adapted to present-day conditions. In this regard, ethnicity is treated as a more or less rational construct (or a cultural tool kit) that can be put to many different uses.[12]

Despite these differences, both these perspectives can become oriented around an ethos of cultural preservation. The social meaning of cultural preservation can be interpreted in different ways by both camps. But putting these differences aside, the social constructionist can still respect the racial boundary lines between minority and majority populations that are taken as a given by the primordialist. So even though social constructionists may explore the ways that immigrants and minorities reconstruct their identities, this does not necessarily mean that they are open to exploring processes that could transform the distinctions that have been used to separate the white majority from nonwhite minority populations. In other words, the various elements of the liberal pluralist mixing bowl never meld. They may learn to coexist with each other. But the presumption is that nothing new will ever emerge from this assortment of cultural differences. Mexican American identities may change over time, but they will remain "Mexican" nonetheless.

It is in this sense that the transformational ambitions of liberal pluralism have been significantly more modest than earlier versions of liberal assimilationist theory. Of course, liberal assimilation theory was not without its shortcomings. It presumed, for example, that cultural change only ran in one direction—requiring immigrants and minorities to blend seamlessly into the culture of the mainstream society. Nevertheless, it contained bolder statements about the need for "old" loyalties and distinctions to be dismantled in order to forge a "new" and more egalitarian collective identity. (A more temperate version of these transformative ambitions has surfaced in recent versions of assimilation theory that have discussed how the mainstream culture is mutually created and transformed by minority and majority populations [Alba and Nee 2005].)

In the next section I look at a minor tendency within the writing of Robert Park that provides a compelling insight into this transformational ethos. Park's writing is significant, if for no other reason that because it provides a striking contrast to the ideas about race, nation, and immigration that informed the Thind decision. But his writing is also compelling because of its ambivalences. Even though it charts a new direction away from the racial common sense of the Jim Crow era, it reproduces (or anticipates) some of the limitations that I point out in my discussion of liberal pluralist theory. I am not turning to his writing because it provides an authoritative solution to the questions that I explore in this chapter. But it does provide an important insight into some of the unresolved tensions—concerning expectations of immigrant integration and the problem of racial marginality—that continue to wrack the U.S. immigration debate.

THE IMMIGRANT AS AN AGENT OF TRANSFORMATION

Five years after the Supreme Court's decision in the case of Bhagat Thind Singh, Park published "Human Migration and the Marginal Man" (1928). Park's essay provided the groundwork for a new field of marginality studies that persisted for several decades.[13] Whereas the Thind decision affirmed the inherent right of a national people to preserve their racial homogeneity, Park offered a theory of modern progress that was bound up with the dynamics of immigration. For Park, this process was epitomized by the marginal individual who transcended race and nationality.

Park used the "mixed race" person as the basis for conceptualizing the modern immigrant experience. Unlike classical sociological theories of alienation, Park did not treat marginality as a social problem.[14] For Park, the marginal type was an agonized individual but he was also on the cutting edge of transformations that would lead to new advances in human civilization. In Park's own words, "It is in the mind of the marginal man that the moral turmoil which new cultural contacts occasion manifests itself in the most obvious forms. It is in the mind of the marginal man—where the changes and fusions of culture are going on—that we can best study the process of civilization and progress" (1928, 893).

These observations on marginality and social change were informed by a social constructionist perspective that was ambitious for its day. Park did not merely argue against biological race theory, he produced an agent that was associated with the forces of deterritorialization. The marginal type transgressed and decomposed cultural, national, and social boundary lines and, in the process, gave rise to new interpretations of familiar narratives, new ways of articulating one's identity, and new social forms.

Like Georg Simmel's stranger, Park's marginal man is a solitary type. The stranger is not accepted by the locals on the basis of a shared heritage or cultural familiarity (Simmel 1971 [1908], 143–149). And as Simmel observed, the unique skill set of the stranger is inextricably bound up with the conditions of his alienation from the local culture. It is possible to see how these same conditions apply to the undocumented migrant worker. Legally speaking, the undocumented worker "shouldn't be here." But the alienness of the undocumented worker justifies the informal labor market practices that allow them to be used as an exploitable commodity. As such, the very reasons that make them useful to the locals also require them to play the role of the outsider (and to take on all the legal hazards that go along with it).

For these reasons, the marginal type appears to violate the assumptions of liberal assimilation theory, including Park's own writing on the subject.[15] The marginality of the immigrant renders her useful to the host society, but this marginality also makes it difficult for her to be fully integrated. So it cannot be assumed that the immigrant becomes modern by assimilating the cultural norms of the host society. The immigrant is already a hypermodern subject by virtue of the dislocation and complex social negotiations that characterize her experience. The immigrant's conditions of living force her to adopt a new orientation toward her inherited culture and the culture of the new land. As a result, the process of assimilation becomes inverted. The host society is only partly successful in assimilating the immigrant to its way of life (and remains ambivalent about incorporating the immigrant as a social equal). But the immigrant innovates new solutions to the antagonisms of modern life that are eventually assimilated by the host society.

Park's writing illustrates how the liberal investment in modern progress results in an identification with the immigrant over the native. This should not be confused with a reverse ethnocentrism that values immigrant cultures more highly than the culture of the native born. Instead, it

is derived from a more abstract set of power relations that have historically informed European ideas about civilization and modernity. The nature of these power relations become clearer on reviewing the etymology
of the word "native."

From the 1600s onward, the word "native" was used by Europeans to
refer to the non-European populations of their colonial holdings and the
earliest meaning of native in the English language refers to a person born
in bondage.[16] These distinctions between natives and colonizers were
closely connected to European ideas about race, but the derogatory meaning of native predates the modern construct of race by several hundred
years.[17] So although the native may always have been viewed as an inferior
type, this inferiority was not always defined in racial terms (even though
nativity, eventually, became racialized). Natives were originally defined by
their boundedness to a place or a traditional culture. Their lowly status
was associated with a proclivity to cling to their "primitive ways." Hence,
the relationship between the colonial society and its natives was often
characterized as a mentor seeking to educate an obstinate pupil.[18]

European colonization also serves as the backdrop for Park's theory
of migration and the marginal man. Park uses a catastrophic theory of
progress to describe the process that produces the marginal type.[19] He argues that the most significant advances in human civilization have been
brought about by points of contact and conflict between cultures that
were driven by the forces of trade, war, and migration. These collisions
produced conditions that gave rise, in turn, to new social types that cannot be reduced to the genetic traits or the apparent cultural similarities
that they happen to share with others.

By identifying the immigrant as an agent of modernization, Park is in-
viting the reader to identify with all of the social types—invaders, mer-
chants, explorers, and others—that have established new points of contact
between cultures. As a result, the immigrant who arrives at Ellis Island at
the turn of the twentieth century and the European colonizer become different faces of the same social process. This reading of history illustrates
how identification with the immigrant can be used to validate the original
acts of conquest that led to the founding of the United States. It also draws
attention to continuities between Park's writing and the way that the matter of race and colonization was dealt with in classical liberal theory. For

example, John Locke's law of enclosures justified the European seizure of Native American lands on the basis of the degree of cultivation of the lands in question (Parekh 1995). This rationale affirmed the natural right of the productive property holder to cultivate lands that were "not in use," rather than affirming the natural right of a superior race to dominate an inferior one.

It is not difficult to see how these distinctions between productive and unproductive types can be folded into ideas about race (and how they might relate to more recent distinctions between "good" productive immigrants and "bad" criminalized immigrants). Liberal intellectuals tend to ignore these connections and are typically opposed to the idea of racial superiority. John Locke, for example, rejected the scientific racism of his day. Park also made a point of distinguishing his explanation of modern progress from biological race theory. Nevertheless, both of these theorists advanced ideas about modern progress that could easily be used to justify the idea of white racial superiority. So although Park's marginal man is someone who "transcends race," it can also be argued that this transcendent capacity has always been a defining feature of white male privilege (Fraser 1992; Pateman 1990).

This problem provides some insight into the evasive way that liberal theorists have dealt with the matter of race (and structural inequality more generally). On one hand, liberal theories of modernity deploy evaluative criteria that make distinctions between more and less advanced types, but they cannot tolerate the inflexible caste distinctions that restrict the freedom of individuals to make decisions about their future development. Hence, liberal theory has been invested in ideas about evolution and progress that continually evoke the specter of race while, at the same time, seeking to unravel these distinctions before they harden into permanent differences that could impose an arbitrary limit on the individual ambition of presumably "raceless" social actors. Even if racial inequality exists as a social fact, it cannot be recognized as a systemic problem—much less a problem that is tied to the antagonisms of liberal thought itself. So it could be argued that the idea of race has posed more of a problem for liberal thought than the problem of existing racial inequality, insofar as liberal thought has actively sought to dismantle the former but has tolerated the latter.

This dilemma provides another insight into the problem of laissez-faire racism. Most important, it demonstrates that what we have come to know as "laissez-faire racism" is not unique to the post–Jim Crow era. It is a manifestation of antagonisms that run through the heart of liberal thought. In this regard, the main limitation of Park's writing on the marginal man is not that it is used to justify racial hierarchies but that it attempts to transcend these hierarchies without directly examining them. Even though Park provides an adventurous interpretation of the dynamics of immigrant integration that flatters the ingenuity of the migrant, he also places most of the burden for overcoming these barriers on the shoulders of this individual. This is a formula for immigrant mobility that foreshadows the "by your bootstraps" model of ethnic mobility that would be revived by liberal pluralist theory in the mid-twentieth century. An important point of difference is that Park believed that this process transcended ethnic culture—as conventionally defined—and could end up transforming the entire society (and not simply the culture of the immigrant). Nevertheless, it is up to the immigrants to find their own way in a society that is reluctant to include them as social equals, and this process is largely driven by the immigrants' willingness to transform themselves.

A NIETZSCHEAN CRITIQUE OF "RACE THINKING"

There is no evidence that Park was a serious reader of Friedrich Nietzsche's writing, but there are some similarities between Park's writing on marginality and migration and Nietzsche's ideas about the process of becoming. Like Park's theory of the marginal man, Nietzsche's ideas ventured outside the mainstream of intellectual thought, and both parted ways with the racial common sense of the Thind decision. Nietzsche's writing is also plagued by antagonisms that raise questions about whether it provides a desirable alternative to the kinds of problems I have outlined. As I argue, however, Nietzsche's writing is most helpful in the way it conceptualizes the "problem of race" and, in this respect, it transcends some of the blind spots of Park's writing.

A good place to start is Nietzsche's critique of Darwinism, and social Darwinism in particular (1967, 243–348). According to Nietzsche, the qualities that define the Darwinian species are only a crude snapshot of

where all of these individuals happen to be located, according to a particular schema of biogenetic development at a particular point in time.
The leveling tendencies of biological racism (which insist that "we are all
equal because we share the same genes") ignore the possibility that individuals who share the same lineage may be developing at different speeds
and in different directions.[20] So for Nietzsche, the problem of race-think-
ing is that it imposed a limitation on the dynamics of transformation.

Like many aspects of Nietzsche's thought, his writing on this matter
was rife with ambiguities, interweaving biological notions of race difference with both praise and criticism of ancestral racial and national
identities. For example, Nietzsche equated the cultural pluralism of nineteenth-century Europe with a kind of barbarism, and he argued that this
condition is one reason why most Europeans had lost the singular vision
required to produce an enduring "higher culture" (1966 [1886], 171–198;
1974 [1882], 158–163). But he also observed that this barbaric mixture of
European cultures was fostering a new type of person, which he sometimes associated with the idea of a new race or with an entirely new kind
of entity that transcended nineteenth-century notions of race and nation
(2009 [1878], 233–234; 1974 [1882], 302–310; 1966 [1886], 171–198). For Nietzsche, however, what was most important was the process of becoming
and not the idea of race as a monolithic collective identity.

His barbaric prototype of the new European race (or for the new postracial European) is not far removed from Robert Park's marginal man.
Both are creatures of "mixed" descent who are becoming something that
has not been preordained by their inherited identities. One notable distinction between these two prototypes is that Nietzsche limits his discussion to the confines of European culture, whereas Park uses a world-historical frame of reference. Park's marginal type is a universal figure that
could emerge from any combination of the human "races," and he makes
this point by using examples from U.S. race relations, the situation of the
Jewish migrant in continental Europe, and the ethnic mixtures produced
by the conquests of the ancient Greeks.

Nietzsche's vision of a new race was, ironically, a more accurate re-
flection of the North American discourse on assimilationism and pluralism. The discourse on assimilation in the nineteenth century often contained allusions to the formation of a new "American race," which was

an underlying motif of the melting pot metaphor (Gerstle 2001). But as the Thind decision illustrates, racial distinctions were used to determine who was allowed to melt into the mainstream. In a similar vein, the earliest treatises on cultural pluralism in the United States and Canada were oriented toward fostering a greater tolerance for the culture of European migrant populations (Day 2000, 146–176; Ratner 1984). In this regard, Nietzsche's writing replicates the exclusionary criteria that were already engrained in the intellectual and popular discourse of his day. By comparison, Park's writing on marginality evokes the egalitarian promise of classical liberal thought. From this perspective, Nietzsche's European exclusivity comes across as an arbitrary, ethnocentric limitation on the scope of this theory. But Nietzsche's writing also sheds light on the limitations of Park's liberalism. Nietzsche was able to see that there was a fatal flaw in most strands of liberal thought that lead it down the same path as social Darwinism.

Nietzsche's argument against social Darwinism (and Darwinism more generally) focuses on the association it makes between survival and the adaptive capacity of an organism (1974 [1882]. 291–292; 1967, 146–147: 343–344). Although Darwinian theory appears to value ingenuity, Nietzsche argues that it also encourages passive traits. Superior types, according to social Darwinism, are those who adapt to the status quo and not those who have developed the audacious capacity to criticize the status quo or envision a new social reality. In this regard, social Darwinism is best understood as a discourse that encourages conformity to existing norms. It does not explain the emergence of other types who manage to thrive by going against the grain of the very same norms and values that define the morality of the "average person."

In a similar vein, Nietzsche criticizes liberalism for promoting a rational individualism that does little more than encourage the subject to conform to existing conditions. British utilitarianism (which had a formative influence on liberal economic theory) was one of the primary targets of this line of criticism (Nietzsche 1966 [1886], 189–192). On this point, Nietzsche argues that the cost-benefit decisions of the rational actor take a number of things as given, including the values that determine the practical and aesthetic worth of things and the structure of authority that has established these values as the norm.

According to Nietzsche, the rationality espoused by the British school of utilitarian thought operates entirely within this prevailing system of values. It is incapable of evaluating the values themselves or of creating new values because this requires the individual to incur costs that may never be recouped. The will to create new values requires a commitment to uphold these values for their own sake, not as a means to an end. Because new values are never the dominant values when they are first created, there must be a commitment to defending them even when the individual is not being rewarded by society for doing so—and even if this means that the individual may never see these values become the prevailing norm in the space of his lifetime.

Nietzsche was unapologetically elitist. So it should be noted that his critique of liberalism and social Darwinism was not informed by a vision of a more egalitarian society. Nevertheless, his critique opens up a space for engaging the antagonisms of liberal thought on the matter of racial inequality. His concern for creating new values provides an insight into the problem that must be confronted if there is to be any resolution to the dilemma of laissez-faire racism.

One of the most ingenious features of Nietzsche's critique is his assertion that ideas about moral and racial superiority are not necessarily organized around an elitist worldview. Instead, according to Nietzsche, they are more often derived from an acquiescent attitude toward an existing structure of authority or an established set of values. This problem is not very different from the limitations of liberal pluralist theory. In this case, the established values are the racial-cultural fault lines that have defined the limits of the majority group identity. Whereas cultural conservatives like Samuel Huntington have sought to preserve these distinctions, liberal pluralism has tended to take them as given.

This tendency to work within the framework of "the known" carries important implications for progressive thought on economic policy, immigrant rights, and the state (Bacon 2009; Chang 2000; Gordon 2007; Marchevsky and Theoharis 2005). One set of policy recommendations that has consistently emerged from this body of writing is the need to strengthen the social, civil, and legal rights that have been eroded by the last few decades of neoliberal restructuring. It is very easy for these policy objectives to be interpreted as calling for a "return" to an earlier paradigm of citizen (and immigrant) rights. It is important to keep in mind, however, that the golden age of the postwar liberal welfare state (when these rights were stronger) overlaps with the late phase of the Jim Crow era (see Katznelson 2006). Efforts to curtail government spending on "wasteful" citizen entitlements became a part of the public lexicon after these entitlements had become associated with black populations (Neubeck and Cazenave 2001). This draws attention to the disturbing fact that citizen rights have grown weaker as the United States has become more racially diverse (and extended formal equality to all people regardless of race). This inverse relationship between racial diversity and citizen rights is, unfortunately, not limited to the United States.[21]

It would seem to follow that any attempt at strengthening citizen and immigrant rights in a society that has become much more diverse over the past several decades would have to actively address (and transform) ideas about race and cultural difference that have historically determined who was most "deserving" of these rights and entitlements. Otherwise, the attempt to strengthen these rights for all could run the risk of inflaming biases and resentments between different segments of the U.S. population that are not accustomed to seeing each other as social equals. On the other hand, if you are not prepared to take on this challenge, you could fashion an agenda for social change that appeals to the cultural (and implicitly racialized hierarchies) that have been historically used to distinguish the deserving and the undeserving. This agenda may be pursued because it reflects the genuinely held ideals of its practitioners or because they feel it is the most practical way of swaying the hearts and minds of a confused and divided people. Either way, it leads the discourse on social progress to operate within the framework of what Nietzsche might have described as the "established values."

The scope of the problem becomes even more apparent on considering that it has also emerged in some strains of Marxist thought. A good example is provided by the writing of Slavoj Zizek, one of the most widely read Marxist writers of the current era. Despite his substantial ideological differences with liberal thought, Zizek's ideal social actor is not far removed from the likes of Park's marginal man. Zizek's Communism is a faithful translation of the forward-looking ideals of the Western enlightenment. It requires, among other things, individuals who are willing to transform and to be transformed. This orientation allows Zizek to view European colonization as a progressive historical event—not because it was justified in its own right but because it was integral to the unfolding of the modern radical political tradition to which he lays claim (Zizek 2009, 114–117). Once again, this is not very different from Park's argument that wars, colonial conquests, trade, and migration have been the incubators of human civilization (with the notable exception that Park does not situate this explanation within a dialectical reading of world history).

Park viewed this as a process that may have played a more formative role in the development of the West compared to other world cultures but that was not unique to the West. He also explained how the process of catastrophic change could emerge from the clashing of any number of different cultural or "racial" mixtures, without privileging one over the other. Zizek, on the other hand, grounds his ideas about social change in a trajectory of political development that is rooted in the West and that he views, in no uncertain terms, as a tradition. So although Zizek evokes the idea of a universal emancipatory struggle that must be waged on behalf of all excluded persons, he is also very clear that this process will require the rest of the world to become progressively Westernized. In this regard, the wheel of social progress only moves in one direction (and can only belong to one culture), which is why Zizek's argument for revolutionary change also translates into a defense of the singularity and inherent superiority of Western values.

Zizek's writing has not directly addressed the question of immigrant integration but he has registered his support for the legalization of unauthorized migrant workers and the strengthening of noncitizen rights (2009, 118–119). He is also critical of nativist and conservative, populist movements that have connected their critiques of the economy and state power to an exclusionary identity politics. In this respect, Zizek's practical views on immigration are not very different from those of many left-leaning proimmigration liberals. The big difference is that Zizek does not believe that the antagonisms of immigration policy (and of the broader political economy) can be resolved within the framework of a liberal capitalist society. It is in this sense that Zizek is opposed to the preservation of the status quo—whether it is defined by discourses on liberal assimilation theory, cultural pluralism. or Samuel Huntington's more spirited defense of an Anglo-Saxon American creed. But there is another way in which the theater of political opposition, which is continually evoked by Zizek's writing, becomes a vehicle for the reproduction of the same.

Zizek's Communist politics allows him to establish a critical distance from the assimilationist discourse of liberals and cultural conservatives. But Zizek's criticism of these perspectives is focused on their political ideology and not with their views on culture per se. Within the framework of his own political project, Zizek is stridently antipluralist. His critique of liberal multiculturalism does not lead in the direction of a radical pluralist project, but toward a new kind of egalitarian unity that liquidates all differences (Zizek 2008, 140–177). Most important, this is a unidirectional process; Zizek allows no room for the prospect of mutual or reciprocal transformations. In this regard, Zizek's views on transformation are very similar to that of early twentieth-century assimilation theory. It is necessary for Others to conform to an already established set of ideals (whether this is a national identity, a traditional ethnic culture, or in Zizek's case, a Western egalitarian-emancipatory tradition).

Zizek's writing contains numerous critical observations about the oppression of black populations and other racial minorities (2009, 86–94). He is much more cautious, however, in his discussions of the political and cultural agency of these populations. His main concern, in his discussion of these matters, is that racial minorities do not "separate" themselves from the West. As a result, he admonishes black and Third World intellectuals that—in his view—have cut themselves off from a Western egalitarian-emancipatory tradition and praises black intellectuals and black political movements that appeared to have embraced this tradition (Zizek 2009, 112–113).[22]

Taken in isolation, there is some validity to all of Zizek's observations, whether they pertain to the dangers of an essentialist identity politics, the influence that Western political values have had on Third World social movements, or the self-serving critiques of Western imperialism that have been advanced by postcolonial governments. But what is most worrisome about Zizek's writing is the direction in which his comments consistently bend. Judging from the themes of Zizek's writing, there is nothing that Western intellectuals could possibly learn from the "non-West." Zizek also implies that there is something inherently problematic about articulations of cultural identity and political interests that do not appear to be clearly derivative of his Western egalitarian-emancipatory tradition. He gives little consideration to the possibility that this Western tradition could itself be open to interpretation. Even though Zizek encourages racial minorities to improve this tradition (by making it more inclusive of their interests and experiences), he sets himself up as the final arbiter of these new interpretations. As a result, it is not clear what he would do with a situation in which an immigrant or minority population is engaging in a form of cultural politics that they view as being in line with Western values but that Zizek strongly believes is an example of cultural separatism or irrational mysticism. It is also not clear what Zizek would do with immigrant and minority populations who insist that the ideals that he locates in his Western tradition are not actually unique to the West and that they have been able to engage this tradition (and push it in new directions) because they have been able to draw on similar ideals that are indigenous to their inherited culture.

There are no formulaic answers to these sorts of questions. They draw attention to the dialogical process through which ideas about Western civilization, national identity, and democratic politics (among other things) are defined—and to the fact that this process does not lend itself to tidy conclusions. The dialogue is unavoidably contentious. There will always be unresolved tensions and differences that cannot be assimilated into the reigning consensus. In order to participate in these sorts of contentious exchanges as a social equal, one needs more than equal rights— one needs to be recognized as an actor who is capable of deliberating on the meaning and desirability of these rights (as opposed to being content with being granted "equal rights," as they have been defined by others). Of course, the historical record shows that the social spaces in which these sorts of egalitarian exchanges have been allowed to occur have always been very exclusive. Race, class, and gender (along with culture, sexuality, and other distinctions) have played a role in determining who is authorized to wield the power of the sovereign decision. Hence there are some social actors who are authorized to operate in the space that exists outside the laws and norms of a given society. These are persons who are actively engaged in the process of rethinking and transforming these laws and norms (and are invested with the authority to do so). And there are others whose place in society is contingent on their obedience to the laws and norms defined by others.

One of the biggest challenges that modern democracies have been faced with is dismantling the arbitrary and ascribed distinctions that have been used to draw the line between active deciders and passive subjects. In the recent past, these distinctions were informed by explicitly articulated gendered and racial ideologies that were actualized by a variety of institutionalized policies and practices. Today, these distinctions appear to be gravitating toward immigration and legal status (and the racial-cultural assumptions about national belonging that are evoked by these distinctions).

The arguments of cultural conservatives (such as those of Samuel Huntington) provide the most straightforward rationalization for why immigrant ethnicity and legal status should define the scope and limits of substantive equality. From his vantage point, participation in the polity cannot be separated from an unqualified acceptance of the core norms and values that have historically defined this polity. This is one of the principal reasons why cultural conservatives and anti-immigrant populists have sought to protect themselves from having to engage immigrant and minority populations in an egalitarian discussion about the norms and values of U.S. society. They have been forthright in insisting that their particular interpretations of U.S. national identity and political culture are nonnegotiable, and there is a direct connection between their concerns about the cultural defense of the West and the need to intensify immigration enforcement (in this regard, English-only ordinances, local immigration laws, and the border control are natural extensions of one another). But this concern for defending the West can also perpetuate racialized distinctions (concerning who really belongs to the West) and cultural hierarchies (concerning whose interpretations of Western values are most authentic) that undermine the very same ideals that are being "defended." This leads to the perverse rationalization that, in order for democratic values to be preserved, they must be defended from themselves (in other words, they must be protected from falling into the wrong hands). The problem, in this case, is not the values themselves but the assumption that they must be protected from spurious interpretations—as opposed to the more heretical possibility that these ideals could be revitalized by an agonistic engagement with this wider world of ideas and that their longevity and world-historical significance flows from this willingness to continually engage the new and unknown.

THE PROBLEM WITH PRACTICALITY

The prior discussion draws attention to points of convergence that operate beneath the more obvious political differences of liberal, conservative, and Marxist intellectuals. This concern for mapping unlikely continuities is, in many respects, the main theme of this book. In each chapter I try to show how a particular set of dynamics (whether they are enforcement practices, legal rationales, or broader governing strategies) has been quietly reinforced by both sides of the debate over immigration policy. In this regard, the political fight over immigration distracts attention from the convergences that underlie these warring perspectives. The problem of immigrant marginality, the unprecedented expansion of the discretionary powers of the state, and—as it concerns this chapter—the defensive undertones of the academic discourse on race, culture, and immigration, cannot be addressed until we shift attention away from the political differences that have defined the mainstream debate and focus our attention on these points of convergence.

Liberal thinkers, ranging from Robert Park to John Locke, have denounced racism as something that is inimical to their enlightened ideals. What is rarely admitted, however, is that racial resentments can be guided by the same kind of utilitarian reasoning that has been promoted by liberal thought . For example, some of the most popular arguments against affirmative action have made the case that these policies work against the practical interests of the white middle class. So even though it can be acknowledged that racism is wrong, policies that attempt to intervene on this history of discrimination are also viewed as being impractical. It follows that the only workable solution is one that eliminates racism without adversely effecting the privileges of the white majority—which leads, once more, to the conundrum of laissez-faire racism. In a similar vein, economic complaints are among the most popular arguments against immigration, whether the arguments focus on immigrants who steal jobs, illegally access public services. or take more from the welfare state than they pay back in taxes.

It is possible to counter these arguments by appealing to the same kind of cost-benefit reasoning. For example, it can be argued that restrictions on legal migration and the mass deportation of unauthorized migrants would not significantly improve the economic situation of the American middle and working class. To whatever extent job stealing actually occurs, it does not account for the steady decline in real wages for the average worker over the past quarter century, the rising costs of health care and education. or the general lack of economic security produced by the casualization of U.S. labor markets. So, the argument goes, it makes more sense to focus on solving these bigger problems rather than scapegoating minorities and immigrants. The economic payoff for solving these problems is much greater than the economic benefits that accrue to the white majority for tolerating existing patterns in racial inequality. The argument can also be made that the long-term costs of racial inequality will actually be more expensive for taxpayers than the short-term inconveniences produced by policies that attempt to protect immigrant rights or promote racial equality. So a rational cost-benefit calculation actually works in favor of the argument for racial equality and progressive social change. But this cost-benefit rationality also tends to cultivate a narrowness of vision. The nature of cost-benefit calculations is that they are based on assessments of known quantities. As a consequence, they lead the rational individual to recoil from disruptions that alter the value of these known quantities—making it more difficult to produce reliable calculations about the likely costs or benefits of a given path of action.

The irony of this line of reasoning is that it cultivates a resistance to change that is the antithesis of the continually evolving, modern individual who has been idealized by other branches of liberal thought. The failings of this shortsighted pragmatism shed some additional light on the rarely acknowledged collusions between liberal reasoning and the racist ideologies disdained by liberal intellectuals. Racism has been guided by its own kind of economic rationality, which has been legitimized by institutional practices that treat racial inequality as the normal state of affairs. And even though most liberal intellectuals have not been racial ideologues, liberal reasoning has nurtured this kind of pragmatic racism by promoting a cost-benefit rationality that becomes invested in perpetuating the inequalities that are taken as given by its calculations.

This is also why liberal thought has often failed to take a principled stand against exclusionary sentiments at moments when these sentiments are on the rise—because the political costs of doing so usually outweigh the immediate benefit of reaching a practical compromise. This is one reason why pragmatic support for mass immigration can be reconciled with a policy agenda that has become increasingly punitive toward immigrants. The economic pressures that lead migrant workers to be recruited as disposable commodities and the political need to appease anti-immigrant anxieties can be informed by the same kind of myopic rationality.

The value of Park's marginal man is that it offers a glimpse into a strand of liberal thought that veers away from this concern for the maximization of self-interest, as this "interest" has been defined by existing conditions. This kind of transformative agent is more consistent with liberal ideas about modernity than the narrow-minded rationalism of *homo economicus* that has been spawned by utilitarian thought. But like many sociologists who have been influenced by liberal thought, Park did not recognize the inherent tension between these two types of individuals. And unlike Nietzsche, Park was unable to acknowledge that his ideas about migrants and modernity pointed toward a theory of the self that would have to transgress the limits of liberal thought.

Nietzsche did not translate his ideas into a coherent theory of society. Even so, his writing has influenced critical theorists who have used his ideas to reconceptualize the meaning of pluralism, democracy, and the dynamics of social change.[23] Many of these scholars have been influenced by Nietzsche's use of genealogical distinctions to describe different trajectories of becoming.[24] Whereas liberal rationality can be criticized for its myopic orientation (which is only able to perceive an already-established reality), genealogical distinctions can be used to engage the dynamics of social change. By making distinctions between different ways of valuing things, genealogical distinctions draw attention to the multiplicity of value systems, which challenges the idea that there is such a thing as a normative reality. The normative reality is revealed to be the historically contingent product of a particular way of valuing things that has prevailed for a period of time—due to the convergence of a variety of political, economic, and cultural factors—but it is never the only possible reality.

This chapter, for example, criticizes the limitations of several bodies of thought. But, more importantly, it outlines distinctions between the various tendencies at work in these bodies of thought. I draw attention to tendencies that collapse the apparent distinctions between liberal pluralism, cultural conservatism, and some forms of Marxism, and I describe other distinctions that have unfolded within liberal thought—between a utilitarian rationality on one hand and a social actor who is involved in a constant process of becoming on the other.

The point of this analysis is not to champion one particular perspective (though my discussion leans in favor of some perspectives over others) but to draw attention to antagonisms that are shared by all of them. I do not blame immigrant marginality or the exclusionary undertones of discourses on Western culture on a specific kind of political ideology. Instead, I treat these problems more like a threshold state that has defined the scope and limits of this field of political discourse. The problem, in this regard, is not that any of these perspectives have openly called for the exclusion of immigrants and minorities (with the notable exception of Huntington's views on Latino migration) but that they have not been very interested in dismantling the discourses and identities that have perpetuated the social exclusion of these populations.

Nietzsche's writing, for example, provides a compelling description of a kind of social actor that could break free of the limitations of the kind of majoritarian identity politics that is evoked by Huntington's writing. But Nietzsche is the most unabashedly elitist and Eurocentric of all of the theorists I discuss. And it would not be very difficult to adapt his ideas to a cultural argument against non-European immigration. Park's marginal man thesis provides a more liberal, egalitarian account of a similar kind of social actor. But his writing places most of the burden of transformation on the migrants themselves—paying little attention to the racial ideologies and structures of institutional discrimination that have perpetuated immigrant marginality. Zizek offers a militant brand of egalitarianism that is more forceful in its condemnation of racism and immigrant marginality, but it is also grounded in an uncompromising defense of Western values that evokes many of the same cultural-civilizational hierarchies that have characterized classical liberal thought (and that beg the question, who gets to define whether or not a particular articulation of political interests is consistent with the Western egalitarian-emancipatory tradition?).

Huntington's ideas about national identity are more stridently defensive than the writing of Zizek and Park, but they are also informed by many of the same egalitarian ideals.

I do not trivialize the differences between these perspectives, but I do question how effective any of them can be in dealing with the problem of immigrant marginality in an era in which U.S. migration flows have become predominantly non-European. Do any of these bodies of thought provide an effective counterpoint to the sorts of commonsense ideas about race and nation that view non-European migration as a cultural and demographic threat to the United States? Consider, for example, how the concern for preserving the singularity of the West has permeated the thought of cultural conservatives like Samuel Huntington and Marxists like Slavoj Zizek. Given the pervasiveness of this way of seeing, is it surprising that defensive concerns about national security, border control, and law enforcement have dominated the policy discourse on immigration?

Neoliberal economic priorities have had a more pronounced influence on the mainstream immigration debate than the ideas of Huntington and Zizek. These priorities have given rise to the proimmigration, proenforcement agenda that has defined U.S. immigration policy for the last several decades. It is also rather telling that these priorities have been mired in a contradiction that is not very different from the one that I describe throughout this chapter. They welcome new migrant flows, on the one hand, while funding the unprecedented expansion of a security-enforcement apparatus that seeks to protect U.S. society from these very same migrant flows (and that sends a powerful message about the symbolic place that the migrant occupies in the national imagination). This problem is much more severe than the limitations of Park's writing on migrants and marginality. Whereas Park avoided a more intensive analysis of the causes of immigrant marginality, the neoliberal priorities guiding U.S. immigration policy have been actively creating the structural-institutional conditions that produce immigrant marginality.

RETHINKING THE NATION: A NEW AMERICAN DILEMMA

The defensive orientation I describe above has become a defining feature of U.S. immigration policy under neoliberalism, but it is not necessarily a defining feature of liberal thought (or Marxist thought for that matter). There are some arguments in favor of immigration that could provide a starting point for the kind of departure that I hint at in this chapter. The distinguishing feature of these arguments, however, is that they are not rooted in an economic pragmatism but in a theory of civic nationalism that views the United States as a nation defined by a shared set of ideals.[25] This perspective is usually contrasted with the flesh and blood nationalism of cultural conservatives, which insists that the nation is better understood as an extended kinship network. Even so, this contrast between an ethnic and a civic nationalism is, itself, rather limiting. It is not enough to say that civic nationalism is the opposite of ethnic nationalism; these ideas about civic nationalism also need to be drawn in new directions.

For example, the idea of the nation does not have to be defined in reference to a collective identity so much as a collective project. This is not quite the same thing as advocating for a new postnational identification (arguing on behalf of an immigrant diaspora or of regional or transnational identities). The principal limitation of these alternatives is that they are not as different from the identity politics of the nation-state as they first appear. They challenge the conventional geopolitical boundaries of the nation, and they offer suggestions for rethinking the relationship between an array of already-established identities. But they do not directly engage the process of becoming, which requires some consideration of how these identities are being transformed—giving rise to entirely new kinds of identities, the elimination of old distinctions, and the emergence of new kinds of distinctions. The main difference, in this case, does not have to do with a national versus a postnational vision of community, but between a fixed identity (defined by an idealized tradition and the imperative of preservation) and another kind of "identity" that is better described as an open-ended project (propelled by an agonistic dialogue between social equals).

One of the principal tasks that this project could take on is the challenge of examining the racial, cultural, and value distinctions that have been used to partition the majority group identity from the rest of society. Ideas about immigration are inextricably bound up with ideas about national identity, and these ideas, in turn, are not far removed from ideas about race, culture, and ethnicity. This is why it is very impractical to treat the immigration debate as if it is just a matter of economics. It is important to consider that the power of the immigration restrictionist argument lies just as much in its vision of U.S. national identity as it does in its more practical arguments about border control and the economic costs of immigration. By comparison, the argument in favor of immigration does not appear to be informed by a clearly defined alternative.

Although civic nationalism lends itself to the idea of the nation as an inclusive, forward-looking project, it is questionable whether it is able to untangle itself from the immigration priorities of the neoliberal state (that also surface in the economic pragmatism of the mainstream policy discourse on immigration). In this regard, the problem is not simply the economic inequalities that have been exacerbated by the last three decades of neoliberal restructuring, but the narrowness of the economic vision that has guided this process.

One of the biggest challenges facing the U.S. immigration debate is the long shadow that was cast by the Supreme Court's decision in the case of Bhagat Singh Thind. The Thind decision (and others like it) clarified the scope and limits of the racial majority identity that is still a feature of U.S. political culture. If there is any hope of moving beyond the enforcement-heavy immigration policies of the current era, one of the questions that will have to be answered is whether it is possible for the United States to move beyond this definition of itself as a white majority society (and also, whether ideas about whiteness and nonwhiteness can be disentangled from popular conceptions of U.S. national identity and cultural diversity). The entire immigration debate does not boil down to these sorts of questions. But it would be a mistake to assume that these questions have nothing to do with the popular resistance to immigration reform or the popularity of immigration enforcement as a solution to the "immigration problems" of the current era. Even so, it is unclear whether the liberal argument for immigration is capable of addressing these questions. Ultimately, the question is whether the liberal argument is truly centered on a forward-looking vision or whether it is organized around a more moderate version of the very same national vision that is espoused by the opponents of immigration. If the latter scenario is the case, then it is likely that the patterns of stratification and immigrant marginality I describe in this book will define the future of race and cultural diversity in the United States.

6

CONCLUSION

THE IMMIGRATION CRUCIBLE

At the time of this writing, the U.S. Congress is gearing up for yet another debate over immigration reform and also for the 2010 midterm elections. Because the outcome of the midterm elections may change the balance of partisan power in the Congress, it could be of immense significance for the next attempt to craft a new immigration law. If the Republican party regains control of the House, it is very likely that we could see a replay of the 2007 immigration debate, which featured a Senate and an Executive Office aligned with a "tough but sensible" path to legalization for unauthorized migrant workers, and a House staunchly opposed to any legalization program (and any attempt to expand the legal flow of migrant labor into the United States). The Republican party has also tried to take advantage of the political momentum of the Tea Party movement.[1] These conservative populist currents could galvanize more support in the halls of Congress for the kind of immigration control agenda that was supported by House Republicans like Tom Tancredo during the 2007 immigration debate (which played a critical role in blocking Republican support for immigration reform).

Of course, U.S. politics can be a very difficult thing to predict and the U.S. immigration debate is certainly no exception. This book, however, is not intended as a manual for predicting the outcome of the next series of

Congressional immigration debates (even though bits and pieces of my analysis may offer some insights into future developments). I am more concerned with examining the unlikely convergences, unresolved tensions, and blind spots that have produced the current immigration status quo. Toward this end, I encourage readers to distance themselves from the presentist orientation of the public debate over immigration, which often takes the form of a series of "shocking developments" (like the controversy surrounding the Arizona immigration law, the Obama administration's decision to send troops to the U.S.-Mexico border, the discovery of yet another recruitment network for unauthorized migrants located in the most unlikeliest of employment sectors and so forth). In most cases, these incidents are not as anomalous as they first appear. And for reasons that are understandable enough, they are often interpreted in light of their significance for the pro- versus anti-immigration positions that have come to define the mainstream immigration debate. But as a result they cannot draw attention to the limitations that are inherent to the entire field of debate.

Some of the most important factors shaping recent trends in immigration policy are not apparent from the surface-level immigration debate. For example, the forms of de facto statelessness I describe in chapter 2 have been shaped by regulatory priorities advanced by proimmigration liberals, immigration control hawks, and fiscal conservatives. And as I explain in chapter 4, the controversy over the Arizona immigration law (and the forms of racial profiling it encourages) distracts attention from other ways that police are being involved in screening immigrants for legal status (which can also lead to racial profiling) that have been much less controversial, meeting with the approval of the federal courts and many federal lawmakers. This is why I have drawn attention to political dynamics, regulatory strategies, legal rationales, and ideas about race and culture that have been unfolding over the course of the past century. I used this historic context to refocus the significance of present-day policy trends. In this chapter, I provide a similar kind of analysis that looks at developments in immigration policy under the Obama administration and situates them in light of issues raised in the previous chapters.

IMMIGRATION POLICY AND ENFORCEMENT
UNDER THE OBAMA ADMINISTRATION

The decision of the Obama administration to sue the government of Arizona for enacting Senate Bill 1070 (its controversial immigration law) provides what is, perhaps, its most striking point of difference with the immigration priorities of the 2000–2008 Bush administration. In this case, it would appear that both administrations are on polar opposite sides of the debate over local immigration laws—given that the Bush administration's internal memos opened the door for immigration laws like the one enacted by the state of Arizona. There are, however, other points of difference (and similarity) between the immigration priorities of both administrations that are not as apparent but are no less significant. The Bush administration's public stance on immigration tended to be more hawkish than its actual policy agenda . Immigration enforcement under the Bush administration was often deployed as a public spectacle, which sent a signal to the general public that the government was getting tough on immigration (see chapters 3 and 4). This distracts attention from the fact that the Bush administration was involved in a protracted fight with House Republicans over its immigration policy platform and that it supported proposals for expanding the legal supply of migrant labor that met with the approval of Democrats in the House and Senate. The Obama administration, on the other hand, appears to have adopted an immigration policy agenda that is more hawkish than the public stance it often takes on immigration policy issues (like, for example, the stance it took on the debate over the Arizona immigration law).

The statements of administration officials have been friendlier to immigrant rights constituencies, but its immigration enforcement agenda has actually been more aggressive than that of the Bush administration. Even though the Obama administration has stopped the Bush administration's high-profile workplace raids, it has increased investigations against employers who are suspected of hiring unauthorized migrants and expanded the use of the E-Verify system (which makes it easier for employers to check the legal status of new hires).[2] In addition to this, the Department of Homeland Security has embarked on a program to expand local police involvement in enforcing immigration laws (Cristina Rodríguez et al. 2010).

The Department of Homeland Security has chosen the 287(g) provisions of the 1996 Immigration Reform Act to pursue this objective, which requires local police to establish a relationship with federal immigration enforcement. This underscores the interest of the Obama administration in supporting local enforcement practices that fall under the cover of federal law. This maneuver could be a sign that the administration will attempt to close the gap between federal legal precedent and local governance that widened under the Bush White House. Before the controversy over the Arizona immigration law, the Obama administration did not give any indication that it was prepared to challenge the legal arguments contained in the memos of the Bush administration that played an instrumental role in widening this gap. But it does appear that the lawsuit it is currently filing against the state of Arizona is setting the stage for a legal argument (and possibly a federal legal precedent) that could be used to challenge the constitutionality of all local immigration laws.[3]

One thing that emerges clearly from all of these developments is that the Obama administration does not want to cater to anti-immigrant hysteria nor does it want to be perceived as "softer" on immigration enforcement than the Bush administration. (Consider, for example, that the decision to send troops to the U.S.-Mexico border occurred shortly after the first critical statements about the controversial Arizona law.)[4] Even so, the administration continues to draw criticism from immigration control advocates who insist that it is moving too slowly on the immigration enforcement front (Kephart 2009). On the face of it, this criticism would seem to be misplaced. However, the continuing dissatisfaction of immigration control advocates with the Obama administration draws attention to a difference that runs deeper than the pragmatic get-tough stance the administration has taken on immigration enforcement. These emerging tensions appear to be a replay of the differences that immigration control advocates had with the Bush administration. The most important difference, in both cases, is that neither the Bush nor Obama administrations had an interest in using immigration enforcement to effect a long-term decline in immigration levels.

One point of consensus that emerged from the last attempt to pass an immigration reform bill was that immigration enforcement needed to be improved before any steps were taken to expand quota levels for guest workers or regularize unauthorized migrant workers. All of the leading immigration reform proposals contained provisions to expand legal migration and the guest worker program that would only be triggered once certain baseline goals for improving immigration enforcement and border security were met (Turner and Rosenblum 2005). These immigration enforcement triggers were one of the tactics used by proimmigration policy makers (concentrated in the Senate) to appease immigration control advocates (concentrated in the House).

Once again, this is a strategic orientation that the Obama administration shares with the last several administrations, which have all taken steps to expand migrant flows and intensify immigration enforcement in tandem with each other. The Reagan-Bush administration was the first to articulate these immigration priorities within a broader strategy for the neoliberal restructuring of the U.S. (and global) economy. But the basic elements of this proimmigration, proenforcement formula can be traced to the immigration reform proposals of the Carter administration (P. Martin 1982) or even, for that matter, to President Roosevelt's strategy for handling Asian migration at the turn of the twentieth century (see chapter 3). In this regard, it would be a mistake to describe the proimmigration, proenforcement strategy as something that is unique to neoliberalism. But it is fair to say that this strategy achieved its mature form during the era of neoliberal restructuring, which has witnessed the largest sustained increase in immigration in U.S. history alongside the largest expansion of immigration enforcement.

There are other signs, however, that immigration enforcement is not just being guided by neoliberal priorities for immigration. Despite the criticism the Obama administration is receiving from immigration control advocates, it has set new records in its prosecutions and deportations of immigration violators.[5] These trends are part of a broader process that is transforming the federal government's strategies for apprehending unauthorized migrants. The border patrol has, historically, been the enforcement agency most responsible for apprehending these migrants. But over the past few decades, the immigration court system has been steadily catching up to the border patrol. In 2009, for example, over 30 percent of all unauthorized migrants who were returned or removed from the United States were channeled through the immigration court system, compared to only 2 percent in 1995.[6] During this same period of time, migrants with noncriminal convictions (most of whom are unauthorized) have overtaken migrants with criminal convictions as the main target of these formal removal proceedings.[7]

Even though these trends are not unique to the Obama administration, the administration's immigration enforcement actions have intensified them. If these enforcement trends continue, the immigration court system could become an integral feature of an interior enforcement strategy oriented toward actively reducing the size of the unauthorized migrant population. In that case, the goals of immigration enforcement would begin to directly challenge the interest in cultivating flows of cheap, migrant labor that has been associated with neoliberal priorities for immigration.

This shift toward a more rigorous kind of immigration enforcement might seem to be an unlikely fit for a Democratic administration. It is consistent, however, with the "grand bargain" immigration control strategies that have been attempted by the center-left administrations of other nations (France being one of the best examples; Hollifield 2004). This approach to immigration reform uses the intensification of immigration enforcement as one feature of a broader strategy to legalize and better regulate immigrant labor markets. The state stems the unauthorized flow of migrant workers. Meanwhile, it creates new avenues for the legal entry of migrant workers, ensuring that they are granted the same rights and privileges as other workers (protecting them from exploitation and also safeguarding wage levels and workplace safety standards for legal resident workers). The trade-off., however, is that the in-flow of migrant labor is not as fluid as it would be under a laissez-faire model that is more amenable to employer interests. So employers would have to settle for a system that is more expensive and (from their perspective) less efficient than the recruitment channels that allow them to access unauthorized migrant labor. But, ideally, this system would be free of inflexible recruitment quotas and arbitrary and punitive enforcement practices that are informed by xenophobic anxieties about the growth of the immigrant population.

This set of priorities outlines a framework for immigration enforcement that could be integrated within a strategy for long-term economic growth that attempts to protect the rights of immigrant workers and improve labor markets for U.S. workers. Some of the trends mentioned above indicate that the Obama administration is trying to pursue an immigration policy that is informed by these principles. If it is successful, this strategy could effect a departure from the laissez-faire labor market priorities that, according to many researchers, have defined the recent history of U.S. immigration policy (Calavita 1992; Massey, Durand, and Malone 2003; P. Martin 2004; Zolberg 2008).

But get-tough immigration enforcement strategies can easily be articulated with laissez-faire (or neoliberal) regulatory priorities. It is seldom acknowledged that the right wing opposition to immigration reform actually perpetuates the underregulation (or laissez-faire regulation) of migrant labor markets. When immigration control advocates call for the intensification of immigration enforcement as the only solution to unauthorized migration (opposing, on principle, any expansion of the legal flow of migrant workers), they create a situation in which unauthorized migration continues to be the main way of bringing low wage migrant workers into the U.S. economy. This is effectively what happened when the last attempt to enact an immigration reform bill was stymied by the resistance of a Republican Congress in the summer of 2007. By the end of that year, the unauthorized migrant population had grown by an additional 400,000 persons (Wasem 2009). The decline in this population that occurred in the subsequent years has been widely attributed to the onset of the U.S. recession (see chapter 2). So it could be argued that business interests that want to keep low wage immigrant labor markets deregulated may not be in a hurry to see a new immigration law enacted. And in a rather perverse way, they may appreciate the impact that immigration control advocates have had on the immigration debate.

In this light, the danger of the grand bargain strategy that is (ostensibly) being attempted by the Obama administration is that it has intensified immigration enforcement in a fractious political climate that may not be conducive to the enactment of a new immigration law. If the political tendencies that derailed the last congressional immigration debate prevail, the efforts of the Obama administration will amount to little more than a replication of the same neoliberal proenforcement, proimmigration priorities that have been implemented by the last several administrations. If this is the case, the intensification of immigration enforcement will only increase the desperation (and exploitability) of the unauthorized migrant workforce and impose arbitrary barriers on the entry and recruitment of migrant labor—similar to what has occurred over the past several years.

IMMIGRATION POLICY, NATIONAL IDENTITY, AND THE LIMITS OF EXECUTIVE AUTHORITY

The public opinion on unauthorized migration is another reason why the Congress has been unable to pass a new immigration reform bill. Even though a broad cross section of the public seems to favor immigration reform, a vocal minority of U.S. citizens are strongly opposed to any attempt to legalize unauthorized migrants.[8] Meanwhile, immigrant rights constituencies have rejected the solutions that the Congress has used to bridge the gap between the pro- and anti-immigrant side of this debate (see NILC 2007).

This polarized political climate sheds some light on the reasons why the immigration system and immigration policy have been subject to the discretionary powers of the executive office. One of the more obvious advantages of this discretionary authority is that it allows the government to make difficult policy decisions without having to engage the public debate over immigration. Policy makers can try their best to craft a new reform law that satisfies the widest possible number of constituents, while reserving the prerogative to adjust the details of this law after it has been enacted.

The problem with this approach is that immigration policy—and unauthorized immigration in particular—has become a focal point for populist outrage against the government. Because of the degree of public attention that has been focused on immigration policy, deviations from the stated intentions of enacted legislation are not likely to go unnoticed for long. So although executive discretion provides the government with an expedient shortcut through the minefields of the immigration debate, the indiscriminate use of this kind of authority can undermine the legitimacy of any policy solution that is arrived at by federal lawmakers.

In addition, the Obama administration is facing a political climate that is extremely sensitive to its use of executive authority. For example, in the summer of 2010, information was leaked about an internal memo being circulated by the U.S. Department of Citizenship and Information Services offering tips for how the administrative powers of the immigration system could be used to prevent the deportation of some noncitizens in the absence of a new immigration reform law.[9] When news of these memos began circulating among Republican pundits and politicians, concerns were immediately raised that they were outlining a strategy for granting amnesty to the entire unauthorized migrant population that would circumvent the Congress. Administration officials confirmed that the DHS did, indeed, approve and circulate these memos, but they have denied that the memos were intended to take the place of a comprehensive immigration reform bill.

These concerns about the unchecked use of discretionary authority are not unreasonable in and of themselves. But the expansion of this discretionary authority has been unfolding for the past 150 years and often with the explicit support of the Congress (see chapter 3). The "dangerous" executive powers that right-wing critics have associated with the Obama administration are by no means unique to this administration. The continuing expansion of executive authority—like the expansion of immigration enforcement—has been propelled by political dynamics that transcend partisan-ideological differences. Nonetheless, there is a tendency for commentaries about executive power to be reduced to a rather narrow partisan critique. For example, many conservative and far right critics of the federal government have portrayed the Obama administration as a "dictatorship."[10] Consistent with the last two decades of conservative discourse on governance, this constituency has advocated for a more decentralized kind of government that gives more power to local citizenries. Ironically, this demand for a decentralized (and smaller) government was also one of the goals of neoliberal restructuring, which actually expanded the executive powers of the federal government. And the legal rationales that have been used to justify racial inequality in the United States have also historically appealed to the idea of a popular or local discretionary authority over the law (see chapters 4 and 5).

If one keeps this history in mind, the complaints about dictatorial state power that are being voiced by conservative populist movements send a rather ambivalent message. In some cases, they appear to be demanding a kind of freedom that idealizes the very same "dictatorial" powers that they believe are being wielded by the state.[11] The incendiary rhetoric of some conservative populists, which can include overtures to violent revolution (and barely veiled assassination threats against federal lawmakers), provides another telling insight into the nature of their politics.[12] What is being asserted, very plainly, is the moral authority to take the life of the Other. One's political opponents are no longer "fellow citizens" but immoral creatures who do not deserve to be protected by the laws of the nation (indeed their very existence is an affront to the values of the nation).[13] As Tim Wise has pointed out, this populist outrage rests on a foundation of white privilege, which makes it possible for the incitement to violence to be viewed as an expression of patriotism—and not as a threat to the public safety.[14]

This problem draws attention to the authoritarian undertones within U.S. political culture that have always existed in an uneasy tension with its democratic ideals. Although, from a liberal perspective, white supremacy is anathema to these ideals, the inflammatory rhetoric of present-day popular nationalist movements also draws attention to the unsettling fact that white supremacy was integral to the sociopolitical foundations of U.S. democracy, and it is still an open question as to whether the U.S. political system will be able to function without it. Ultimately, this rests on the question of whether it is possible for the United States to become a genuinely postracial society (or a genuine "racial democracy") in which racial difference is no longer the main fault line that defines the political interests of the electorate. In other words, is it possible for racial inequalities to be eliminated and for racial minorities to become more involved in the political system without appearing to threaten the interests of the white majority? Is it possible for this to be viewed as a natural extension of the democratic ideals of the United States, or will it instigate a new movement to "preserve" U.S. democracy that views these ideals as something that is culturally exclusive to the white population? Of course, both of these tendencies are already a feature of U.S. political culture, and the conflict between them has already been playing out in the struggle over civil rights legislation, affirmative action, and antidiscrimination policies in the post–Jim Crow era (J. Daniels 2009; Higham 1999; Wise 2010).

The conflict between these radically different perspectives on race, nation, and the meaning of democracy is also poised to play itself out in the continuing debate over the direction of U.S. immigration policy. Arguments about the economic benefits of immigration can be used to side-step the discussion of these broader issues. But, as a result, they tend to acquiesce to the commonsense ideas about race and nation that have been used to portray immigrants as a racialized demographic threat. It is possible to counter these arguments with data showing that immigrants actually contribute more to the public tax base than they take in services, that they are replenishing an aging workforce, and that they fill important labor niches (Dowell Meyers 2008)—but this is not the same thing as constructing an alternative vision that makes it possible for new immigrants be seen as "one of us." Much of the anger about rising immigration levels has to do with the fear of being outnumbered by people who are not—and as Samuel Huntington has argued can never become—"like us."

One of the big questions facing federal lawmakers is whether the immigration debate can be used as an opportunity to foster a more engaged and informed public dialogue on immigration or whether public opinion will be viewed as an obstacle to reform. Despite all of the hazards of such a dialogue, that is what I favor. Instead of retreating from the public debate—or simply tolerating the status quo—more effort should be made to open up and pluralize this field of debate. For example, the public should be exposed to arguments that demonstrate that conservative populists are not the only ones who are frustrated with the current immigration situation, and that it is possible to be in favor of strengthening immigrant rights and be critical of the neoliberal priorities that have influenced the last three decades of U.S. immigration policy. And instead of merely opposing or tacitly catering to the flesh and blood nationalism of the anti-immigrant pundits, the public could be exposed to other ideas about national belonging and be encouraged to become actively involved in a discussion about "who we are" as a national people. The value of this kind of discussion is that it could put the primordialist vision of U.S. national identity in context, alongside other ideas that are probably just as popular but that may not receive as much exposure. And just as important, the process of actively discussing these ideas can become part of the process whereby the popular concept of the nation can be interrogated and transformed.

Admittedly, this is an ambitious project. The struggle over the meaning of democracy, national identity, and the continuing legacy of race in the United States raises a number of thorny questions that cannot be solved simply by adopting a particular political standpoint or ideology. It requires an engagement across lines of difference that has the potential to transform the perspectives of all parties that are involved in the encounter. This is why I have drawn attention to antagonisms within the racial and cultural discourse of liberal pluralism that are shared by cultural conservatives and some variants of Marxist thought (see chapter 5). The point of this discussion is not to brand all of these bodies of thought as Eurocentric or racist. Instead, I pay more attention to the limitations of the preservationist ethos that undergird all of them and try to explain how this desire to preserve (to avoid being transformed) can end up reproducing the very same racial-cultural hierarchies they have disclaimed.

This critique draws attention to a kind of conflict that has to do with the struggle to define the very meaning of things. For example, even if we all agree that we are in favor of a more just and democratic society, who gets to define what these terms mean? Will there be a commitment to ensuring that the process through which the meaning of democracy will be defined will itself be an open, democratic process? And at what point does this willingness to be perpetually open to new voices and new interpretations run the risk of collapsing into an incoherent relativism? Is it possible to have "too much" democracy? Is the democratic process strengthened or depleted by this practice of being willing to continually expand the dialogue over the scope and meaning of democracy?

A thorough exploration of these questions is beyond the scope of this book (though I align myself unambiguously with the idea that it is necessary to expand the scope and limits of existing democracy). But the way these questions are answered carries important implications for the immigration debate. One of the most important political functions of race in U.S. history is that it provided a very practical solution to the "problem of democracy." Whiteness was an important precondition for membership in the national political community and, in turn, defined the scope and limits of U.S. democracy. European immigrants did not just passively assimilate into the white mainstream. The popular discourse on whiteness and the institutional mechanisms that protected the privileges of the white native-born population had to be restructured to incorporate these immigrants. Even though the policies and practices that have been used to

incorporate black populations have always been controversial, the institutional and political transformations that made it possible for Jews, the
Irish, and Italians to be accepted as "fellow whites" were just as ambitious
and interventionist (as well as being much more successful and much less
controversial; Brodkin 1998; Katznelson 2006; Massey 2007, 51–112; Roediger 2006). These interventions were the crucible that forged the white
majority formation that is viewed, today, as the traditional citizenry of the
United States—and European migration flows were an integral part of this
process.

The major stumbling block for immigrants in the current era is that
the United States has become reliant on a level of mass immigration that
is comparable to the great European migrant waves of the early 1900s,
but there is no indication that it is willing to undergo the same process
of transformation that was needed to produce the new majority of that
era. This is a problem that cannot be separated from the legacy of white
racial identity in the United States but that is also, in some respects, bigger than the issue of race. This is why I do not just focus on the problem
of racism and racial inequality. Once again, the main point of distinction
is not between white and nonwhite or immigrant and native born, but
between a defensive, preservationist type of identity politics and a more
open, transformational understanding of political-cultural identity. This
latter kind of identity (or project) requires an openness to new interpretations of what could be broadly defined as the U.S. national identity. This
latter kind of "identity politics" is grounded in an understanding of progressive development and social change that is consistent with some interpretations of the egalitarian-emancipatory ideals of Western political
culture. For example, the distinction I make between a preservationist
and transformational orientation is not very different from the distinction
that Benedict Anderson makes between a bounded and an open seriality
(Anderson 1998). In this regard, the danger of the temptation to fall into
an uncompromising defense of Western values—whether it is associated
with a liberal pluralist or cultural conservative worldview—is that it gravitates in the direction of a kind of identity politics that becomes tradition-
alist in the most unfortunate sense of the word. Ironically, this trenchant
defense of the West may be the threshold that defines the immanent limits of the sequence of forward-looking transformations that has histori-

cally defined the Western enlightenment project (converting these ideals into a religious dogma).

It is also important to emphasize that this transformational process carries implications that extend far beyond the process of immigrant acculturation—which tends to presume that "culture" is synonymous with "ethnicity." The process has much more to do with the ongoing struggle to transform and redemocratize the national political culture, and it requires a willingness to see how discourses on race and ethnic identity have been used to define the scope and limits of this political culture. So it is important to consider how the politics of race in the United States has helped to create (and obscure) a set of governing arrangements that gave rise to unchecked discretionary authority (see chapter 3). It is also important to consider how the expansion of this kind of authority is related to the centralization of state power in the executive office and a new, more extreme kind of class stratification and corporate dominance of the domestic and global economy. As it concerns immigration, this analysis directs our attention toward the kinds of issues that I examine in this book—including the expansion of the immigration enforcement apparatus and the various forms of de facto statelessness that describe the contemporary migrant experience. But immigrant marginality is just one manifestation of a type of legal-political marginality that is shared by a growing number of legal residents and native-born persons. Simply put, the same policy developments that have weakened immigrant rights have also weakened the social, civil, and legal rights of all U.S. residents. So the goal of transforming the political culture to make it more inclusive of new immigrant populations can also be connected to a broader project of regenerating a political culture that does a better job of including and safeguarding the rights of the entire U.S. population.

This is a project that requires a critical race analysis but that is not just oriented toward fixing racial inequalities. There must also be a willingness to examine and reconstruct popular ideas about whiteness and the cultural difference of immigrants, among other things. Unfortunately, the postracial rhetoric of the Obama era has made this already difficult task even more daunting. One of the strengths of the Obama campaign was its ability to appeal to the desire for a nationalism that transcended partisan, cultural, and racial differences. The subtle message sent by Obama's campaign speeches is that systemic racial inequalities can be addressed, in a way that avoids divisive racial politics (R. Smith and King 2009). As some researchers have noted, this strategy of positioning oneself above the fray of race has been used by other black candidates to avoid being caught in the dilemma of responding to racial controversies that could alienate them from the white mainstream (Jones and Clemons 1993; Wright 1995).

The problem with this strategy when it is translated into a policy stance is that it predisposes the executive office to continually underemphasize the significance of race. This makes it more difficult to assess how much of the popular resistance to immigration reform is being fueled by negotiable concerns about labor markets and border security and how much of this resistance is being fueled by a more intransigent fear of racial Others. It also becomes difficult to provide a convincing counterargument to these latter concerns if they are not formally recognized as concerns but are allowed to proliferate within the public sphere through a coded discourse that makes hard and fast distinctions between immigrants and "traditional Americans."

Even though Jim Crow is now a closed chapter in U.S. legal history, there is still a romantic attachment within the popular culture to images of national community that stem from this era. These romantic attachments are enmeshed in a conflicted set of desires that, on one hand, insist that the American public has a right to preserve this idea of the national community while, on the other hand, avoid any discussion of the racial exclusions that were required to sustain it. The desire to create a truly postracial public culture requires a willingness to let go of these romanticized images of the past. To do this requires having something equally compelling with which to replace it. The pragmatic interests driving U.S. immigration policy have been unable to engage these broader questions. The immigration debate does not need to be subjected to yet another round of practical solutions informed by these same priorities. It needs a paradigm shift that is guided by an entirely new understanding of practicality.

1. INTRODUCTION: AN UNTIMELY INTERVENTION ON THE U.S. IMMIGRATION DEBATE

1   This brief description summarizes the outcome of the 2007 congressional de-
    bate over immigration reform, which culminated in a Senate proposal that was
    cosponsored by President Bush and Senator Ted Kennedy. The right wing im-
    migration restrictionists in the House (led by Representative Tom Tancredo)
    were the most vocal in opposing the bill—but it was also rejected by immigrant
    rights constituencies who were concerned that its proposed methods for le-
    galizing unauthorized migrant workers were too draconian. See David Bacon,
    "Who Killed the Immigration Bill; Who Wants It Back?" (Truthout, June 11,
    2007: www.truthout.org/article/david-bacon-who-killed-immigration-bill-
    who-wants-it-back [accessed March 29, 2010]). Also see Robert Pear and Carl
    Hulse, "Immigration Bill Fails to Survive Senate Vote," *New York Times,* June
    28, 2007.

2   Massachusetts, for example, would have experienced a significant population
    decline from the 1980s onward had it not been for immigration. Immigration is
    the driving force behind workforce replenishment and population stability in
    the state—making up for the out-migration of native-born populations over the
    past several decades (Sum et al. 2006).

3   For example, in March 2010 the well-known anti-immigration pundit Glenn
    Beck advised television viewers to avoid churches that adopted a program of

social and economic justice (equating such aims with Communism and Nazism). See David Sessions, "Glenn Beck Urges Listeners to Leave Churches That Preach Social Justice" (*Politics Daily,* March 8, 2010). Beck was not simply critical of social justice programs that might help immigrants. He objected, in principle, to any program that calls into question structural inequalities in wealth and income, consistent with the antiwelfarist orientation of other conservative, anti-immigrant pundits (Buchanan 2001).

4   For one example of how proimmigrant arguments can be combined with these sorts of narratives see, *Assimilation, American Style* (Salins 1997).

5   For an example, see Ed Rubenstein's July 2, 2010, report on VDare.com ("June Jobs: Immigrants Displacing American Workers . . . Again," http://www.vdare.com/rubenstein/100702_nd.htm). Rubenstein uses Hispanic employment levels as a proxy for all immigrant labor. Hence, Hispanic persons are presumed to be immigrants by virtue of their ethnicity (irrespective of their actual status under the law). In addition to being a grossly inaccurate measure, it contributes to the commonsense discourse on race and nationality that has come to define the immigration control movement (in which "Latino" and "American" are treated as mutually exclusive constructs).

6   Some of my own research has been subjected to such interpretations. I was surprised to find that an article I had written in favor of repealing the immigrant welfare restrictions imposed by the 1996 welfare reform laws (Kretsedemas 2005) had been cited as an example of a left-leaning argument against labor migration (Lyons 2007, 4, 28). The author of the article was arguing that advocates for unauthorized migrants should look to international law for helpful legal precedents to protect the rights of these migrants. In contrast, my article argued (by implication, because it did not directly address international law) that the most important conflicts over the future of immigrant rights were unfolding within the sphere of national law. I also pointed out that any argument for reinstating the social and legal rights that were taken away from immigrants by the 1996 reform laws will have to tackle the legal developments that have weakened social and legal/civil rights of all U.S. residents. In this context, my observations about immigrant recruitment strategies that were geared toward cultivating flows of exploitable labor were used to make comparisons with the policy and structural transformations that have casualized labor markets for lower-income U.S. workers. I used this comparison to point out that these issues must be addressed in tandem with each other (requiring stronger coalitions between immigrant and native-born populations), because their aims are not mutually exclusive. The point of this critique was not to argue against labor migration (with the aim of restricting it) but to draw attention to the need for policy and labor market reforms that could improve

the living and working conditions of migrant workers (but not *only* migrant workers).

7   See Spencer Hsu, "Little New in Obama's Immigration Policy: While Embracing Bush's Programs, President Says Nuance Makes the Difference" (*Washington Post,* May 20, 2009), and Cam Simpson, "Obama Hone's Immigration Policy" (*Wall Street Journal,* July 21, 2009).

8   This ratio is derived from spending levels for 2011 Department of Homeland Security budget. The entire budget for all three branches of the immigration system (which fall under the DHS) is approximately $19.8 billion, whereas the budget for the wing of this system that is primarily responsible for immigration services (U.S. Citizenship and Immigration Services) is $2.8 billion. The other $17 billion of the immigration systems budget is allotted to Immigration and Customs Enforcement (ICE) and Customs and Border Protection (CBP) (DHS 2010). Most of these funds (approximately $11.2 billion) have been allotted to the CBP, but ICE (which handles interior enforcement and is primarily responsible for tracking immigration violators into deportation proceedings) has been the fastest growing wing of the immigration system over the past twenty-five years. It experienced its fastest growth between 1985 and 2002—its budget quintupling from $1 billion to $4.9 billion—and has continued to grow at a steady but slower pace since that time (Migration Policy Institute 2005).

9   It has been estimated that of the approximately 193,000 jobs the federal government expected to create between 2007 and 2009, over 83,000 (or approximately 43 percent) were for the Department of Homeland Security and that security/enforcement-related jobs were expected to grow the most across all government agencies. Within the immigration wing of the DHS, the biggest spike in job growth was for border patrol agents (Partnership for Public Service 2007).

10 Over the past several decades immigration policy has been used to expand the recruitment of high-skilled migrant workers. But as some researchers have pointed out it has also been used to introduce security measures and other kinds of controls that impose an arbitrary limitation on the ability of these workers to become permanent settlers or to remain gainfully employed in the United States (see Papademetriou et al. 2009; Skeldon 2008).

2. A DIFFERENT KIND OF IMMIGRATION, A NEW KIND OF STATELESSNESS

1   The earlier boom period spanned 1880–1924. Between 1879 and 1880 the annual inflow of immigrants almost tripled, from 177,000 to over 450,000 persons, beginning a forty-five-year period of expansion. The peak years of this

boom (years in which immigration exceeded 1 million persons per annum) all occur within a ten-year period (between 1905 and 1914). The immigration levels of the current era are comparable, but peak levels (of over 1 million people per year) have been sustained for a much longer period of time. Over the past twenty years, for example, the annual growth of the immigrant population has averaged close to 1 million persons per year (DHS 2009a).

2   This is a brief summary of trends that are discussed in more depth later in this chapter. Readers who want to skip ahead to this data should see figures 2.1 and 2.2.

3   In 2009 over 36 million nonimmigrants were admitted to the United States whereas 1.1 million noncitizens were granted legal permanent residence (DHS 2009a, 2009d). Please note that this estimate of the nonimmigrant flow is derived from I-94 admissions only. For an explanation of the difference between nonimmigrants who enter with I-94 forms and those who do not see nn10, 11 in this chapter.

4   Most nonimmigrants are admitted as nonresidents, with visas that last no longer than ninety days. But a small minority are admitted as short- or long-term residents with visas that can span one to six years and may grant the nonimmigrant the right to apply for legal permanent residence. In 2009, over 36 million nonimmigrants were admitted to the United States and 32.5 million of these persons (or 90 percent) were admitted as nonresidents, the remaining 10 percent being admitted as longer term, nonimmigrant residents (DHS 2009d).

5   It is extremely difficult to develop an accurate count of this population. This 10 percent estimate follows from the estimate that approximately 10 percent of nonimmigrants are admitted as short- or long-term residents. Most of these nonimmigrant residents are professional-class workers who are allowed to enter the United States with their spouses and children and are also granted the right to apply for legal permanent residence. Of course, all of these persons do not end up applying for legal residence. But it also bears noting that some of the nonimmigrants admitted as nonresidents (i.e., as tourists or business visitors) also attempt to seek permanent residence through some other means (e.g., through marriage to a U.S. citizen). The Government Accountability Office has estimated that as many as two to three hundred thousand persons per year overstay their visas (most of whom were admitted as nonresidents). By the GAO's own admission, this is a conservative estimate because it is focused on visa overstayers who enter the U.S. via air travel, but does not account for the incidence of visa overstaying within the much larger flow of nonimmigrants who enter the U.S. via the Canadian or Mexican land-border (GAO 1995; 2008).

6 Many professional-class migrants are allowed to enter the United States with H1B visas that allow them to apply for permanent residence. But only a relatively small number of these persons are awarded permanent resident status in any given year. In 2009, for example, the number of persons who entered the United States with professional-class work visas was almost nine times larger than the number of people who adjusted from these visas to legal permanent resident status (DHS 2009c; 2009d). U.S. policy has become even more stringent on the matter of granting pathways to permanent residence for asylum seekers (Welch 2002, 83–102). There are also many nonimmigrants who would like to become permanent residents but are not eligible to apply due to the terms of their visas (e.g., persons admitted with student visas, H3 visas for professional trainees, H2 visas for low-skilled workers), The visa overstayer population is a testament to the limited pathways to permanent resident status that exist for these migrants.

7 The Supreme Court's decision on *Zadvydas v. Davis* (533 U.S. 678 [2001]) has provided one of the most recent deliberations on remedies for the hazards of statelessness under U.S. law. This decision limited the capacity of the immigration system to indefinitely detain noncitizens who cannot be deported because of their stateless legal situation.

8 Existing legal remedies under U.S. law are also rather weak. Even though the Supreme Court's *Zadvydas v. Davis* decision (533 U.S. 678 [2001]) limited the capacity of the immigration system to indefinitely detain stateless persons, it also outlined criteria by which limitations on detention could be extended (in ninety-day intervals) at the discretion of immigration officials.

9 Michel Foucault's discussion of positive power stems from the distinction that he makes between the sovereign authority of the feudal monarch and the disciplinary power that emerges under modern capitalism. Whereas the first kind of power tends to exert itself through the power to deprive (to take life), the latter attempts to shape and manage living organisms through punishments and coercions intended to cultivate particular kinds of behaviors and capacities in its subjects. And instead of merely depriving the subject, it manifests itself through acts of provision (which are granted contingent on obedience; Foucault 1995).

10 I-94 forms are used to document the arrival of nonimmigrants of all visa categories (including tourists and business visitors who enter the United States under the visa waiver system). However, they are primarily used to document arrivals by air and sea. Most nonimmigrant entries occur by land (across the U.S.–Mexico and U.S.–Canada borders), and the vast majority of these entries

do not involve the filing of I-94 forms. The current ratio of non-I-94 entries to I-94 entries is approximately 4.5 to 1 (DHS 2009d).

11 Mexican nationals with border crossing cards and Canadian tourists and business visitors are the main populations of nonimmigrants who are exempt from filing I-94 forms. Hence, the vast majority of I-94 entries are air and sea entries by nonimmigrants entering from outside of the North American continent (although a relatively small number of Mexican and Canadian nationals also enter the United States under various specialty visa categories). All nonimmigrant residents (who are granted the right of temporary residence in the United States for a period of a year or more, along with spouses and children) are required to file I-94 forms regardless of national origin, port of entry, or means of entry (DHS 2009d).

12 The number of noncitizens who marry U.S. citizens is usually between 30 and 40 percent of the annual number of new adjustees. When accounting for all adjustments that have something to do with family reunification or sponsorship, the number of these types of adjustments increases to well over 50 percent (even though adjustments for noncitizen spouses of U.S. citizens is still by far the largest category in this group). For an overview of trends for 1986–2009, see DHS, 2009c (rows 38–41) and DHS, 2004a (rows 27–31, but note that this latter table does not disaggregate family sponsored LPRs by new arrivals and adjustees).

13 In 2009 temporary workers and their families accounted for only 1.7 million of the more than 36 million nonimmigrants admitted to the United States (I-94 entries only; DHS 2009d).

14 The annual inflow of tourists and business visitors increased from 10.6 million in 1981 to 36.2 million by 2009. The annual inflow of nonimmigrant workers increased from approximately 217,000 to over 1.7 million during this same time period (DHS 2004c; 2009d).

15 In 2009 temporary workers (and their families) accounted for approximately 48 percent of all persons admitted as nonimmigrant residents. The remaining 52 percent were primarily international students, exchange visitors, and diplomats—and a very small minority of persons who are spouses, fiancés, or children of U.S. citizens (DHS 2009d).

16 Unauthorized migrants are overwhelmingly concentrated in low-skilled employment sectors (food preparation, janitorial services, construction, and agricultural sectors). The majority of unauthorized migrants (over 70 percent) are not agricultural workers, but the agricultural and fishing industries appear to have the largest share of unauthorized migrants, relative to the size of the entire employment sector. According to data from 2006, unauthorized migrants make up 11 percent of all agricultural/fishery workers, compared to only 6 per-

cent of all construction workers, and 9 percent of all low-skilled service workers (Pew Hispanic Center 2006).

17 The annual inflow is different from the net growth (which as been estimated at between 470,000 and 525,000 persons). Government estimates have been generally more conservative than the estimates of the Pew Hispanic Center. Whereas the center's reports have documented an inflow of up to 800,000 persons per year in the 2000–2004 period, government estimates are closer to 625,000 per year for the same period. These tendencies also surface in government and Pew Hispanic Center estimates in the average net growth of the unauthorized migrant population—though both sources agree that the annual inflow and net growth have decreased substantially since 2007 (Hoefer, Rytina, and Baker 2008; Passel and Cohn 2008). Also see Wasem (2009).

18 This ratio is based on a conservative estimate of the size of the unauthorized migrant population of 10 million persons. (As of January 2009, this population was estimated at 10.8 million persons [Wasem 2009].) It is also based on a very generous estimate of the size of the H2 worker population, which doubles the size of the annual recruitment level for this population in 2009 (amounting to over 400,000 persons, accounting for the likelihood that there is a degree of overlap in the expiration dates of the visas granted in the prior year). It is important to emphasize, however, that because of the one-year visa span, the H2 workforce is a rotating population and not a steadily accumulating one.

19 One of the strongest years for the growth of the unauthorized population occurred in 2001. According to Passel and Cohn (2008), the unauthorized population grew by 1 million between 2000 and 2001. In contrast, the annual inflow of nonimmigrants (I-94 only) during this same period of time was 33 million persons, and approximately 2.5 million nonimmigrants were admitted as either short- or long-term residents (DHS 2001b).

20 The estimate of the Mexican unauthorized population is for the 1998–2007 period, derived from, Passel and Cohn (2008). The estimate of the Mexican nonimmigrant population for the same period is derived from tables presented in the 1998–2009 Immigration Yearbooks (Department of Homeland Security) that document nonimmigrant admissions (I-94 only) by class of admission and nationality. See table 2.4 for a full citation of these sources.

21 Data has not been collected (or at least not made publicly available) on the nationality of nonimmigrants who enter the United States by land without filing I-94s. It is known, however, that the number of arrival events of this nature per year is usually between 120 and 150 million persons (derived from subtracting the total number of nonimmigrant arrivals from I-94 arrivals only; DHS 2009d). It is also known that all of these non I-94 arrivals involve persons who

are entering via the U.S.-Canada or U.S.-Mexico border. Even when using the very conservative estimate that Mexican nationals only account for 10 percent of these additional arrivals (or an additional 15 million arrivals per year), the annual inflow of Mexican nonimmigrants increases from 47 million (for those filing I-94s) to over 200 million arrival events (total count).

22 Ngai observes that the United States was recruiting as many as 200,000 Bracero workers and 35,000 "regular immigrants" from Mexico per year during the early 1960s. The 1965 Immigration Act imposed a very restrictive annual quota of 20,000 on immigration from Mexico—setting the tone for huge disparities between the legal pathways to migration and the actual size of the Mexican migration flow, which continues to this day (Ngai 2005, 260–263).

23 The largest number of people removed for these reasons in recent years (according to available data) was in 1997 and only amounted to thirty cases. After that time no more than fifteen people were removed for national security reasons each year (but it bears noting that 2005 was the last year that this data was published by the Department of Homeland Security; DHS 2005).

24 The annual number of removals (or deportations) has increased tenfold from 1925 to 2009; DHS 2009h). The deportable alien population—which includes all persons with deportable violations that have been apprehended by federal enforcement personnel—has grown even more precipitously during this same period of time (from 22,000 in 1925 to over 1 million per year from 1976 onward, notwithstanding a decline from 2006 to 2009; DHS 2009f). It bears noting that persons who are apprehended and counted as part of the deportable alien population are not necessarily deported in that year. There is also some overlap between the deportable alien population, voluntary departures (which are focused on unauthorized entrants who are apprehended near the border) and formal removals. Even so, it does provide a helpful insight into the intensification of immigration enforcement over time.

25 In 1989, 830,890 persons were subjected to voluntary departures compared to 580,107 in 2009. The peak years for voluntary departures (ranging between 1.5 and 1.6 million per year) were 1996 to 2000. These levels decreased significantly (but erratically) from 2001 onward (DHS 2009h; note that most "returns" described in this table are voluntary departures).

26 Deportations expanded from 34,427 in 1989 to 393,389 in 2009 (DHS 2009h).

27 See Saskia Sassen's discussion of how the state denationalizes flows of capital in the era of global economic expansion (Sassen 2007, 45–96).

28 Since the mid-1990s Indian nationals have consistently been the single largest national origin category among H1B visa holders. Indian nationals usually account for 25 to 40 percent (and sometimes as much as 50 percent) of all H1B admissions in a given year (Lowell 2000, 11; Barr, Jefferys, and Monger 2008, 5).

29 Admittances for European nationals must also be explained in light of preexisting corporate linkages, trade relations, and diplomatic ties between the United States and western European nations that, according to many scholars, serve as the institutional infrastructure for economic globalization as we know it today (Bello 2005; Giddens 2003; Sassen 2007). It is not possible to completely separate the historical embeddedness of European and U.S. institutional networks from national origin preferences that have been historically biased in favor of European migrants (especially from the UK and northwestern Europe), but it is also important not to radically reduce the former to the latter.

30 This statement only refers to nonimmigrants admitted with I-94 forms, not the much larger flow of nonimmigrants who cross the U.S.-Mexico and U.S.-Canada border without filing I-94s. There is no concrete national origin data on persons who enter the United States without filing I-94s but it is very likely that entries (and frequency of visits during the course of the typical fiscal year) are much higher for U.S.-Canada entries, because Canada is a larger trading partner with the United States than Mexico and because the U.S.-Canada border is not as heavily policed by federal enforcement officers as the United States' southern border with Mexico. When one also accounts for the fact that the Canadian population is comprised of a much larger majority of white, Anglo-Saxon heritage persons than the United States, the results are generally consistent with European national dominance of I-94 nonimmigrant flows. So whether one is looking only at I-94 entries or developing a cruder estimate of all nonimmigrant flows, it still appears very likely that white, European-heritage persons are the single largest racial-ethnic category.

31 See Kevin Bohn, "Report: Security on U.S.–Canada Border Fails Terror Test" (CNN.com, September 27, 2007, www.cnn.com/2007/US/09/27/border.security/index.html [accessed May 8, 2010]) and Bill Porter, "Lack of Funding Blurs Border Between U.S., Canada: Washington Is Urged to Pay Share of Upkeep" (*Boston Globe,* April 1, 2007).

32 Caribbean migrants (most of whom hail from Afro-Caribbean nations) are the national-origin group most often deported for criminal reasons rather than any other reason. And criminal deportation rates for Caribbean nationals are typically 25 to 40 percent higher than criminal deportation rates for other national origin groups (Nopper 2008, 222–223).

33 The details of Jean-Baptiste's deportation charges are summarized in *United States v. Lionel Jean-Baptiste,* U.S. Court of Appeals, 11th Circuit. 395 F.3d 1190, January 4, 2005.

34 Jean-Baptiste's conviction was based on the testimony of a federal agent who insisted that he attempted to arrange a cocaine sale for her. This crucial segment of their exchange was not picked up by the agent's hidden recorder that

she had been using to tape her conversation with Jean-Baptiste, as discussed in Jennifer Kay, "Haitian-American Stripped of U.S. Citizenship Awaits Fate" (Associated Press, December 9, 2006).

35 Between 600,000 and 700,000 nonimmigrants adjust to legal permanent resident status each year, compared to 33 to 36 million nonimmigrants admitted to the United States on an annual basis (DHS 2009c, 2009d).

36 With the exception of the 2008–2009 downturn in the size of the unauthorized migrant population (see table 2.2), this population has been growing at a rate of 500 to 800,000 persons per annum for the past several years. Using the most conservative estimates, 25 percent of this increase would amount to more than 100,000 persons (Passel 2006, 16; Passel and Cohn 2008).

37 *United States v. Lionel Jean-Baptiste,* U.S. Court of Appeals, 11th Circuit.

38 For a review of the exclusionary nature of U.S. policy toward Haitian migrants from the 1970s to the late 1990s see Lennox (2003). For a brief discussion of Haitian interdiction policies under the 2000–2008 Bush administration see, Kretsedemas (2004).

39 In some instances, the executive branch has sent military officers and high-ranking federal officials to attend immigration trials in which it has taken a special interest. The point of this exercise is to make sure the immigration judges are aware that they are being observed. Mark Dow (2008) has explained that this strategy was used to influence immigration court cases involving Haitian asylum seekers that had the potential to set important legal precedents.

3. THE SECRET LIFE OF THE STATE

1 See Beale (1956, 192–199). For a discussion of the history of Asian exclusions, see Hing (2003, 28–50).

2 See Pauley (2001) and Dodds (2003).

3 U.S. Supreme Court, *Fong Yue Ting v. United States,* 149 U.S. 698 (1893). Nos. 1345, 1346, 1347, decided May 15, 1893.

4 A good example is the controversy that surrounded the Council on American Islamic Relations, which endorsed George W. Bush's candidacy in 2000, and was later accused of (but not formally charged with) providing material support for Islamic terrorist organizations. See Neil MacFarquhar, "Muslim Groups Oppose a List of 'Co-Conspirators,'" *New York Times,* August 16, 2007.

5 Dodds describes executive orders as "documents that the president designates as such and which enable him or her to make legally binding policies by a mere stroke of the presidential pen" (Dodds 2003, 2). Executive orders are considered legally valid only insofar as they do not directly contradict existing legis-

lation or judicial decisions. In practice, however, executive orders can be used to establish special operations, committees, and legal agreements that have the ability to influence and reinterpret existing legal precedent. Since executive orders allow the president to take immediate action, it can often take years before the actions authorized by a particular executive order are subjected to judicial review. The U.S. Constitution contains no language that explicitly authorizes the use of executive orders (although it does not expressly prohibit their issuance). As Giorgio Agamben (2005, 19–23) has noted, the United States is one of the few Western democracies that has left the exercise of executive authority largely unregulated.

6   Agamben draws heavily from the writing of the Italian jurist, Romano, in making this argument. He points out that Romano viewed necessity as a "state of affairs" that both precedes the law and is the "first and originary source of all law." Following this, Romano argues that all exceptions to the law are guided by an "unwritten positive law" that is superior to the written law, noting that "there are norms that cannot or should not be written; there are others that cannot be determined except when the circumstances arise for which they must serve" (Agamben 2005, 28–29).

7   Agamben only discusses the exercise of executive authority over the law as it applies to Napoleon (Agamben 2005, 4–5). Romano's discussion of the innate logic of "revolutionary law" could apply just as easily to the French Revolution under the Reign of Terror, during which Robespierre was accused of acting as a de facto dictator. For an account see David Andress (2006).

8   Robespierre's actions under the Reign of Terror are a suitable example. So are the authoritarian tendencies of Communist movements (often criticized as vanguardism or Stalinism). These authoritarian tendencies are sometimes treated as political contradictions that betray the egalitarian ideals of the movement. But they are also an organizational response to the radically indeterminate conditions (the dissolution of the law, the dismantling of the "old" norms and authority structures) that have been produced by revolutionary violence. Hence, radical disruptions of the status quo tend to be accompanied by an equally extreme recentralization of authority that, in some cases, takes shape as a political reaction to the revolutionary movement but that can also be justified as an attempt to translate the revolutionary agenda into a permanent, sustainable model of governance.

9   Foucault describes raison d'etat as a logic of governance that becomes abstracted from the notion of a transcendent divine will and is oriented, instead, toward preserving and expanding the state as an end in and of itself. Raison d'etat is, essentially, a discourse on necessity that transcends the law. Foucault

notes that it is an administrative/managerial form of power rooted in the authority of the sovereign that is alien to the notion of "justice" and the norms and policies of the juridical sphere (Foucault 2007, 262–310; 2008, 1–6).

10 In the introduction to *Homer Sacer,* Agamben explains that his analysis complements Foucault's but also explores a terrain in which Foucault rarely ventured: the relationship between the micropolitics of governmentality and the practice of the law. But outside of this acknowledgment, he does not explore the matter further—leaving aside the larger question of how his argument concerning sovereign power complicates Foucault's understanding of the transition from sovereign and disciplinary power, which Foucault believed was one of the most significant transformations in the modern art of governance (Agamben 1995, 3–12).

11 There is evidence that Lincoln harbored suspicions about the racial inferiority of blacks (McPherson 2002). Nevertheless, Lincoln made several public statements in support of abolition prior to becoming president, and there is evidence that he was persistently lobbied by abolitionists after assuming the presidency (Poinsatte and Poinsatte 1984).

12 A decision to free enslaved Africans in Union states would have been a more consistent expression of Lincoln's abolitionist ideals, but it also would have compromised the very nature of the authority that he used to justify the decision—which would have resulted in an even more ambitious expansion of the discretionary authority of the executive office. Under these conditions, Lincoln could not have used his authority as commander in chief to justify the issuance of the Emancipation Proclamation (since the rationale for freeing enslaved populations in Confederate states was that Lincoln was confiscating the "property" of enemy forces). Instead, he would have had to invoke a much broader interpretation of executive authority that would have ceded to the president the authority to revoke or instate any law of his choosing for reasons of moral conscience.

13 Some of the suspended due process rights and expanded surveillance powers authorized by the USA PATRIOT Act were introduced as temporary measures that could be extended by future legislation. Other surveillance powers (such as the authority to monitor private citizens' public library and Internet usage without warrant or notification) were introduced as measures that would be permanent unless revoked by future legislation (Etzioni 2004).

14 See Jeff Muskus, "Democrats Spar With Obama DoJ over PATRIOT Act" (Huffington Post, September 23, 2009, www.huffingtonpost.com/2009/09/23/democrats-spar-with-obama_n_296280.html [accessed May 12, 2010]). Notably, three years earlier, the federal courts decided a case that awarded Brandon

Mayfield a $2 million settlement for breaches of his civil liberties that occurred during the course of an FBI investigation (Ifitikhar 2008). This is the only instance when a U.S. citizen has been successful in pressing charges against the U.S. government for surveillance and enforcement practices connected to the post-9/11 war on terror. The Obama administration's decision concerning the PATRIOT Act would make it nearly impossible for U.S. citizens to bring these sorts of cases against the government in the future.

15 This process has also been characterized as the conversion of the public sphere from a critical dialogical space into a passive consumerist spectacle. Most of these critical perspectives, however, place more weight on the corporatization and commercialization of public life than on the expanded power of the state itself (Robbins 1993).

16 This reference to "what existed before" refers to the welfare state just prior to the New Deal era. As Theda Skocpol (1995) has pointed out, the United States had a relatively well-funded system of welfare and citizen entitlements in the nineteenth century. Even so, the guiding priorities of the U.S. welfare state have historically been organized around a model of liberal individualism and relief for the poor that shied away from engaging in macroeconomic interventions—like the corporatist and democratic-socialist welfare states of Europe. However, the political turmoil of the Depression era forced the federal government to significantly expand its social welfare programs, laying the groundwork for the liberal welfare state that would persist for the better part of the twentieth century (until being significantly downsized in the mid-1990s). For an overview of these events see Piven and Cloward. (1971, 45–79). For an overview of liberal, corporatist and social-democratic welfare states see Peck (2001, 74–76).

17 For an overview of how these principles have been used to downsize and restructure the postwar liberal welfare state see Peck (2001).

18 This is generally consistent with Saskia Sassen's and Manuel Castell's arguments about how globalization has been guided by the strategic interventions and investments of the state (Sassen 2001; Castells 2009). Two specific examples include government subsidies and tax breaks that were granted to multinational corporations to help them relocate their manufacturing plants to take advantage of cheaper labor (and a more employer-friendly regulatory climate) in other parts of the world and the role of government funding, policy, and public-private sector consortiums in shaping the emergency of new technologies. See Eitzen and Zinn (1989).

19 For an account of how these strategies guided the formation of the Department of Homeland Security see D. Cohen, Cuellar, and Weingast (2006).

20 Invoking a fraternal solidarity in defiance of a despotic paternal figure is part
    of the "deep culture" of liberal democracy (Pateman 1990). Originally, the pa-
    ternal despot was the absolute monarch of the old feudal order. In more recent
    times conservatives have portrayed the despotic state as a maternal figure.
    Hence, the neoliberal argument for reducing "welfare dependency" is one that
    tends to contrast masculinized self-sufficiency against feminizied (and racial-
    ized) pathological codependency (A. Smith 2007).

21 For an overview of the growth of the U.S. state bureaucracy (and federal spend-
    ing) over the course of the twentieth century see Garrett and Rhine (2006).
    Most sociological and economic theories of this process are markedly different
    from the explanation I advance in this chapter. The most proximate theories
    are ones that focus on the monopolistic tendencies of state bureaucratic forms
    (akin to the arguments famously advanced by Robert Michels), but even these
    theories usually lack an analysis of power relations or of particular techniques
    of state power (see Garrett and Rhine's discussion). In this regard, they tend
    to be more concerned with analyzing the expansion of the state bureaucracy
    (a concern that can easily dovetail with neoclassical arguments against "big
    government") and not with the expansion of state authority in and of itself.

22 There is a point of intersection between Agamben's critique of executive au-
    thority and the left critique of Stalinist Communism. According to the latter,
    Russian Communism devolved into a system of authoritarian "state capital-
    ism," in which the "dictatorship of the proletariat" became a thin rationale for
    the consolidation and expansion of centralized state power that was concen-
    trated in the hands of an exclusive bureaucratic elite (James with Dunayevs-
    kaya and Lee 1986).

23 This includes the Telecommunications Act of 1996, which eliminated most
    regulations on media ownership; the Depository Institutions Deregulation
    and Monetary Control Act of 1980 and the Garn–St. Germain Depository In-
    stitutions Act of 1982, which deregulated interest rates and expanded merger
    options in the banking sector; and the 1996 Personal Responsibility Work Op-
    portunity and Reconciliation Act and the 1998 Quality Housing and Work Re-
    sponsibility Act, which gave state and local governments more control over the
    administration of welfare and public housing services—which also included
    more freedom to subcontract the management of these services to private sec-
    tor and nongovernment organizations.

24 See David Sirota's probing commentary, "Truth About UAE Port Security
    Scandal Quietly Leaks Out" (Huffington Post, February 22, 2006, www.huff-
    ingtonpost.com/david-sirota/truth-about-uae-port-secu_b_16133.html [ac-
    cessed May 12, 2010]).

25 See Neil King and Gregg Hitt, "Dubai Ports World Sells U.S. Assets: AIG Unit Buys Operations That Ignited Controversy As Democrats Plan Changes" (*Wall Street Journal,* December 12, 2006).

26 See Zolberg (2008, 383). Also see, Executive Order 12889, Implementation of the North American Free Trade Agreement, signed, December 27, 1993, William J. Clinton, Executive Orders Disposition Tables, Federal Register, National Archives.

27 Between 2005 and 2007 the Bush administration made several attempts at supporting (and in the some cases directly sponsoring) bipartisan immigration reform bills that would have increased quotas for guest workers and expanded temporary legal status options for some unauthorized migrants. All these efforts failed, primarily due to opposition from Republicans in the House. See the White House press release "President Bush Disappointed by Congress's Failure to Act on Comprehensive Immigration Reform," Office of the Press Secretary, June 28, 2007, www.whitehouse.gov/news/releases/2007/06/20070628-7.html (accessed January 9, 2009).

28 This peak amounted to 1.67 million border enforcement actions for 2000. See n29 below for more detail on these trends.

29 This amounts to an average of 1.56 million border enforcement actions (mostly voluntary departures) during the second term of the Clinton administration, compared to an average of 1.03 million actions for the 2000–2008 Bush presidency. The recession was probably responsible for the low number of border enforcement actions in 2007 and 2008 (as the overall unauthorized migrant population began to shrink) but it bears noting that the drop in border enforcement actions occurs at the very beginning of the Bush presidency. In the last year of the Clinton presidency, border enforcement actions reached an all-time high of 1.67 million, dropping to 1.35 million by the end of the first year of the Bush presidency (2001). This 1.35 million figure was the high point in border enforcement actions for the Bush administration. Border enforcement actions continued to drop throughout the Bush presidency (DHS 2008h; "returns" in this chart can be read as estimates of border control actions).

30 Between 2000 and 2008 (the span of the Bush presidency) the unauthorized migrant population grew from 8.4 to a historic high of 12.5 million persons. The pace of growth was comparable to the growth of the unauthorized population under the 1992–2000 Clinton administration (increasing by approximately 5 million persons, compared to an increase of approximately 4 million persons during the Bush years). But the absolute size of the unauthorized migrant population in the Bush years was much higher. Although there were some year-to-year fluctuations in the size of this population, at no point did

its size revert to prior 2000 levels. The population only began to decrease in 2007–2008 (to 11.9 million persons), largely due to the recession—but even this number is a historic high compared to the size of this population prior to the Bush administration's tenure (Wasem 2009, 3).

31 The term "militarized" is used very loosely (hence the scare quotes). All of the immigration reform proposals that were considered by the Congress in 2007 required some degree of intensification in immigration enforcement (including an increase in armed border patrol officers) but Congressman Tom Tancredo was the only lawmaker to put forward a proposal that literally involved U.S. military troops (Migration Policy Institute 2006).

32 In the mid-1950s it was possible for the Republican senator Pat McCarran (coauthor of the 1952 Immigration Nationality Act) to acknowledge during a Senate hearing that "a farmer can get a wetback and he does not have to go through that red tape. . . . We might as well just face this thing realistically. The agricultural people, the farmers . . . want this help. They want this farm labor, they just can't get along with out it" (Ngai 2005, 255: original source, Hadley 1956, 337). For a contemporary discussion of unauthorized migration that makes a similar point see Hanson (2005).

33 The actions of the executive office during the Clinton administration serve as a good example of these priorities in action. In this case, the discretionary authority of the executive office is used to deflect movements to restrict noncitizen rights that are rising from the Congress, even as the executive is also playing a leading role in restructuring and weakening social rights for all U.S. residents (via welfare reform; Singer 2004). To a lesser extent the 2000–2008 Bush administration played a similar role by sponsoring legislation that was opposed by immigration control hard-liners in the House of Congress (see n27 this chapter. But whereas the Clinton administration used its discretionary authority fairly consistently to protect immigrant rights (or at least, to minimize curtailments of those rights), the Bush administration used its discretionary authority to expedite enforcement strategies that required further curtailments of immigrant rights. These proenforcement maneuvers had a much greater impact on policy than the Bush administration's tepid affirmations of immigrant rights (Kretsedemas 2008a).

34 For one example of these sorts of arguments see Juan Mann, "Time for Operation Wetback II" (VDare.com, February 8, 2003, www.vdare.com/mann/operation_wetback.htm [accessed January 10, 2009]).

35 Peak annual removals under Operation Wetback, including formal deportations and voluntary departures, approached 1.1 million (1954). Between 1976 and 2007, immigration enforcement deported 1 million or more persons per

year. In only five years during this period were removals below 1 million per annum, the lowest point being 910,000 removals in 1980 (DHS 2009g; "returns" in this chart can be read as estimates of voluntary departures or border control actions).

36 This memo was exposed by a Freedom of Information Act query filed by the ACLU. See the American Civil Liberties Union press release "Secret Immigration Enforcement Memo Exposed," September 7, 2005, www.aclu.org/immigrants-rights/secret-immigration-enforcement-memo-exposed (accessed May 8, 2010).

37 These laws do not all pertain to police involvement in enforcing immigration laws and they are not uniformly restrictive. However, a sizable number (over 50 percent) authorize police and other local authorities (and private citizens) to check people for legal status for a variety of reasons (NCSL 2009a). The scope and variation of these laws are discussed in more detail in chapter 4 (see table 4.1).

38 See Tom Barry, "U.S. Immigration Debate Splits Conservatives" (ILW.com, August 2, 2007, www.ilw.com/articles/2006%2C0821-barry.shtm [accessed May 12, 2010]).

4. CONCERNED CITIZENS, LOCAL EXCLUSIONS:
LOCAL IMMIGRATION LAWS AND THE LEGACY OF JIM CROW

1 For examples of news stories that make similar arguments, see Roberto Lovato, "Juan Crow in Georgia" (*Nation*, May 8, 2008), and Roberto Rodriguez, "The New Jim Crow: Sham Trials the Norm for Mexicans in Arizona" (New America Media, January 19, 2009).

2 For examples of news stories that have made these connections, see the following reports (focusing on the local immigration law enacted by the Arizona state government in 2010): *Newsweek* (Arian Campos-Flores, "Will Arizona's Immigration Law Lead to Racial Profiling?" April 27, 2010), *The New York Times* (Randall Archibold, "Arizona Enacts Stringent Law on Immigration," April 23, 2010) and *ABC News* (Huma Khan, "Legalizing Racial Profiling? Arizona Bill Draws Fire," April 22, 2010).

3 *Gonzales v. City of Peoria*, 722 F.2d 468 (9th Cir. 1983).

4 *United States v. Vasquez-Alvarez*, 176 F.3d 1294 (10th Cir. 1999); *United States v. Santana-Garcia*, 264 F.3d 1188 (10th Cir. 2001).

5 There is evidence, however, that law enforcement is becoming a more popular theme among local immigration laws. These kinds of laws were among the most popular being proposed and enacted at the state and local level in the

first quarter of 2010 (ranking fourth among all categories of local immigration laws, not counting resolutions; NCSL 2010).

6   A good example is local immigration laws that address education, health, and human trafficking. Only seven of the twenty-eight education-related state laws enacted in 2009 were used to restrict educational services and funding to citizens and lawful permanent residents (and only one of these seven bills—Missouri bill, H 390—expressly forbade unauthorized migrant children from receiving education-related financial aid). The remaining twenty-one laws were used, in various ways, to better serve and incorporate immigrant students and noncitizen educators. Health care–related state laws for 2009 were more varied. Twelve of the twenty-eight laws enacted that year imposed new legal status restrictions on access to health care services or health care career opportunities; three laws went as far to limit some services and employment positions to citizens only (Minnesota bills H 1503 and H 1988 and Nevada bill S 54). The remaining sixteen health-related bills attempted to improve service access for immigrants and support immigrant-related health care services (NCSL 2009b).

7   In recent years, many of the state laws listed under the miscellaneous category have been related to budget appropriation issues. The diversity of these miscellaneous bills is more apparent when looking at laws enacted in 2005–2007 (NCSL 2005, 2006, 2007).

8   The 1996 immigration reform law merely expanded the options for state governors to arrange these memoranda, but these memoranda arrangements were in existence prior to the 1996 law (Appleseed 2008, 17–20).

9   As John Cell has explained, however, this consensus was also made possible by a small but strategically important contingent of black leaders (Cell 1982, 171–191).

10 Ironically, Wilson has also been very influential in advancing these skills-mismatch arguments and other structural explanations of the marginalization of the urban, black poor (Wilson 1990). In this regard, his analysis of black exclusion during the Jim Crow era seems to provide a richer account of the politics of racial formation and racial marginality than his analysis of the contemporary black situation.

11 As Michael Omi and Howard Winant (1994, 82) have explained, Mexican and Chinese migrant populations in the nineteenth and twentieth century complicated the U.S. system of racial classification—introducing crises that threatened to realign some its coordinates. To a lesser extent, the racialization of some European migrant groups (the Irish as well as some Germanic and southern European populations) produced complications that—at the time—

were viewed as essential differences that separated them from native-born whites (Roediger 2008).

12 As John Cell (1982, 119–121) has observed, the southern planters and the leadership of the Democratic party often viewed the white populists as a threat—and a target for disenfranchisement—that was just as important to their political objectives as the marginalization of the black population.

13 Edna Bonacich's (1975) split labor market theory is a primary example of these kinds of neo-Marxist arguments. It is important to note that Bonacich is describing a political process, but it is a political process that is oriented, primarily, around the struggle over the emerging form of national labor markets, which is narrower in focus than the political process I describe.

14 See Joe Chapman, "Ku Klux Klan Plans Amarillo Rally. Event Aimed at Immigration Laws" (*Amarillo Globe News*, July 12, 2006). For a broader overview see Southern Poverty Law Center, "Patriot Groups, Militias Surge in Number Last Year," March 2, 2010, www.splcenter.org/get-informed/news/splc-report-number-of-patriot-groups-militias-surges-by-244-in-past-year (accessed April 14, 2010).

15 The 1980 census was the first to separate the Hispanic category from the other "racial" categories—thus giving Latinos the opportunity to select "Hispanic" and then go on to decide whether they were "white," "black," or "other" (Clara Rodriguez 2000). But the implications of this change for the racial demographics of the U.S. were not explored by many academics until a decade or two later (Grieco and Cassidy 2001).

16 See Brentin Mock, "Smokescreen: Activists Say a Black Anti-Immigrant Movement Is Gathering Steam, But It Seems to be Largely the Creation of White People," *Intelligence Report,* no. 123 (2006): 18–23.

17 This quote is from a *Newsday* special report titled "Farmingville: A Suburb's Struggle" (from the section "Getting Hired," January 29, 2006).

18 See the discussion in chapter 2 for more detail on disparities in border enforcement actions under the Bush and Clinton administrations. For more information on the intensification of border control under the Clinton administration see Nevins (2010). For an overview of the intensification of immigration workplace raids under the latter years of the 2000–2008 Bush administration, see Stewart Powell, "Bush Administration Steps Up Immigration Raids, Election Year Aside, ICE Vows to Go Full Force" (*Houston Chronicle,* May 31, 2008).

19 Also see the CNN report "Operation Tarmac Sweep Widens." April 24, 2002, http://edition.cnn.com/2002/TRAVEL/NEWS/04/24/airports.sweep/?related (accessed May 12, 2010).

20 This interpretation of illegality is consistent with functionalist and social constructionist theories of deviance that have explained how the deviant defines
the norm and is, in many respects, constitutive of the norm from which it is
ritually excluded (S. Cohen 2003; Merton 1938).

21 The distribution of local immigration laws documented by the Migration Policy Institute is instructive (Laglaron et al. 2008). States with larger and more
politically influential immigrant constituencies have been more likely to pass
local laws that enhance immigrant rights, whereas the local laws enacted in
new destination states are more uniformly oriented toward screening immigrants for legal status and restricting immigrant rights. Changes in state administration can also be instrumental in determining what kind of political
constituencies are likely to shape state-level immigration policy. For example,
the shift from a Republican to Democratic governor in Massachusetts in 2006
resulted in the revocation of the memorandum of understanding between state
police and immigration enforcement that had been signed by the former governor. See Jonathan Saltzman, "Governor Rescinds Immigration Order: Frees
Police from Arrest Pact" (*Boston Globe*, January 12, 2007).

22 For a concise summary of variations and themes in Jim Crow laws by state see,
"Interactive Maps: Jim Crow Laws," PBS, The Rise and Fall of Jim Crow, www.
pbs.org/wnet/jimcrow/maps.html (accessed May 12, 2009).

23 Comparisons between apprehension data and size of the undocumented population (by ethnicity) are derived from a more extensive discussion in Kretsedemas (2008b).

24 *Mena v. City of Simi Valley*, 226 F.3d 1031 (9th Cir., 2000). *Muehler et al. v.
Mena*, 544 U.S. 93 (2005).

25 For commentary on the overly aggressive nature of the search and detainment
see Judge Stevens' statement. Judge Stevens positioned this commentary as a
concurring—not a dissenting—opinion. 544 U.S. 93 (2005), J. Stevens, concurring in judgment.

26 544 U.S. 93 (2005), Opinion of the Court, 7.

27 For a discussion of the Arizona law see, Randal Archibold, "Arizona Enacts
Stringent Law on Immigration" (*New York Times*, April 23, 2010). A comparable local immigration law is Georgia Senate Bill 529 (Georgia Immigration/
Security Compliance Act) that was enacted in 2006. One notable distinction is
that the Georgia law did not give local police the same broad leeway to screen
suspected unauthorized migrants as the Arizona law, but it did introduce
a fairly comprehensive system of guidelines for screening legal status that
spanned law enforcement and the public and private sector.

28 Specifically, the lawsuit challenges the Arizona law on the grounds that it violates the supremacy of federal law, that it preempts federal law (violating the Constitution's preemption clause) and also that it violates the Constitution's commerce clause. The lawsuit was filed by Attorney General Eric Holder on July, 6 2010. The United States of America, Plaintiff, v. the State of Arizona; and Janice K. Brewer, Governor of the State of Arizona, in Her Official Capacity.

29 See, Peter Nicholas, "Obama Criticizes Arizona Immigration Law," *Los Angeles Times*, April 28, 2010.

30 For information about the DoJ lawsuit, see n28 this chapter. Other suits include *Friendly House v. Whiting* (May 17, 2010), *League of United Latin American Citizens v. State of Arizona* (July 9, 2010), *National Coalition of Latino Clergy and Christian Leaders v. State of Arizona* (April 29, 2010), and *Salgado v. Brewer* (April 29, 2010). Federal supremacy (and preemption) arguments are central to all of these lawsuits. By comparison, complaints about due process and unlawful search and seizure practices appear in only two of them (in the suits filed by the League of United Latin American Citizens and the National Coalition of Latino Clergy and Christian Leaders).

31 See the Associated Press, "Arizona Immigration Law Sections Struck Down by Federal Judge" (July 28, 2010).

32 See n28 this chapter.

33 The City of Hazleton, Illegal Immigration Relief Act Ordinance (2006, Ordinance 18).

34 See n2 this chapter for examples of news stories that have raised the question of racial profiling in connection with the Arizona immigration law. For example of a report that has made similar connections between racial profiling and the Hazleton law, see Hispanic News Network, "U.S. Federal Appeals Court Rules City of Hazleton Illegal Immigration Relief Act Unconstitutional," September 9, 2010, http://hispanicnewsnetwork.blogspot.com/2010/09/us-federal-appeals-court-rules-city-of.html (accessed October 20, 2010).

35 U.S. District Court, Middle District of Pennsylvania, 2007, *Lozano et al. v. the City of Hazleton*, no: 3:06, cv1586.

36 The Pennsylvania court's decision on the Hazelton case referenced the Fourteenth Amendment to justify its decision concerning the rights of unauthorized migrants to enter into lease agreements with local landlords, arguing that "the city may not burden their right to contract more than that of other persons." However, most of the court's arguments against Hazelton's local immigration laws focused on the way it contradicted preexisting state and federal laws. The decision never broached the issue of racial profiling or Fourth

Amendment arguments that equated aggressive legal screenings with unreasonable search and seizure practices (U.S. District Court, Middle District of Pennsylvania, 2007, *Lozano et al. v. the City of Hazleton*, 186).

37 U.S. Third Circuit Court of Appeals. *Lozano et al. v. City of Hazleton*. No: 07-3531. Argued October 9, 2008. Decided September 9, 2010.

38 See the *Washington Post* report by Senators Romano Mazzoli and Alan Simpson, "Enacting Immigration Reform, Again" (September 15, 2006).

39 See the *Washington Post* report by Michael Barbaro, "Wal-Mart to Pay $11 Million" (March 19, 2005).

40 In May 2011 the Supreme Court upheld this employer sanctions law, which had also met with the approval of the 9th Circuit Court of Appeals in an earlier, 2008 decision.

41 For an overview of some of this pending and prospective legislation see Daniel, Wood, Christian Science Monitor report by Daniel Wood ("After Arizona: Why Are 10 States Considering Immigration Bills?" May 10, 2010).

42 According to the Office of National Drug Control Policy, there is no significant difference in illegal drug use between whites and blacks (see Minorities and Drugs: Facts and Figures, www.whitehousedrugpolicy.gov/drugfact/minorities/minorities_ff.html [accessed October 10, 2010]). Nonetheless blacks are sentenced for drug-related crimes at a much higher rate than whites (with drug-related violations accounting for the majority of sentences against blacks; Human Rights Watch 2008). In recent years, however, there has been a sharp decline in the drug incarceration rates for blacks (Mauer 2009).

5. RACE, NATION, IMMIGRATION: STRANDED AT THE CROSSROADS OF LIBERAL THOUGHT

1 *Ozawa v. United States,* 260 U.S. 178 (1922).

2 *United States v. Bhagat Singh Thind,* 261 U.S. 204 (1923).

3 For various perspectives on the social-historical construction of race from a genetics perspective, see, Koenig, Lee, and Richardson (2008).

4 The Court reasoned that "Aryan" denoted a cultural-linguistic heritage that could have been shared by persons of diverse "racial" ancestries. Hence, the Aryan strains in Thind's cultural heritage did not provide sufficiently clear evidence of a Caucasian biological lineage (*United States v. Bhagat Singh Thind,* 261 U.S. 204 [1923]).

5 The following excerpt summarizes the rationale that guided the Court's decision: "In the endeavor to ascertain the meaning of the statute we must not fail to keep in mind that it does not employ the word 'Caucasian,' but the

words 'white persons,' and these are words of common speech and not of scientific origin. . . . Indeed, as used in the science of ethnology, the connotation of the word is by no means clear, and the use of it in its scientific sense as an equivalent for the words of the statute, other considerations aside, would simply mean the substitution of one perplexity for another. But in this country, during the last half century especially, the word by common usage has acquired a popular meaning, not clearly defined to be sure, but sufficiently so to enable us to say that its popular as distinguished from its scientific application is of appreciably narrower scope. *It is in the popular sense of the word, therefore, that we employ it as an aid to the construction of the statute,* for it would be obviously illogical to convert words of common speech used in a statute into words of scientific terminology when neither the latter nor the science for whose purposes they were coined was within the contemplation of the framers of the statute or of the people for whom it was framed" (*United States v. Bhagat Singh Thind,* 261 U.S. 204 [1923]; emphasis added).

6   These trends toward restricting immigrant and citizen rights are discussed in chapters 2 and 3, but for more context see Buff (2008) and Kretsedemas and Aparicio (2004). Restrictions on immigrant and citizen rights have often occurred in tandem with each other. For example, the 1996 welfare reform act ended welfare as a long-term (or "lifetime") form of assistance for all U.S. residents in addition to imposing special restrictions on immigrant welfare use. And the same legislation that was used shortly after 9/11 to facilitate counterterrorism investigations that targeted immigrants also expanded government surveillance powers over all U.S. residents.

7   According to Bobo (1999) laissez-faire racism "involves staunch rejection of an active role for government in undoing racial segregation and inequality, an acceptance of negative stereotypes of African Americans, a denial of discrimination as a current societal problem and attribution of primary responsibility for black disadvantage to blacks themselves." Although Bobo refers specifically to the situation of black populations, this belief system describes dispositions toward race and the role of government that can easily be extended to other racial minorities (including Latino/a immigrants).

8   This was especially true of the writing of Robert Park (2005).

9   See Omi and Winant (1994, 14–23, 95–112) and S. Steinberg (2001). As other critics have argued, this reasoning replicates the preexisting racial bias of liberal assimilation theory (Jung 2009).

10 For an overview of liberal objections to the introduction of these kinds of structural pluralist arrangements in the United States, see Michael Walzer and

Anthony Appiah's response to Charles Taylor's argument in favor of structural pluralism in C. Taylor (1994).

11 For an example of how these observations apply to the Tea Party movement see Khalil Gibran Muhammad's commentary at the Defender's Online, "The Ballot or the Bullet?" April 13, 2010, www.thedefendersonline.com/2010/04/13/the-ballot-or-the-bullet/ (accessed May 25, 2010).

12 Social constructionist theories of ethnicity do not always tend in this direction, but there is a point of similarity between the rationalist presumptions of social constructionism and explanations of the framing and construction of collective action frames that have been developed by social movement theorists. Social movement literature on collective action frames was driven by an interest in developing better explanations of how cultural identities and narratives shaped the interest-seeking behavior of movement actors (Gamson 1992; Swidler 1986).

13 In many respects, the study of marginality and marginalization is as integral to the sociological discipline today as it ever has been. But the particular thesis introduced by Park, and the various debates and translations that it inspired, had disappeared from the sociological literature by the early 1970s.

14 Park's perspective on alienation and social change is much closer to that of Simmel than to Marx or Durkheim (Simmel 1971 [1908], 217–226). Despite their profound theoretical and political differences, both Marx and Durkheim treated alienation as a problematic condition produced by macrostructural forces (Durkheim 1933 [1893], 291–309; Twining 1980). In contrast, the alienation of Park's marginal man was inextricably bound up with the dynamics of modern progress. As such, it can be regarded as a kind of alienation that was inextricably bound up with the agency of the social actor. Moreover, it is a kind of alienation that cannot be eliminated without arresting the processes of intercultural contact and social change.

15 The best known example is Park's cycle of race relations, which describes the stages through which new populations become assimilated and amalgamated within the population of the host society. Peter Kivisto has argued, however, that Park's writing on assimilation was much more nuanced than it has been given credit for—noting that Park did not necessarily view assimilation as a final end point or as a unilateral, unidirectional process. Kivisto also notes that Park's writing on assimilation is often used as a straw man for sociologists who are critical of the underlying assumptions of mainstream assimilation theory (Kivisto 2005, 3–32).

16 Charles Mills (1997. 42–45) has observed that the distinction between savages and civilized people was integral to the racial distinctions between whites and

nonwhites that took shape in the early colonial era—but also that the European discourse on "savagery" can be traced to the medieval era. Many of the traits that Mills associates with the "savage" (or "wild man") are similar to those that were eventually associated with the colonial-era "native." But whereas the "savage" was defined by the absence of civilized traits, the "native" was defined, primarily, by his subjugation. According to one source, the earliest European usage of "native," in noun form, can be traced to 1450, referring to a "person born in bondage," and from 1535 onward as a general reference to a "person who has always lived in a place." As of 1652 "native" became more closely associated with the non-European, referring to the original inhabitants of the non-European lands where Europeans hold political power. Online Etymology Dictionary, www.etymonline.com/index.php?term=native (accessed May 17, 2009).

17   The earliest derivation of the term "native" can be traced to the early 1400s and carries a meaning that is similar to that of the ancient Latin term "genus." The idea of the native as a "person born in bondage" can be traced to 1450 (see n16 this chapter). The term "race" also has an ancient pedigree that can be traced to the writings of Herodotus (*The History of Herodotus*, 440 BC), who often referred to Greeks, barbarians, and Persians as distinct races. Modern definitions of race, which established the phenotype distinctions with which we are familiar today, did not take shape until the late seventeenth and early eighteenth century. The Swedish naturalist Carl Linnaeus has been credited with developing the first widely influential taxonomy of the "human races" with the publication of the tenth edition of his *Systemae Naturae* in 1758.

18   This paternalistic mindset is captured by Rudyard Kipling's 1899 poem *The White Man's Burden*. J. A Hobson's *Imperialism: A Study* (1965[1902]), which was published just a few years later, provides an insightful Marxist analysis of the historical and politico-economic context for Kipling's poem.

19   Park also used this theory of catastrophic progress to contradict racist theories that associated the rise of civilization with "racial preservation," observing that "if it is true that races are the product of isolation and inbreeding, it is just as certain that civilization, on the other hand, is a consequence of contact and communication. The forces which have been decisive in the history of mankind are those which have brought men together in fruitful competition, conflict and cooperation. Among the most important of these influences have been—according to what I call the catastrophic theory of progress—migration and the incidental collisions, conflicts and fusions of people and cultures which they have occasioned" (Park 1928, 882).

20 On this matter, Nietzsche's thought is limited by his adherence to biological race theory. In contrast, Park's catastrophic theory of change is capable of describing fluid trajectories of social and cultural development that are impossible to capture with a biological theory of race.

21 In their review of immigration and the politics of welfare reform in Europe, Michael Bommes and Andrew Geddes (2000, 1–12) make a similar observation about the growing racial-cultural diversity of European societies and controversies over social rights.

22 A notable example is his admonishment of the black identity politics of Stokely Carmichael (Kwame Toure) and his approving observations about Frantz Fanon's embrace of Western ideals (Zizek 2009, 120, 117–118).

23 For one of the best examples, see Connolly (1995). The writing of Hardt and Negri (2005) could also be included in this category insofar as the influence of Nietzsche is recognized in their applications of Deleuzian theory. For more insights into how Nietzschean-inspired poststructuralist theory has been used to connect questions of philosophy to questions of political practice see Deleuze (2003) and Guattari (1995). Zizek has been very critical of the political credentials of these intellectuals, portraying their brand of neo-Marxian theory (or post-Marxist theory in the case of Deleuze and Guattari) as an accommodationist response to the capitalist status quo (Zizek 2008, 2009). This is yet another example of Zizek's concern for purging his political tradition of spurious influences. From this vantage point, any approving acknowledgment of difference "within the ranks" amounts to a compromise with an alien perspective that is ultimately, aligned with the "enemy." It bears noting, however, that these theorists have also been very critical of the despotic-authoritarian tendencies within Lacanian Marxism that have influenced Zizek's writing.

24 Michel Foucault has, arguably, done more than any other scholar to translate the Nietzschean understanding of genealogy into an analytic method (Foucault 1994). Also see Deleuze (2003, 141–142).

25 There are many variations of this thesis, ranging from conservative arguments (Salins. 1997) to others that are more consistent with classical liberal views on the civic culture (Almond and Verba 1989) and still others that articulate this civic nationalism with a social democratic agenda (Skocpol. 1995). The perspective that is most consistent with the argument I provide in this chapter combines aspects of this social-democratic agenda with some of the more adventurous "postethnic" ruminations of David Hollinger's (1995) treatise on the subject.

6. CONCLUSION: THE IMMIGRATION CRUCIBLE

1   The Tea Party movement seems to be largely concentrated among U.S. citizens who are part of the grassroots base for the Republican party (see Kate Zernike and Megan Thee-Brenan, "Poll Finds Tea Party Backers Wealthier and More Educated," *New York Times*, April 14, 2010). This probably explains why Republican party leaders have attempted to win over Tea Party sympathizers (see Steve Holland, "McCain Says Tea Party Concerns Worth Addressing," Reuters, September 30, 2010; Tenille Tracy, "Top Republican Cites Concerns for GOP's Senate Chances," *Wall Street Journal*, September 19, 2010). Of course, it is always convenient for the party that is not in control of the executive office to align itself with populist forces that are critical of the government, but it also appears that Republican overtures to the Tea Party are being motivated by an interest in holding together its base constituency.

2   See Cam Simpson, "Obama Hones Immigration Policy" (*Wall Street Journal*, July 21, 2009).

3   The broader significance of the lawsuit is referenced in a statement issued by the Department of Justice (DoJ) that quotes the following from the legal brief filed by the DoJ to challenge the Arizona law: "The Constitution and federal law do not permit the development of a patchwork of state and local immigration policies throughout the country." The DoJ statement also goes on to observe that "a patchwork of state and local policies would seriously disrupt federal immigration enforcement. Having enacted its own immigration policy that conflicts with federal immigration law, Arizona 'crossed a constitutional line'" (DoJ 2010).

4.   President Obama's first critical statements about the Arizona law occurred in late April. The decision to send troops to the U.S. border occurred in late May (and was followed only a few days later by the decision to file a lawsuit against the Arizona law). See Peter Nicholas, "Obama Criticizes Arizona Law," Los Angeles Times, April 28, 2010; Patricia Zengerle, "Obama Sending 1200 Troops to Mexico Border," Reuters, May 25, 2010; Paul Davenport and Peter Yost, "Obama Administration Signals Lawsuit Over Arizona Immigration Law," Huffington Post, May 29, 2010.

5   The Bush administration ended its final year in office with a record high of 358,886 deportations (for 2008). In its first year in office, the Obama administration exceeded this number by over 10 percent (reaching more than 390,000 deportations for 2010; DHS 2009g). In addition to this emphasis on deportations, the Obama administration has set new records in federal prosecutions of noncitizens for immigration violations (TRAC 2009).

6   In 1995 over 1.3 unauthorized migrants were apprehended by border patrol (most of whom are returned to their countries of origin via the voluntary departure procedure that bypasses the immigration court system; see chapter 2) but only 25,000 were processed through formal removal proceedings (DHS 2004d, 2004e). In 2009 over 613,000 unauthorized migrants were apprehended by border patrol (DHS 2009g), but over 201,000 were processed through formal removal proceedings (DHS 2009i). Because the DHS stopped providing data on noncriminal removals by category of offense in 2005, it is not possible to give a precise estimate of noncriminal removals tied to unauthorized presence in 2009. Between 1996 and 2005, however, 76 percent of all noncriminal removals were tied to some form of unauthorized presence in the United States (DHS 2005). This percentage was used to estimate the number of unauthorized migrants processed through noncriminal removals in 2009. This 76 percent estimate (from 2005 data) may be rather conservative, since all signs indicate that the Obama administration has intensified the federal government's efforts to use all existing enforcement channels to apprehend and prosecute civil immigration violators.

7   Since 1997 the number of noncitizens removed from the United States for noncriminal reasons has outnumbered the number of noncitizens removed for criminal reasons. In 1997 the number of noncriminal removals was approximately 15 percent larger than the number of criminal removals (61,000 noncriminal removals compared to 53,000 criminal removals). By 2009 the number of noncriminal removals was more than 200 percent larger than the number of criminal removals (261,000 noncriminal removals compared to only 97,000 criminal removals) (DHS 2009i; INS 1999). See n6 this chapter for the estimation that was used to determine that most of these noncriminal removals involve unauthorized migrants.

8   Public opinion on this matter, as in all things, is mixed. There is substantial support for immigration reform and the implementation of a "tough but fair" pathway to legalization for unauthorized migrants. On the other hand, there is also fairly broad-based support for extremely aggressive immigration enforcement measures. Polls show that more than 60 percent of the general public favor legalization for unauthorized migrants; they also show that a slight majority (51 percent) favor the controversial immigration law that was enacted by Arizona in 2010 (America's Voice 2010; USC/Los Angeles Times Poll 2010).

9   See Jason Ryan, Matthew Jaffe and Devin Dwyer, "Obama 'Scheming' on Immigrant Amnesty? Memo Draws Republican Fire," ABC News, July 30, 2010.

10 For two examples, see RightPundits.com. ("Paul Brown: Obama Dictatorship," November 10, 2006, www.rightpundits.com/?p=2392 [accessed May 1, 2010]),

and Amanda Terkel, "Rep. Steve King: Obama Will Make America a 'Totalitarian Dictatorship'" (Think Progress, October 28, 2008, http://thinkprogress.org/2008/10/28/king-obama-dictator/ [accessed May 1, 2010]).

11 For a discussion of some of these authoritarian tendencies, see Bill Hare, "Tea Bag Movement: Harbinger of Fascism?" (Political Cortex, February 10, 2010, www.freerepublic.com/focus/f-bloggers/2450994/posts [accessed May 1, 2010]).

12 See Nico Pitney, "Tea Bag Terror: Protests Causing Scares, Evacuations at Congressional Offices" (Huffington Post, April 15, 2009, www.huffingtonpost.com/2009/04/14/tea-bag-terror-protests-c_n_186596.html [accessed May 12, 2010]).

13 This is a view of the Other that is very similar to Giorgio Agamben's discussion of *homer sacer* (Agamben 1995).

14 See Wise's essay "Imagine If the Tea Party Was Black" (One Utah, April 24, 2010, http://oneutah.org/2010/04/24/imagine-if-the-tea-party-was-black-tim-wise/ (accessed May 1, 2010).

BIBLIOGRAPHY

Adler, Rachel. 2008. *Yucatecans in Dallas, Texas: Breaching the Border, Bridging the Distance.* Pearson.

Agamben, Giorgio. 1995. *Homer Sacer: Sovereign Power and Bare Life.* Stanford, CA: Stanford University Press.

———. 2005. *State of Exception.* Translated by Kevin Attell. Chicago: University of Chicago Press.

Alba, Richard, and Victor Nee. 2005. *Rethinking the American Mainstream: Assimilation and Contemporary Immigration.* Cambridge, MA: Harvard University Press.

Alexander, Michelle. 2010. *The New Jim Crow: Mass Incarceration in the Age of Colorblindness.* New York: New Press.

Allen, Theodore. 1994. *The Invention of the White Race.* London: Verso.

Almond, Gabriel, and Sydney Verba. 1989. *The Civic Culture: Political Attitudes and Democracy in Five Nations.* New York: Sage.

America's Voice. 2009. "Polls Show Most Americans Support Comprehensive Immigration Reform." Washington, DC: National Immigration Forum. http://amvoice.3cdn.net/aed609a4968f2d0380_h6m6bn79o.pdf (accessed May 1, 2010).

Anderson, Benedict. 1998. "Nationalism, Identity, and the World-in-Motion: On the Logics of Seriality." In Pheng Cheah and Bruce Robbins, eds., *Cosmopolitics: Thinking and Feeling Beyond the Nation,* 117–133. Minneapolis: University of Minnesota Press.

Andress, David. 2006. *The Terror: The Merciless War for Freedom in Revolutionary France*. New York: Farrar Straus and Giroux.

Angelo, Michael. 1997. *The Sikh Diaspora: Tradition and Change in an Immigrant Community*. New York: Routledge.

Appadurai, Arjun. 1996. *Modernity at Large: Cultural Dimensions of Globalization*. Minneapolis: University of Minnesota Press.

Appleseed Foundation. 2008. "Forcing Our Blues Into Gray Areas: Local Police and Federal Immigration Enforcement." Washington, DC: Appleseed Foundation.

Arditti, J., J. Lambert-Shute, and K. Joest. 2003. "Saturday Morning at the Jail: Implications of Incarceration for Families and Children." *Family Relations* 52: 3: 195–204.

Arthur, John. 2000. *Invisible Sojourners: African Immigrant Diaspora in the United States*. Westport, CT: Praeger.

Ashfaq, Abira. 2008. "Invisible Removal, Endless Detention, Limited Relief: A Taste of Immigration Court Representation for Detained Noncitizens." In David Brotherton and Philip Kretsedemas, eds., *Keeping Out the Other: A Critical Introduction to Immigration Enforcement Today*, 179–203. New York: Columbia University Press.

Bacon, David. 2009. *Illegal People: How Globalization Creates Migration and Criminalizes Immigrants*. New York: Beacon Press.

Banerjee, P. 2010. "Transnational Subcontracting, Indian IT Workers, and the U.S. Visa System." *Women's Studies Quarterly* 38: 1–2: 89–110.

Barber, James. 1998. *Theodore Roosevelt: Icon of the American Century*. Washington, DC: Smithsonian Institution.

Barr, Macreadie, Kelly Jefferys, and Randall Monger. 2008. "Nonimmigrant Admissions to the United States: 2007." Annual Flow Report. Washington, DC: Department of Homeland Security.

Bashi, Vilna. 2004. "Globalized Anti-Blackness: Transnationalizing Western Immigration Law, Policy, and Practice." *Ethnic and Racial Studies* 27: 4: 584–606.

——. 2007. *Survival of the Knitted: Immigrant Social Networks in a Stratified World*. Stanford, CA: Stanford University Press.

Bashi, Vilna, and Antonio McDaniel. 1997. "A Theory of Immigration and Racial Stratification." *Journal of Black Studies* 27: 5: 668–682.

Beale, Howard. 1956. *Theodore Roosevelt and the Rise of America to World Power*. Baltimore, MD: Johns Hopkins University Press.

Bedi, S. 2003. "The Constructed Identities of Asian and African Americans: A Story of Two Races and the Criminal Justice System." *Harvard BlackLetter Law Journal* 19: 181–199.

Bello, Walden. 2005. *Deglobalization: Ideas for a New World Economy*. New York: Zed Books.

Bennett, Lerone, Jr. 1975. *The Shaping of Black America: The Struggles and Triumphs of African-Americans, 1619–1990s.* Chicago: Johnson.

Bobo, Lawrence. 1999. "The Color Line, the Dilemma, and the Dream: Race Relations in America at the Close of the 20th Century." In John Higham, ed., *Civil Rights and Social Wrongs: Black-White Relations Since World War II*, 33–55. University Park: Pennsylvania State University Press.

Bommes, Michael, and Andrew Geddes. 2000. "Introduction: Immigration and the Welfare State." In Michael Bommes and Andrew Geddes, eds., *Immigration and Welfare: Challenging the Borders of the Welfare State*, 1–12. New York: Routledge.

Bonacich, E. 1975. "Abolition, the Extension of Slavery, and the Position of Free Blacks: A Study of Split Labor Markets in the United States, 1830–1863." *American Journal of Sociology* 81: 3: 601–628.

Bonilla-Silva, Eduardo. 2002. "We Are All Americans! The Latin Americanization of Racial Stratification in the USA." *Race and Society* 5: 3–17.

———. 2009. *Racism Without Racists: Colorblind Racism and the Persistence of Racial Inequality in America.* New York: Rowman and Littlefield.

Boothe, Demico. 2010. *Why Are So Many Black Men in Prison?* Memphis, TN: Full Surface Publishing.

Borjas, G. 2006. "Making It in America: Social Mobility in the Immigrant Population." *Future of Children* 16: 2: 55–71.

Bosniak, L. 2000. "Citizenship Denationalized." *Indiana Journal of Global Legal Studies* 7: 2: 447–510.

Brimelow, Peter. 1996. *Alien Nation: Common Sense About America's Immigration Disaster.* New York: Harper Perennial.

Brodkin, Karen. 1998. *How Jews Became White Folks: And What That Says About Race in America.* Piscataway, NJ: Rutgers University Press.

Brotherton, David, and Luis Barrios. 2004. *The Almighty Latin King and Queen Nation: Street Politics and the Transformation of a New York City Gang.* New York: Columbia University Press.

Brotherton, David, and Philip Kretsedemas, eds. 2008. *Keeping Out the Other: A Critical Introduction to Immigration Enforcement Today.* New York: Columbia University Press;

Buchanan, Patrick. 2001. *The Death of the West: How Dying Populations and Immigrant Invasions Imperil Our Country and Civilization.* New York: Thomas Dunne Books.

———. 2007. *State of Emergency: The Third World Invasion and Conquest of America.* New York: St. Martin's Griffin.

Buff, Rachel, ed. 2008. *Immigrant Rights in the Shadow of Citizenship.* New York: New York University Press.

Burton, David. 1997. *Theodore Roosevelt, American Politician: An Assessment.* Cranbury, NJ: Associated University Presses.

Butcher, K., and J. Dinardo. 2002. "The Immigrant and Native-Born Wage Distributions: Evidence from U.S. Censuses." *Industrial and Labor Relations Review* 56: 1: 97–121.

Butcher, Kristin, and Anne Piehl. 2005. "Why Are Immigrants' Incarceration Rates So Low? Evidence on Selective Immigration, Deterrence, and Deportation" Working Paper 19. Chicago: Federal Reserve Bank of Chicago.

Calavita, Kitty. 1992. *Inside the State: The Bracero Program, Immigration, and the INS.* New York: Routledge.

———. 2005. *Immigrants at the Margins: Race, Law, and Exclusion in Southern Europe.* London: Cambridge University Press.

Capetillo-Ponce, Jorge. 2008. "Framing the Debate on Taxes and Undocumented Workers: A Critical Review of Texts Supporting Proenforcement Policies and Practices." In David Brotherton and Philip Kretsedemas, eds., *Keeping Out the Other: A Critical Introduction to Immigration Enforcement Today,* 314–333. New York: Columbia University Press.

Carey, J. 1946. "Some Aspects of Statelessness Since World War I." *American Political Science Review* 40: 1: 113–123.

Carter, A. 2001. "The Architecture of Government in the Face of Terrorism." *International Security* 26: 3: 5–23.

Castells, Manual. 2009. *Network Society: A Cross-Cultural Perspective.* New York: Wiley-Blackwell.

Catanzarite, L. 2002. "Brown-Collar Jobs: Occupational Segregation and Earnings of Recent-Immigrant Latinos." *Sociological Perspectives* 43: 1: 45–75.

Cell, John W. 1982. *The Highest Stage of White Supremacy: The Origins of Segregation in South Africa and the American South.* New York: Cambridge University Press.

Chang, Grace. 2000. *Disposable Domestics: Immigrant Women Workers in the Global Economy.* Boston: South End Press.

Charles, C. Z. 2003. "The Dynamics of Racial Residential Segregation." *Annual Review of Sociology* 29: 167–207.

Chavez, Leo. 1997. *Shadowed Lives: Undocumented Immigrants in American Society.* Wadsworth.

———. 2008. *The Latino Threat: Constructing Immigrants, Citizens, and the Nation.* Stanford, CA: Stanford University Press.

Chesteen, R. 1971. "Bibliographical Essay: The Legal Validity of Jim Crow." *Journal of Negro History* 56: 4: 284–293.

Cohen, D. K., M. F. Cuellar, and B. Weingast. 2006. "Crisis Bureaucracy: Homeland Security and the Political Design of Legal Mandates." *Stanford Law Review* 59: 3: 673–759.

Cohen, Jean, and Andrew Arato. 1994. *Civil Society and Political Theory*. Cambridge, MA: MIT Press.

Cohen, Stan. 2002. *Folk Devils and Moral Panics*. New York: Routledge.

Cole, David. 2000a. "Georgetown University Law Center On the Use of Secret Evidence in Immigration Proceedings and HR. 2121." Testimony before the House Judiciary Committee, May 23.

———. 2000b. *No Equal Justice: Race and Class in the American Criminal Justice System*. New York: New Press.

———. 2005. *Enemy Aliens: Double Standards and Constitutional Freedoms in the War on Terrorism*. New York: New Press.

Connolly, William. 1995. *The Ethos of Pluralization*. Minneapolis: University of Minnesota Press.

Cornelius, Wayne. 2008. "Controlling Unauthorized Immigration from Mexico: The Failure of 'Prevention through Deterrence' and the Need for Comprehensive Reform." June. Center for Comparative Immigration Studies, University of California, San Diego.

Cornelius, Wayne, Takeyuki Tsuda, Philip Martin, and James Hollifield, eds. 2004. *Controlling Immigration: A Global Perspective*. Stanford, CA: Stanford University Press.

Crowley, M., D. Lichter, and Z. Qian. 2006. "Beyond Gateway Cities: Economic Restructuring and Poverty Among Mexican Immigrant Families and Children." *Family Relations* 55: 3: 345–360.

Daniels, Jessie. 2009. *White Supremacy Online and the New Attack on Civil Rights*. Lanham, MD: Rowman and Littlefield.

Daniels, Roger. 2004. *Guarding the Golden Door: American Immigration Policy and Immigrants Since 1882*. New York: Hill and Wang.

Darner, Katherine, Robert Baird, and Stuart Rosenbaum, eds. 2004. *Civil Liberties vs. National Security in a Post-9/11 World*. Amherst, NY: Prometheus Books.

Day, Richard. 2000. *Multiculturalism and the History of Canadian Diversity*. Toronto: University of Toronto Press.

De Genova, Nicholas. 2005. *Working the Boundaries: Race, Space, and Illegality in Mexican Chicago*. Durham, NC: Duke University Press.

Deleuze, Gilles. 2003. *Desert Islands and Other Texts, 1953–1974*. Translated by Michael Taormina. Cambridge, MA: Semiotext(e)/MIT Press.

———. 2006. *Nietzsche and Philosophy*. New York: Columbia University Press.

Department of Homeland Security (DHS). 1998. Table 38, "Nonimmigrants Admitted by Selected Class of Admission and Region and Country of Citizenship: Fiscal Year 1998." *Fiscal Year 1998 Statistical Yearbook.*

———. 1999a. Table 2, "Immigration by Region and Selected Country of Last Residence: Fiscal Years 1820–1999." *Fiscal Year 1999 Statistical Yearbook.*

———. 1999b. Table 36, "Nonimmigrants Admitted by Selected Class of Admission and Region and Country of Citizenship: Fiscal Year 1999." *Fiscal Year 1999 Statistical Yearbook.*

———. 1999c. Table 38, "Nonimmigrants Admitted as Temporary Workers, Exchange Visitors, and Intracompany Transferees by Region and Country of Citizenship: Fiscal Year 1999." *Fiscal Year 1999 Statistical Yearbook.*

———. 2000. Table 36, "Nonimmigrants Admitted by Selected Class of Admission and Region and Country of Citizenship: Fiscal Year 2000." *Fiscal Year 2000 Statistical Yearbook.*

———. 2001a. Table 36, "Nonimmigrants Admitted by Selected Class of Admission and Region and Country of Citizenship: Fiscal Year 2001." *Fiscal Year 2001 Statistical Yearbook.*

———. 2001b. Table 41, "Nonimmigrants Admitted by Selected Class of Admission and State of Destination: Fiscal Year 2001." *Fiscal Year 2001 Statistical Yearbook.*

———. 2002. Table 25, "Nonimmigrants Admitted by Selected Class of Admission and Region and Country of Citizenship: Fiscal Year 2002." *Fiscal Year 2002 Statistical Yearbook.*

———. 2003. Table 23, "Nonimmigrants Admitted by Selected Class of Admission and Region and Country of Citizenship: Fiscal Year 2003," *Yearbook of Immigration Statistics 2003.*

———. 2004a. Table 4, "Immigrants Admitted by Type and Selected Class of Admission: Fiscal Years 1986–2004." *Yearbook of Immigration Statistics 2004.*

———. 2004b Table 23, "Nonimmigrants Admitted by Selected Class of Admission and Region and Country of Citizenship: Fiscal Year 2004," *Yearbook of Immigration Statistics 2004.*

———. 2004c. Table 24, "Nonimmigrants Admitted by Class of Admission: Selected Fiscal Years 1981–2004." *Yearbook of Immigration Statistics 2004.*

———. 2004d. Table 38, "Principal Activities and Accomplishments of the Border Patrol: Fiscal Years 1993–2004." *Yearbook of Immigration Statistics 2004.*

———. 2004e. Table 42, "Aliens Removed by Administrative Reason for Removal: Fiscal Years 1991–2004." *Yearbook of Immigration Statistics 2004.*

———. 2005. Table 40, "Aliens Formally Removed by Administrative Reason for Removal: Fiscal Years 1996 to 2005." *Yearbook of Immigration Statistics 2005.*

———. 2009a. Table 1, "Persons Obtaining Legal Permanent Residence: Fiscal Years 1820–2009." *Yearbook of Immigration Statistics 2009.*

———. 2009b. Table 2, "Persons Obtaining Legal Permanent Residence by Region and Selected Country of Last Residence: Fiscal Years 1820–2009." *Yearbook of Immigration Statistics 2009.*

———. 2009c. Table 6, "Persons Obtaining Legal Permanent Resident Status by Type and Major Class of Admission: Fiscal Years 1998 to 2009." *Yearbook of Immigration Statistics 2009.*

———. 2009d. Table 25, "Nonimmigrant Admissions by Class of Admission: Fiscal Years 1999 to 2009." *Yearbook of Immigration Statistics 2009.*

———. 2009e. Table 26, "Nonimmigrant Admissions (I-94 Only) by Region and Country of Citizenship: Fiscal Years 2000 to 2009," *Yearbook of Immigration Statistics 2009.*

———. 2009f. Table 33, "Deportable Aliens Located: Fiscal Years 1925 to 2009." *Yearbook of Immigration Statistics 2009.*

———. 2009g. Table 35. "Deportable Aliens Located by Program and Border Patrol Sector and Investigations Special Agent in Charge (SAC) Jurisdiction: Fiscal Years 2000–2009." *Yearbook of Immigration Statistics 2009.*

———. 2009h. Table 36. "Aliens Removed or Returned: Fiscal Years 1892 to 2009." *Yearbook of Immigration Statistics 2009.*

———. 2009i. Table 38. "Aliens Removed by Criminal Status and Region and Country of Nationality: Fiscal Years 2000–2009." *Yearbook of Immigration Statistics 2009.*

———. 2010. Fiscal Year 2011 Budget in Brief. www.dhs.gov/xlibrary/assets/budget_bib_fy2011.pdf (accessed October 21, 2010).

Department of Justice (DoJ). 2010. "Citing Conflict With Federal Law, Department of Justice Challenges Federal Immigration Law. " July 6, News Release. Washington, DC: Department of Justice Office of Public Affairs.

Dodds, Graham. 2003. "Modernizing the Presidency: Theodore Roosevelt and Executive Orders." Presented at the annual meeting of the American Political Science Association. Philadelphia Marriott Hotel, Philadelphia, PA. www.allacademic.com/meta/p64739_index.html (accessed September 6, 2008).

Dow, Mark. 2005. *American Gulag: Inside U.S. Immigration Prisons.* Berkeley: University of California Press.

———. 2008. "Unchecked Power Against Undesirables: Haitians, Mariel Cubans, and Guantánamo." In David Brotherton and Philip Kretsedemas, eds., *Keeping Out the Other: A Critical Introduction to Immigration Enforcement Today,* 29–43. New York: Columbia University Press.

Durkheim, Emile. 1933 [1893]. *The Division of Labor in Society.* New York: Macmillan.

Dunn, Timothy. 2010. *Blockading the Border and Human Rights: The El Paso Operation That Remade Immigration Enforcement*. Austin: University of Texas Press.

Edwards, James. 2003. "Officers Need Backup: The Role of State and Local Police in Immigration Enforcement." April. Washington, DC: Center for Immigration Studies.

Edwards, John. 2003. "Up to the Challenge." *Foreign Policy* 135: 52–54.

Eitzen, Stanley, and Maxine Baca Zinn, eds. 1989. *The Reshaping of America*. Englewood Cliffs, NJ: Prentice Hall.

Etzioni, Amitai. 2004. *How Patriotic Is the Patriot Act? Freedom Versus Security in the Age of Terrorism*. New York: Routledge.

Fanon, Frantz. 1967. *Black Skin, White Masks*. New York: Grove Press.

Feagin, Joe, and Eileen O'Brien. 2004. *White Men on Race: Power, Privilege, and the Shaping of Cultural Consciousness*. Boston: Beacon Press.

Fenton, Steve. 2003. *Ethnicity*. Cambridge, UK: Polity.

Fernandes, Deepa. 2007. *Targeted: Homeland Security and the Business of Immigration*. New York: Seven Stories Press.

Fiscal Policy Institute. 2009. "Immigrants and the Economy: Contribution of Immigrant Workers to the Country's 25 Largest Metro Areas." December. New York: Fiscal Policy Institute.

Fix, Michael, and Wendy Zimmerman. 1999. *All Under One Roof: Mixed-Status Families in an Era of Reform*. Washington, DC: Urban Institute.

Fleras, Augie, and Jean Leonard Elliot. 2002. *Unequal Relations: An Introduction to Race and Ethnic Dynamics in Canada*. 4th edition. Scarborough, Ontario: Prentice Hall.

Foucault, Michel. 1994. *The Order of Things: An Archeology of the Human Sciences*. New York: Vintage.

———. 1995. *Discipline and Punish: The Birth of the Prison*. New York: Vintage.

———. 2007. *Security, Territory, Population: Lectures at the College de France, 1977–1978*. New York: Macmillan-Palgrave.

———. 2008. *The Birth of Biopolitics: Lectures at the College de France, 1978–1979*. New York: Macmillan-Palgrave.

Fraser, Nancy. 1992. "Rethinking the Public Sphere: A Contribution to the Critique of Actually Existing Democracy." In Craig Calhoun, ed., *Habermas and the Public Sphere*, 109–142. Cambridge, MA: MIT Press.

Fraser, Nancy, and Linda Gordon. 1998. "Contract versus Charity: Why Is There No Social Citizenship in the United States?" In Gershon Shafir, ed., *The Citizenship Debates: A Reader*, 113–130. Minneapolis: University of Minnesota Press.

Fuchs, Lawrence. 1990. *The American Kaleidoscope: Race, Ethnicity, and the Civic Culture*. Middletown., CT: Wesleyan University Press.

Gallagher, C. 2003. "Color-blind Privilege: The Social and Political Functions of Erasing the Color Line in Post-Race America." *Race, Gender, and Class* 10: 4: 22–37.

Gamson, William. 1992. "The Social Psychology of Collective Action." In Aldon Morris and Carol McClurg Mueller, eds., *Frontiers in Social Movement Theory*, 53–76. New Haven, CT: Yale University Press.

Gans, Herbert. 1999. "The Possibility of a New Racial Hierarchy in the Twenty-First Century United States." In Michele Lamont, ed., *The Cultural Territories of Race: Black and White Boundaries*, 371–90. Chicago: University of Chicago Press.

Garrett, T., and R. Rhine. 2006. "On the Size of Growth of Government." *Federal Reserve Bank of St. Louis Review* 88: 1: 13–30.

Gelatt, Julia. 2005. "Schengen and the Free Movement of People Across Europe." October. Washington, DC: Migration Policy Institute.

Genovese, Michael A. 2001. *The Power of the American Presidency, 1789–2000*. Oxford, UK: Oxford University Press.

Gerstle, Gary. 2001. *American Crucible: Race and Nation in the Twentieth Century*. Princeton, NJ: Princeton University Press.

Gerth, H. H., and C. Wright Mills, eds. 1946. *From Max Weber: Essays in Sociology*. New York: Oxford University Press.

Giddens, Anthony. 2003. *Runaway World: How Globalization Is Shaping Our Lives*. New York: Routledge.

Gilens, Martin. 2000. *Why Americans Hate Welfare: Race, Media, and the Politics of Antipoverty Policy*. Chicago: University of Chicago Press.

Gladstein, Hannah, Annie Lai, Jennifer Wagner, and Michael Wishnie. 2005. "Blurring the Lines: A Profile of State and Local Police Enforcement of Immigration Law Using the National Crime Information Center Database, 2002–2004." December. Washington, DC: Migration Policy Institute.

Glazer, Nathan, and Daniel Patrick Moynihan. 1970 [1963]. *Beyond the Melting Pot: The Negroes, Puerto Ricans, Jews, Italians, and Irish of New York City*. 2nd edition. Cambridge, MA: MIT Press.

Goldsmith, P. R., R. Rubio-Goldsmith, M. Escobedo, and L. Khoury. 2009. "Ethno-Racial Profiling and State Violence in a Southwest Barrio." *Aztlán: A Journal of Chicano Studies* 34: 1: 93–123.

Gordon, Jennifer. 2007. *Suburban Sweatshops: The Fight for Immigrant Rights*. Cambridge, MA: Belknap Press of Harvard University Press.

Government Accountability Office (GAO). 1980. *Controls Over Nonimmigrant Aliens Remain Ineffective*. September. Washington, DC: GAO.

———. 1992. "Immigration and the Labor Market: Nonimmigrant Alien Workers in the United States." April. Washington, DC: GAO.

———. 1995. "Illegal Immigration: INS Overstay Estimation Methods Need Improvement." September. Washington, DC: GAO.

———. 2008. "Visa Waiver Program: Actions Are Needed to Improve Management of the Expansion Process and to Assess and Mitigate Program Risks." September. Washington DC: GAO.

Greeley, Andrew. 1974. *Ethnicity in the United States: A Preliminary Reconnaissance*. New York: John Wiley and Sons.

Grieco, Elizabeth M, and Rachel C. Cassidy. 2001. "Overview of Race and Hispanic Origin." 2000 U.S. Census Brief. Washington, DC: U.S. Census.

Guattari, Felix. 1995. *Chaosophy*. Cambridge, MA: Semiotext(e)/MIT Press.

Hadley, E. 1956. "A Critical Analysis of the Wetback Problem." *Law and Contemporary Problems* 21: 334–357.

Haney López, Ian. 2006. *White by Law: The Legal Construction of Race*. New York: NYU Press.

Hanson, Gordon. 2005. *Why Does Immigration Divide America? Public Finance and Political Opposition to Open Borders*. Washington, DC: Institute for International Economics.

———. 2007. *The Economic Logic of Illegal Immigration*. Washington, DC: Brookings Institution Press.

Hardt, Michael, and Antonio Negri. 2005. *Multitude: War and Democracy in the Age of Empire*. Cambridge, MA: Harvard University Press.

Harris, David. 2003. *Profiles in Injustice: Why Racial Profiling Cannot Work*. New York: New Press.

Harvey, David. 2005. *A Brief History of Neoliberalism*. Oxford University Press.

Higham, John, ed. 1999. *Civil Rights and Social Wrongs: Black-White Relations Since World War II*. University Park: Pennsylvania State University Press.

Hing, Bill. 2003. *Defining America Through Immigration Policy*. Philadelphia, PA: Temple University Press.

Historical Statistics of the United States: Earliest Times to the Present, Millennial Edition. 2006. Edited by Susan Carter, Scott Sigmund Gartner, Michael Haines, Alan Olmstead, Richard Sutch, and Gavin Wright. Table Ad1014–1022, "Nonimmigrants Admitted, by Class of Admission: 1925–1996." New York: Cambridge University Press.

Hobson, J. A. 1965 [1902]. *Imperialism: A Study*. Ann Arbor: University of Michigan Press.

Hoefer, Michael, Nancy Rytina, and Bryan Baker. 2008. "Estimates of the Unauthorized Immigrant Population Residing in the United States: January 2007." *2007 Immigration Yearbook: Population Estimates*. Washington, DC: Department of Homeland Security.

Hofstadter, Richard. 1992 [1955]. *Social Darwinism in American Thought*. New York: Beacon Books.

Hollifield, James. 2004. "France: Republicanism and the Limits of Immigration Control." In Wayne Cornelius, Takeyuki Tsuda, Philip Martin and James Hollifield, eds., *Controlling Immigration: A Global Perspective*, 2nd ed., 183–214. Stanford, CA: Stanford University Press.

Hollinger, David. 1995. *Postethnic America: Beyond Multiculturalism*. New York: Basic Books.

Human Rights Watch. 2008. "Targeting Blacks: Drug Law Enforcement and Race in the United States." May. New York: Human Rights Watch.

Huntington, Samuel P. 1998. *The Clash of Civilizations and the Remaking of World Order*. New York: Simon and Schuster.

——. 2004. "The Hispanic Challenge." *Foreign Policy* 141: 30–45.

——. 2005. *Who Are We? The Challenges to America's National Identity*. New York: Simon and Schuster.

Ibrahim, M. 2005. "The Securitization of Migration: A Racial Discourse." *International Migration* 43: 5: 163–187.

Ichijo, Atsuko, and Gordana Uzelac. 2005. *When Is the Nation? Towards an Understanding of Theories of Nationalism*. New York: Routledge.

Ifitikhar, Arsalan. 2008. "Presumption of Guilt: September 11 and the American Muslim Community." In David Brotherton and Philip Kretsedemas, eds., *Keeping Out the Other: A Critical Introduction to Immigration Enforcement Today*, 108–137. New York: Columbia University Press.

Ignatiev, Noel. 1995 *How the Irish Became White*. New York: Routledge.

Immigration and Nationality Service (INS). 1999. Table 63: Aliens Removed by Criminal Status and Region and Country of Nationality. Fiscal Year 1999 Statistical Yearbook.

Inda, Jonathan Xavier. 2005. *Targeting Immigrants: Government, Technology, and Ethics*. Malden, MA: Blackwell.

Jacobson, Robin. 2008. *The New Nativism: Proposition 187 and the Debate over Immigration*. Minneapolis: University of Minnesota Press.

James, C. L. R., with Raya Dunayevskaya and Grace Lee. 1986. *State Capitalism and World Revolution*. Chicago: Charles H. Kerr.

Jayasuriya, Laksiri, and Jan Gothard, eds. 2003. *Legacies of White Australia: Race, Culture, and Nation*. Crawley, Perth: University of Western Australia Press.

Johnston, James. 1970. *Race Relations in Virginia and Miscegenation in the South, 1776–1860*. Amherst: University of Massachusetts.

Jones, Charles, and Michael Clemons. 1993. "A Model of Racial Crossover Voting: An Assessment of the Wilder Victory." In Georgia Persons, ed., *Dilemmas of*

Black Politics: Issues of Leadership and Strategy, 128–146. New York: Harper Collins.

Jung, M. K. 2009. "The Racial Unconscious of Assimilation Theory." *Du Bois Review* 6: 2: 375–395.

Kanstroom, Dan. 2010. *Deportation Nation.* Cambridge, MA: Harvard University Press.

Kateel, Subhash, and Aarti Shahani. 2008. "Families for Freedom: Against Deportation and Delegalization." In David Brotherton and Philip Kretsedemas, eds., *Keeping Out the Other: A Critical Introduction to Immigration Enforcement Today,* 258–290. New York: Columbia University Press.

Katznelson, Ira. 2006. *When Affirmative Action Was White: An Untold Story of Racial Inequality in the Twentieth Century.* New York: W. W. Norton.

Kelley, Robin. 1998. *Yo' Mama's Dysfunktional! Fighting the Culture Wars in Urban America.* Boston: Beacon Press.

Kephart, Janice. 2009. "E-Verify: Challenges and Opportunities." Testimony for the Record Before the U.S. House Committee on Oversight and Government Reform. July 23.

Kerber, L. 2005. "Toward a History of Statelessness in America." *American Quarterly* 57: 3: 727–749.

Kivisto, Peter, ed. 2005. *Incorporating Diversity: Rethinking Assimilation in a Multicultural Age.* London: Paradigm.

Koenig, Barbara, Sandra Soo-Jin Lee, and Sarah Richardson, eds. 2008. *Revisiting Race in a Genomic Age.* New Brunswick, NJ: Rutgers University Press.

Koopmans, R., and P. Statham. 1999. "Challenging the Liberal Nation-State? Postnationalism, Multiculturalism and the Collective Claims-Making of Migrants and Ethnic Minorities in Britain and Germany." *American Journal of Sociology* 105: 652–696.

Kretsedemas, Philip. 2004. "Avoiding the State: Haitian Immigrants and Welfare Services in Miami-Dade County." In Philip Kretsedemas and Ana Aparicio, eds., *Immigrants, Welfare Reform, and the Poverty of Policy,* 107–136. Westport, CT: Greenwood-Praeger.

——. 2005. "Reconsidering Immigrant Welfare Restrictions: A Critical Review of Post-Keynesian Welfare Policy." *Stanford Law and Policy Review* 16: 2: 463–480.

——. 2008a. "Immigration Enforcement and the Complication of National Sovereignty: Understanding Immigration Enforcement as an Exercise in Neoliberal Governance." *American Quarterly* 60: 3: 553–573.

——. 2008b. "What Does an Undocumented Immigrant Look Like? Local Enforcement and the New Immigrant Profiling." In David Brotherton and Philip

Kretsedemas, eds., *Keeping Out the Other: A Critical Introduction to Immigration Enforcement Today*, 334–364. New York: Columbia University Press.

Kretsedemas, Philip, and Ana Aparicio, eds. 2004. *Immigrants, Welfare Reform, and the Poverty of Policy*. Westport, CT: Greenwood-Praeger.

Kymlicka, Will. 1996. *Multicultural Citizenship: A Liberal Theory of Minority Rights*. London: Oxford University Press.

Laglaron, Lauren, Cristina Rodriguez, Alexa Silver, and Sirithon Thanasombat. 2008. "Regulating Immigration at the State Level: Highlights from the Database of 2007 State Immigration Legislation and the Methodology." October. Washington, DC: Migration Policy Institute.

Lennox, M. 2003. "Refugees, Racism, and Reparations: A Critique of the United States' Haitian Immigration Policy." *Stanford Law Review* 45: 3: 687–724.

Li, Peter. 1999. "Race and Ethnicity." In Peter Li, ed., *Race and Ethnic Relations in Canada*, 3–20. London: Oxford University Press.

Liu, Hiaming. 2005. *The Transnational History of a Chinese Family*. Piscataway, NJ: Rutgers University Press.

Loescher, G., and John Scanlan. 1984. "Human Rights, U.S. Foreign Policy, and Haitian Refugees." *Journal of Interamerican Studies and World Affairs* 26: 3: 313–356.

Lowell, Lindsey. 2000. "H-1B Workers: Estimating the Population." Working Paper 12. Comparative Center for Immigration Studies. University of California San Diego.

Lyons, B. 2007. "Tipping the Balance: Why Courts Should Look to International and Foreign Law on Unauthorized Immigrant Worker Rights." *University of Pennsylvania Journal of International Law* 29: 1: 169–242.

Major Cities Chiefs. 2006. "MCC Immigration Committee Recommendations for the Enforcement of Immigration Laws by Local Police Agencies." June. Columbia, MD: Major Cities Chiefs Immigration Committee.

Marchevsky, Alejandra, and Jeanne Theoharis. 2006. *Not Working: Latina Immigrants, Low-Wage Jobs, and the Failure of Welfare Reform*. New York: New York University Press.

Martin, David. 2005. "Twilight Statuses: A Closer Examination of the Unauthorized Population." June. Washington, DC: Migration Policy Institute.

Martin, Philip. 1982. "Select Commission Suggests Changes in Immigration Policy—A Review Essay." February. *Monthly Labor Review*.

———. 2004. "The United States: The Continuing Immigration Debate." In Wayne Cornelius, Takeyuki Tsuda, Philip Martin, and James Hollifield, eds., *Controlling Immigration: A Global Perspective*, 51–85. Stanford, CA: Stanford University Press.

Martin, Philip, and J. Edward Taylor. 1991. "Immigration Reform and Farm Labor Contracting in California." In Michael Fix, ed., *The Paper Curtain: Employer Sanctions' Implementation, Impact, and Reform*, 239–261. Washington, DC: Urban Institute Press.

Massey, Douglas. 2008. *Categorically Unequal: The American Stratification System*. New York: Russell Sage Foundation.

Massey, Douglas, Jorge Durand, and Nolan Malone. 2003. *Beyond Smoke and Mirrors: Mexican Immigration in an Era of Economic Integration*. New York: Russell Sage Foundation.

Mauer, Mark, 2009. "Changing Racial Dynamics of the War on Drugs." April. Washington, DC: Sentencing Project.

McPherson, J. 2002. "How President Lincoln Decided to Issue the Emancipation Proclamation." *Journal of Blacks in Higher Education* 37: 108–109.

Merton, R. 1938. "Social Structure and Anomie." *American Sociological Review* 3: 672–82.

Meyers, Deborah. 2003. "Does 'Smarter' Lead to Safer? An Assessment of the Border Accords with Canada and Mexico." June. Washington, DC: Migration Policy Institute.

———. 2005. "One Face at the Border: Behind the Slogan." June. Washington, DC: Migration Policy Institute.

Meyers, Dowell. 2008. "Thinking Ahead About Our Immigrant Future: New Trends and Mutual Benefits in Our Aging Society." Washington, DC: Immigration Policy Institute.

Migration Policy Institute. 2005."Immigration Enforcement Spending Since IRCA." Immigration Facts. November, No. 10. www.migrationpolicy.org/IT-FIAF/FactSheet_Spending.pdf (accessed March 29, 2010).

———. 2006. "Side by Side Chart for Major Legislation Pending in the 109th Congress: Enforcement Provisions." www.gcir.org/system/files/legislation_jan06.pdf (accessed April 5, 2010).

Mills, Charles. 1997. *The Racial Contract*. Ithaca, NY: Cornell University Press.

Mindiola, Tatcho, Yolanda Flores Niemann, and Nestor Rodriguez, 2003. *Black-Brown Relations and Stereotypes*. Austin: University of Texas Press.

Mitchell, K. 2003. "Educating the National Citizen in Neoliberal Times: From the Multicultural Self to the Strategic Cosmopolitan." *Transactions of the Institute of British Geographers* 28: 4: 387–403.

Muchetti, A. 2005. "Driving While Brown: A Proposal for Ending Racial Profiling in Emerging Latino Communities." *Harvard Latino Law Review* 8. www.law.harvard.edu/students/orgs/llr/vol8/mucchetti.php (accessed May 12, 2010).

National Conference of State Legislators (NCSL). 2005. Immigration Legislation in 2005. Washington, DC: NCSL.

———. 2006. State Legislation Related to Immigration: Enacted and Vetoed. Washington, DC: NCSL.

———. 2007. State Enacted Legislation Related to Immigrants and Immigration. Washington, DC: NCSL.

———. 2008. Overview of State Legislation Related to Immigrants and Immigration: January–March 2008. Washington, DC: NCSL.

———. 2009a. State Laws Related to Immigrants and Immigration: January 1–December 31, 2009. Washington, DC: NCSL.

———. 2009b. Immigration Database. www.ncsl.org/default.aspx?TabId=19209 (accessed May 12, 2010).

———. 2010. Immigration-Related Bills and Resolutions in the States: January–March 2010. Washington, DC: NCSL.

National Immigration Law Center (NILC). 2007. "NILC's Statement on the Senate–White House Immigration Reform Proposal." May 21. www.nilc.org/immlawpolicy/CIR/cir022.htm (accessed May 12, 2010).

Ndaula, Malik, with Debbie Satyal. 2008. "Rafiu's Story: An American Immigrant Nightmare." In David Brotherton and Philip Kretsedemas, eds., *Keeping Out the Other: A Critical Introduction to Immigration Enforcement Today,* 241–257. New York: Columbia University Press.

Neubeck, Kenneth J., and Noel A. Cazenave. 2001. *Welfare Racism: Playing the Race Card Against America's Poor.* New York: Routledge.

Neumayer, E. 2006. "Unequal Access to Foreign Spaces: How States Use Visa Restrictions to Regulate Mobility in a Globalized World." *Transactions/ Institute of British Geographers* 31: 72–84.

Nevins, Joseph. 2010. *Operation Gatekeeper and Beyond: The War on "Illegals" and the Remaking of the U.S.–Mexico Boundary.* New York: Routledge.

Ngai, Mae. 2005. *Impossible Subjects: Illegal Aliens and the Making of Modern America.* Princeton, NJ: Princeton University Press.

Nguyen, Mai Thi, and Hannah Gill. 2010. "The 287(g) Program: The Costs and Consequences of Local Enforcement in North Carolina Communities." Chapel Hill: University of North Carolina at Chapel Hill and the Latino Migration Project, Institute for the Study of the Americas.

Nietzsche, Friedrich. 1956 [1872]. *The Birth of Tragedy.* New York: Anchor Books.

———. 1966 [1886]. *Beyond Good and Evil.* New York: Vintage.

———. 1967. *The Will to Power.* New York: Vintage.

———. 1974 [1882]. *The Gay Science.* New York: Vintage.

———. 2009 [1878]. *Human, All Too Human.* New York: Prometheus Books.

Nopper, Tamara. 2008. "Why Black Immigrants Matter: Refocusing the Discussion on Racism and Immigration Enforcement." In David Brotherton and

BIBLIOGRAPHY

Philip Kretsedemas, eds., *Keeping Out the Other: A Critical Introduction to Immigration Enforcement Today,* 204–237. New York: Columbia University Press.

Numbers USA. 2010. "The Need for State and Local Immigration Law Enforcement of Immigration Laws." www.numbersusa.com/content/learn/attrition-through-enforcement/interior-/need-state-and-local-immigration-law-enf.html (accessed April 15, 2010).

Oboler, Suzanne, ed. 2009. *Latino/as and Prison in the United States.* New York: Palgrave MacMillan.

Omi, Michael, and Howard Winant. 1994. *Racial Formation in the United States: From the 1960s to the 1990s.* New York: Routledge.

Papademetriou, Demetrious, Doris Meissner, Marc Rosenblum, and Madeleine Sumption. 2009. "Aligning Temporary Immigration Visas with U.S. Labor Market Needs: The Case for a New System of Provisional Visas." Washington, DC: Migration Policy Institute.

Parekh, Bhikhu. 1995. "Liberalism and Colonialism." In Jan Nederveen Pieterse and Bhikhu Parekh, eds., *The Decolonization of Imagination: Culture, Knowledge, and Power.* London: Zed Books.

Parenti, Christian. 2000. *Lockdown America: Police and Prisons in the Age of Crisis.* New York: Verso.

Park, Robert. 1928. "Human Migration and the Marginal Man." *American Journal of Sociology* 33: 6: 881–893.

———. 2005. "Racial Assimilation in Secondary Groups with Particular Reference to the Negro." In Peter Kivisto, ed., *Incorporating Diversity: Rethinking Assimilation in a Multicultural Age,* 33–46. London: Paradigm.

Partnership for Public Service. 2007. "Where the Jobs Are: Mission Critical Opportunities for America." Washington, DC: Partnership for Public Service.

Passel, Jeffrey. 2006. "Size and Characteristics of the Unauthorized Migrant Population in the U.S." March. Pew Hispanic Center.

Passel, Jeffrey, and D'Vera Cohn. 2008. "Trends in Unauthorized Immigration: Undocumented Inflow Now Trails Legal Inflow." Washington, DC: Pew Hispanic Center.

———. 2009. "A Portrait of Unauthorized Immigrants in the United States." April 14. Washington, DC: Pew Hispanic Center.

Pateman, Carole. 1990. *The Disorder of Women: Democracy, Feminism, and Political Theory.* Stanford, CA: Stanford University Press.

Pauley, Garth E. 2001. *The Modern Presidency and Civil Rights: Rhetoric on Race from Roosevelt to Nixon.* College Station: Texas A&M University Press.

Peck, Jamie. 2001. *Workfare States.* New York: Guilford Press.

Perea, Juan, ed. 1996. *Immigrants Out! The New Nativism and the Anti-Immigrant Impulse in the United States.* New York: NYU Press.

Peri, Giovanni. 2009. "The Effect of Immigration on Productivity: Evidence from U.S. States." November. Working Paper No. 15507. Cambridge, MA: National Bureau of Economic Research.

Petit, B. and B. Western. 2004. "Mass Imprisonment and the Life Course: Race and Class Inequality in U.S. Incarceration." *American Sociological Review* 69: 2: 151–169.

Pew Hispanic Center. 2006. "The Labor Force Status of Short-Term Unauthorized Workers." April. Washington, DC: Pew Hispanic Center.

———. 2008. "One in 100: Behind Bars in America 2008." Washington, DC: Pew Hispanic Center.

Phillips, J. and D. Massey. 1999. "The New Labor Market: Immigrants and Wages After IRCA." *Demography* 36: 2: 233–246.

Piven, Francis Fox, and Richard Cloward. 1971. *Regulating the Poor: The Functions of Public Welfare*. New York: Vintage.

Poinsatte, C., and A. M. Poinsatte. 1984. "Augustin Cochin's 'L'Abolition de l'esclavage' and the Emancipation Proclamation." *Review of Politics* 46: 3: 410–427.

Portes, Alejandro. "Introduction: Immigration and Its Aftermath." *International Migration Review* 28: 4: 632–639.

Portes, Alejandro, and Alex Stepick. 1993. *City on the Edge: The Transformation of Miami*. Berkeley: University of California Press.

Portes, Alejandro, and Min Zhou. 1993. "The New Second Generation: Segmented Assimilation and Its Variants." *Annals of the American Academy of Political and Social Science* 530: 74–96.

Povinelli, Elizabeth. 2002. *The Cunning of Recognition: Indigenous Alterities and the Making of Australian Multiculturalism*. Durham NC: Duke University Press.

Prado, C. G. 2000. *Starting with Foucault: An Introduction to Genealogy*. Boulder, CO: Westview.

Rabinowitz, Howard. 1978. *Race Relations in the Urban South, 1865–1890*. New York: Oxford University Press.

Ratner, S. 1984. "Horace M. Kallen and Cultural Pluralism." *Modern Judaism* 4: 2: 185–200.

Reagan, Patrick. 2000. *Designing a New America: The Origins of New Deal Planning, 1890–1943*. Boston: University of Massachusetts Press.

Rees, Richard. 2007. *Shades of Difference: A History of Ethnicity in America*. Lanham, MD: Rowman and Littlefield.

Reider, Jonathan, ed. 2003. *The Fractious Nation? Unity and Division in Contemporary American Life*. Berkeley: University of California Press.

Reiman, Jeffrey. 2006. *The Rich Get Richer and the Poor Get Prison: Ideology, Class, and Criminal Justice*. New York: Allyn and Bacon.

Reitz, Jeffrey. 1999. *Warmth of the Welcome: The Social Causes of Economic Success in Different Nations and Cities*. Boulder, CO: Westview.

Robbins, Bruce, ed. 1993. *The Phantom Public Sphere*. Minneapolis: University of Minnesota Press.

Rodríguez, Clara. 2000. *Changing Race: Latinos, the Census, and the History of Ethnicity in the United States*. New York: New York University Press.

Rodríguez, Cristina, Muzaffar Chishti, Randy Capps, and Laura St. John. 2010. "A Program in Flux: New Priorities and Implementation Challenges for 287(g)." Washington, DC: Migration Policy Institute.

Rodrik, D. 1998. "Why Do More Open Economies Have Bigger Governments." *Journal of Political Economy* 106: 5: 997–1032.

Roediger, David. 2006. *Working Toward Whiteness: How America's Immigrants Became White: The Strange Journey from Ellis Island to the Suburbs*. New York: Basic Books.

——. 2008. *The Wages of Whiteness: Race and the Making of the American Working Class*. New York: Verso.

Rogin, Michael. 1988. *Ronald Reagan The Movie: And Other Episodes in Political Demonology*. Berkeley: University of California Press.

Root, Maria, ed. 1996. *The Multiracial Experience: Racial Borders as the New Frontier*. New York: Sage.

Rosenzweig, M. 2006. "Global Wage Differences and International Student Flows." *Brookings Trade Forum* 57–86.

Rothenberg, Daniel. 2000. *With These Hands: The Hidden World of Migrant Farmworkers Today*. Berkeley: University of California Press.

Rumbaut, Rubén. 2008. "The Coming of the Second Generation: Immigration and Ethnic Mobility in Southern California." *Annals of the American Academy of Political and Social Science* 620: 196–236.

Rumbaut, Rubén, and Walter Ewing. 2007. "The Myth of Immigrant Criminality." Border Battles: The U.S. Immigration Debate. New York, Social Science Research Council. http://borderbattles.ssrc.org/Rumbault_Ewing/ (accessed May 12, 2010).

Sagarin, R. 2003. "Adapt or Die." *Foreign Policy* 138:68–69.

Salins, Peter. 1997. *Assimilation, American Style*. New York: Basic Books.

Samore, W. 1951. "Statelessness as a Consequence of the Conflict of Nationality Laws." *American Journal of International Law* 45: 3: 476–494.

Sampson, R. 2008. "Rethinking Crime and Immigration." *Contexts* 7:28–33.

Sampson, R., S. Raudenbush, and F. Earls. 1997. "Neighborhoods and Violent Crime: A Multilevel Study of Collective Efficacy." *Science* 277:918–24.

Sandoval, Carlos. 2003. *Farmingville*. Directed by Carlos Sandoval and Catherine Tambini. Camino Bluff Productions.

Sassen, Saskia. 2000. *Guests and Aliens*. New York: New Press.

———. 2001. *The Global City*. Princeton, NJ: Princeton University Press.

———. 2006a. *Territory, Authority, Rights: From Medieval to Global Assemblages*. Princeton, NJ: Princeton University Press.

———. 2006b. "The Bits of a New Immigration Reality: A Bad Fit with Current Policy." Border Battles: The U.S. Immigration Debate. New York: Social Science Research Council. http://borderbattles.ssrc.org/Sassen/ (accessed August 25, 2010).

———. 2007. *A Sociology of Globalization*. New York: W. W. Norton.

Segal, Elizabeth, and Keith Kilty, eds. 2006. *The Promise of Welfare Reform: Political Rhetoric and the Reality of Poverty in the Twenty-First Century*. New York: Routledge.

Shahani, Aarti, and Judith Greene. 2009. "Local Democracy on ICE: Why State and Local Governments Have No Business in Federal Immigration Law Enforcement." February. New York: Justice Strategies.

Sheikh, Irum. 2008. "Racializing, Criminalizing, and Silencing 9/11 Deportees." In David Brotherton and Philip Kretsedemas, eds., *Keeping Out the Other: A Critical Introduction to Immigration Enforcement Today*, 81–107. New York: Columbia University Press.

Simmel, Georg. 1971 [1908]. *Georg Simmel on Individuality and Social Forms*. Chicago: University of Chicago Press.

Simons, S. 1901. "Social Assimilation. VII. Assimilation in the Modern World." *American Journal of Sociology* 7: 2: 234–248.

Singer, Audrey. 2004. "Welfare Reform and Immigrants: A Policy Review." In Philip Kretsedemas and Ana Aparicio, eds., *Immigrants, Welfare Reform, and the Poverty of Policy*, 21–34. Westport CT: Greenwood-Praeger.

Skeldon, R. 2008. "Of Skilled Migration, Brain Drain, and Policy Responses." *International Migration* 47: 4: 3–29.

Skocpol, Theda. 1995. *Social Policy in the United States: Future Possibilities in Historical Perspective*. Princeton, NJ: Princeton University Press.

Smith, Anna Marie. 2007. *Welfare Reform and Sexual Regulation*. Cambridge, UK: Cambridge University Press.

Smith, Robert. 2005. *Mexican New York: Transnational Lives of New Immigrants*. Berkeley: University of California Press.

Smith, Rogers M., and Desmond S. King. 2009. "Barack Obama and the Future of American Racial Politics." *Du Bois Review* 6:25–35.

Somers, Margaret. 2008. *Genealogies of Citizenship: Markets, Statelessness, and the Right to Have Rights*. Cambridge, UK: Cambridge University Press.

Soysal, Yasmin. 1998. "Toward a Postnational Model of Membership." In Gershon Shafir, ed., *The Citizenship Debates: A Reader*, 189–217. Minneapolis: University of Minnesota Press.

Spencer, H. 1857. "Progress: Its Law and Causes." *Westminster Review* 67: 445–465.

Steinberg, James. 2003. Statement to the National Commission on Terrorist Attacks Upon The United States. October 14. Washington, DC: National Commission on Terrorist Attacks Upon the United States.

Steinberg, Stephen. 2001. *The Ethnic Myth: Race, Ethnicity, and Class in America.* New York: Beacon.

———. 2007. *Race Relations: A Critique*. Stanford, CA: Stanford University Press.

Stonequist, Everett. 1937. *The Marginal Man: A Study in Personality and Culture Conflict*. New York: Charles Scribner's Sons.

Subcommittee on International Law, Immigration, and Refugees. 1994. "Haitian Asylum Seekers." Committee on the Judiciary, House of Representatives, 103rd Congress. 2nd Session on HR 4114 and HR 4264. June 15.

Sum, Andrew, Ishwar Khatiwada, Sheila Palma, and Paulo Tobar. 2006. "New Foreign Immigrant Inflows into Massachusetts, 2000–2005: An Assessment of Their Size, Characteristics, and Impacts on State Population and Labor Force Growth." Boston: Center for Labor Market Studies, Northeastern University.

Sweet, Frank. 2005. *Legal History of the Color Line: The Rise and Triumph of the One-Drop Rule*. Palm Coast, FL: Backintyme.

Swidler, A. 1986. "Culture in Action: Symbols and Strategies." *American Sociological Review* 51: 273–286.

Takaki, Ronald. 1994. "Reflections on Racial Patterns in America." In Ronald Takaki, ed., *From Different Shores: Perspectives on Race and Ethnicity in America*, 24–40. New York: Oxford University Press.

Taylor, Charles. 1994. *Multiculturalism: Examining the Politics of Recognition*. Edited by Amy Gutmann. Princeton, NJ: Princeton University Press.

Taylor, J. Edward, Philip L. Martin, and Michael Fix. 1997. *Poverty Amid Prosperity: Immigration and the Changing Face of Rural California*. Washington, DC: Urban Institute Press.

Tichenor, Daniel. 2002. *Dividing Lines: The Politics of Immigration Control in America*. Princeton, NJ: Princeton University Press.

Tonry, Michael. 1996. *Malign Neglect: Race, Crime, and Punishment in America*. Cambridge, UK: Oxford University Press.

Transactional Records Access Clearinghouse (TRAC). 2009. "Immigration Prosecutions at Record Levels in FY 2009."

TRAC Reports. Syracuse, NY: Syracuse University. http://trac.syr.edu/immigration/reports/218/ (accessed August 25, 2010).

Turner, Eliot, and Marc R. Rosenblum. 2005. "Solving the Unauthorized Migrant Problem: Proposed Legislation in the U.S." September. Washington, DC: Migration Policy Institute.Twining, J. 1980. "Alienation as a Social Process." *Sociological Quarterly* 21: 3: 417–428.

U.S. Census Population Estimates. 2008. Table 3, "Annual Estimates of the Resident Population by Sex, Race, and Hispanic Origin for the United States." Washington, DC: U.S. Bureau of the Census.

U.S. Citizen and Immigration Services (USCIS). 2008. "H1B Benefit Fraud and Compliance Assessment." September. Washington, DC: Department of Homeland Security.

———. 2009. "Cap Count for H-1B and H-2B Workers for Fiscal Year 2010." August 17. Washington, DC: Department of Homeland Security. www.aila.org/content/fileviewer.aspx?docid=28663&linkid=208196 (accessed May 8, 2010).

USC/Los Angeles Times Poll. 2010. Conducted by Greenberg Quinlan Rosner Research for the *Los Angeles Times* and the University of Southern California College of Letters, Arts and Sciences. www.greenbergresearch.com/index.php?ID=2520 (accessed October 18, 2010).

U.S. Department of State (USDS). 2008. "Returning H2B (H2R) Workers." http://travel.state.gov/visa/laws/telegrams/telegrams_2764.html (accessed December 16, 2008).

U.S. 9/11 Commission. 2004. "The U.S. 9/11 Commission on Border Control." *Population and Development Review* 30: 3: 569–574.

Vaca, Nicolas. 2004. *Presumed Alliance: The Unspoken Conflict Between Latinos and Blacks and What It Means for America.* New York: HarperCollins.

VanHook, J., S. Brown, and M. Kwenda. 2004. "A Decomposition of Trends in Poverty Among Children of Immigrants." *Demography* 41: 4: 649–670.

Walzer, Michael. 1984. *Spheres of Justice: A Defense of Pluralism and Equality.* New York: Basic Books.

Wasem, Ruth Ellen. 2005. "U.S. Immigration Policy on Haitian Migrants." Congressional Research Service Reports for Congress. http://trac.syr.edu/immigration/library/P960.pdf (accessed August 25, 2010).

———. 2006. "Immigration Policy for Intracompany Transfers (L Visa): Issues and Legislation." Congressional Research Service Reports for Congress. www.ieeeusa.org/policy/reports/CRSL1visa.pdf (accessed August 25, 2010).

———. 2009. "Unauthorized Aliens Residing in the U.S.: Estimates Since 1986." Washington, DC: Congressional Research Service Report. http://trac.syr.edu/immigration/library/P4001.pdf (accessed August 25, 2010).

Wasem, Ruth Ellen, and Karma Ester. 2008. "Temporary Protected Status: Current Immigration Policy Issues." Congressional Research Service Reports for

Congress. Library of Congress. http://trac.syr.edu/immigration/library/P332. pdf (accessed August 25, 2010).

Waters, Mary. 2001. *Black Identities: West Indian Immigrant Dreams and American Realities*. Cambridge, MA: Harvard University Press.

Weis, P. 1962. "The United Nations Convention on the Reduction of Statelessness, 1961." *International and Comparative Law Quarterly* 11: 4: 1073–1096.

Welch, Michael. 2002. *Detained: Immigration Laws and the Expanding INS Complex*. Philadelphia, PA: Temple University Press.

——. 2006. *Scapegoats of September 11th: Hate Crimes and State Crimes in the War on Terror*. Piscataway, NJ: Rutgers University Press.

Western, Bruce. 2007. *Punishment and Inequality in America*. New York: Russell Sage Foundation.

Willen, S. 2007 "Exploring 'Illegal' and 'Irregular' Migrants' Lived Experiences of Law and State Power." *International Migration* 45: 3: 2–7.

Wilson, William Julius. 1976. "Class Conflict and Jim Crow Segregation in the Postbellum South." *Pacific Sociological Review* 19: 4: 431–446.

——. 1990. *The Truly Disadvantaged: The Inner City, the Underclass, and Public Policy*. Chicago: University of Chicago Press.

Wise, Tim. 2010. *Colorblind: The Rise of Post-Racial Politics and the Retreat from Racial Equality*. San Francisco: City Lights.

Woodward, C. Vann. 1955. The Strange Career of Jim Crow. New York: Oxford University Press.

Wright, S. 1995. "Electoral and Biracial Coalition: Possible Election Strategy for African American Candidates in Louisville, Kentucky." *Journal of Black Studies* 25: 6: 749–758.

Zamudio, M., and F. Rios. 2006. "From Traditional to Liberal Racism: Living Racism in the Everyday." *Sociological Perspectives* 49: 4: 483–501.

Zentella, A. C. 1997. "The Hispanophobia of the Official English Movement in the U.S." *International Journal of the Sociology of Language* 127: 71–86.

Zhou M. 1997. "Growing Up American: The Challenge Confronting Immigrant Children and Children of Immigrants." *Annual Review of Sociology* 23: 63–95.

Zizek, Slavoj. 2008. *Violence: Six Sideways Reflections*. New York: Picador.

——. 2009. *First as Tragedy, Then as Farce*. New York. Verso.

Zolberg, Aristide. 2008. *A Nation by Design: Immigration Policy in the Fashioning of America*. Cambridge, MA: Harvard University Press.

House of Representatives, 67, 72, 137, 139, 141. *See also* Congress
Huntington, Samuel, 113–15, 124, 129, 134

illegal or illegality, 7, 9, 15, 29–30, 37–38, 44; alien, 9, 88; becoming illegal, 27, 37, 44; discourse on illegal immigration, 74, 83; drug trade, 102; illegalized labor or illegalization, 31, 89–90; legal migrants and, 10, 24, 103; local enforcement and, 97; migrant worker, 9, 30; nonimmigrant flow and, 16; state of exception and, 51. *See also* unauthorized migrant
Illegal Immigration Reform and Immigrant Responsibility Act. *See* immigration, policy
immigrant or migrant: acculturation, assimilation, or integration, 11, 13–14, 74, 85–86, 117, 121, 126, 100–101, 150; African, 38–39, 40, 42, 94; Arab-Muslim, 35–36, 48; Asian, 41–42, 47–49, 63, 94, 104–105, 108, 141; black, 37–39, 42–43; Caribbean, 38–40, 42, 94; European, 38–40, 42, 94, 109–111, 123, 133, 148, 149; flow, 2, 4, 8, 15–17, 19, 21, 29–31, 34–35, 39, 41–42, 45, 63, 71, 86, 91, 134, 141; Haitian, 43–45, 62; Indian, 36; Iranian, 35; Japanese, 48; Jewish, 122; labor markets, 2–4, 7–8, 14, 19–20, 24–32, 37, 39, 41–43, 45, 58, 63, 66, 68, 70, 84–86, 103, 118, 131, 142–43, 151; Latin American, 39–42, 98–99, 105; marginality, 4, 12, 19, 20–21, 74, 107, 117–18, 121, 130, 133–34, 136, 150; Mexican, 28–29, 30, 51; networks, 14, 16, 29–30, 33,

110, 112; racial profiling, 7, 10–11, 36, 74, 78, 94–96, 98–100, 102, 138; recruitment, 7, 9, 24, 26–31, 37, 39, 63, 69, 75, 87, 138, 142, 144; rights and rights activists, 1, 2, 4–5, 19, 43, 62, 63, 65, 67, 68, 74, 78, 80, 91, 97, 99–101, 105–106, 124, 125, 126, 131, 139, 142, 144, 147, 150; settlement, 15; undocumented (*see* unauthorized migrant or migration)
—crime or incarceration, 5, 42–44, 45–46, 92, 100–101; Latinos and, 94, 100–101
—Latino/a, 2, 28–31, 41, 75, 84; cross-border networks of, 30; ethnic job sectors, 75; permanent residents, 42; unauthorized migrants, 42 88; second-generation, 101
immigration: control, 3–4, 6, 67–69, 71, 72, 73, 87, 89, 91, 97–98, 113, 137–38, 140–43; debate (U.S.), 1, 5, 8–9, 11–12, 74, 82, 91, 101, 117, 134–36, 137–38, 143–44, 147–48, 151; demographic threat, 113, 134, 147; economy and, 1–5, 7, 13, 27, 30; enforcement (*see* immigration enforcement); liberalizing flows, 6, 8, 33, 48; quotas, 28, 30, 63, 99, 105, 140, 142; restrictionists, 1–2, 6, 8, 41, 47–48, 65, 67–68, 135; system, 6, 8, 15–16, 18, 24, 35, 36, 46, 49, 62, 68–71, 73, 77, 103, 144–45
—policy, 2, 4–5, 7–9, 11–12, 16, 38, 41–42, 47–49, 62, 67, 69, 72, 73, 83, 92, 103, 105, 126, 130, 134, 138–39, 143–44, 147, 151; Illegal Immigration Reform and Immigrant Responsibility Act, 4, 66, 70, 81, 96, 140; Immigration and Nationality Act, 79; Im-

WARREN TWP LIBRARY
42 MOUNTAIN BLVD

FEB 2 3 2012

WARREN, NJ 07059
908-754-5554